THE SCIENCE OF GOD

THE SCIENCE OF GOD

An Introduction to Scientific Theology

Alister E. McGrath

WILLIAM B. EERDMANS PUBLISHING COMPANY
GRAND RAPIDS, MICHIGAN

© 2004 T&T Clark International
A Continuum imprint
All rights reserved

Published 2004
in Great Britain by
T&T Clark International
The Tower Building, 11 York Road, London SE1 7NX
www.tandtclark.com

and in the United States of America,
under license from T&T Clark Ltd, by
Wm. B. Eerdmans Publishing Co.
255 Jefferson Ave. S.E., Grand Rapids, Michigan 49503
www.eerdmans.com

Manufactured in Great Britain

09 08 07 06 05 04   7 6 5 4 3 2 1

ISBN 0-8028-2815-9

Contents

v

Preface

The publication of the three volumes of *A Scientific Theology* (2001–3) has generated a high degree of interest in its themes and distinctive approach. It is already being described as 'one of the best systematic theologies in recent years'. The three volumes – subtitled *Nature*, *Reality* and *Theory* respectively – set out an approach to theology which respects the unique nature of that discipline, while at the same time drawing on the insights of the natural sciences in a process of respectful and principled dialogue. The projects represent the most sustained and extended attempt to date by a single author to 'explore the interface between Christian theology and the natural sciences, on the assumption that this engagement is necessary, proper, legitimate and productive' (1:xviii).[1] While the work can be read both as a treatise on the relation of Christian theology and the natural sciences and a full-blown work on theological methodology, it is probably best seen as a defence of the entire theological enterprise itself. Christian theology is argued to be a distinct legitimate intellectual discipline in its own right, with its own sense of identity and purpose, linked

with an appreciation of its own limitations and distinctive emphases within the human quest for wisdom as a whole.

Nothing appeals so powerfully to the imagination as the sense
that one is drawing aside a veil on something that is immense,
beautiful and true. That deep sense of conviction has been the
driving force behind this project. I believe that the approach I
adopt is workable, and offers Christian theology a means to
reconstruct its priorities and tasks in the light of the failures of
some of the paths it has explored in recent decades, leading to a
recovery of its purpose and place.

As will become clear, the 'scientific theology' trilogy concerns
itself almost entirely with issues of theological method. As the
Princeton ethical philosopher Jeffrey Stout once commented,
writing on method is a bit like clearing your throat before beginning a lecture. You can only go on for so long before the audience
starts to get a little restless. However, I suspect that it is not really
necessary for me to apologize for this shortcoming. Systematic
theology simply cannot be done without a preliminary engagement with issues of method. Before dealing with the classic
themes of Christian dogmatics, it is thus entirely proper to reas-
sure its intended audience of the intellectual viability of Christian
theology as a serious participant in the long human search for
wisdom and enlightenment.

This book is designed to introduce the distinctive themes and
emphases of this scientific theology to a wider readership. It aims
to introduce the leading themes of a scientific theology without
making unrealistic assumptions about its users. There are four
obvious reasons why such an introduction is needed, each of
which rests on a characteristic of the original three-volume work
which required modification for the purposes of such an introduction.

1. Its *level.* The three volumes of *A Scientific Theology* are
   written on the assumption that its readers are familiar with
   the theological, philosophical and scientific issues being
   addressed, and can hence identify the significance of the
   particular approach I adopt. Yet many would value an introduction to the general context against which the work
   has been written, and an explanation of the distinctive
   approach adopted. For example, the implicit assumption
   throughout the work is that the Enlightenment project has
   failed. Many, however, would appreciate an explanation of
   what that project actually was, why it is believed to have
   failed, and what its implications are for anyone doing theology in the twenty-first century. This introduction aims to
   provide that additional level of support.

2. The *style* of the original work. *A Scientific Theology* is written
   in an academic style which makes no allowance for those
   not used to this way of writing. A more accessible style is
   required for such an introductory book. This introduction
   is more than an abbreviated version of the three original
   volumes; it includes new sections, written specifically with
   a different audience in mind. While faithful to the ideas and
   approach of the original volumes, the present introduction
   aims to achieve a relatively high degree of explanatory
   clarity.

3. The *length* of the original work. The three volumes of *A
   Scientific Theology* take up one thousand pages of closely set
   type. The chapters are often long – sometimes as long as a
   hundred pages. It is clearly important to have a considerably shorter introduction, which will help readers to understand the points being made, without the need for long
   scholarly footnotes or extended discussions of some points
   of fine detail.

4. The extensive use of *case studies* from the history of science or historical theology. The original volumes include many such 'case studies' to illuminate or justify points of importance, and are an integral aspect of the approach being adopted. Yet for some readers, they will simply slow down the argument. Although important for the readership of the project as a whole, there is no reason why they should be considered in detail at an introductory stage. These case studies will occasionally be noted briefly, and their relevance explained – but they will not be developed in detail. It is hoped that readers of this shorter work will feel encouraged to explore these case studies from the original volumes at a later stage, once their purpose has become clearer.

This book opens by considering the background against which the 'scientific theology' project was written. The opening chapter explains how the distinctive approach was developed over a period of roughly twenty years (1976–96), locating this work against the development of my career as a theologian and my various writing projects, and explains what I hoped to achieve in writing it. The following chapters deal with each of the four major subdivisions of the work, as outlined below:

Volume 1. Nature
     Part 1. Prolegomena
  1. The Legitimacy of a Scientific Theology
  2. The Approach to be Adopted
     Part 2. Nature
  3. The Construction of Nature
  4. The Christian Doctrine of Creation
  5. Implications of a Christian Doctrine of Creation
  6. The Purpose and Place of Natural Theology

This layout, with the chapters numbered continuously, is intended to reinforce the point that volume 2 cannot be read independently of volume 1, nor volume 3 independently of volume 1 *and* volume 2. The argument for a scientific theology is developed in a linear manner throughout the entire work, and foundations are laid in earlier sections of the work for arguments which occur in later sections. The argument is linear and cumulative; none of its many aspects are discrete or independent; and must be set against the overall trajectory of the coherent vision of Christian theology which it sets out.

Space does not permit every aspect of the debate to be summarized; at times, only brief accounts of a discussion can be provided. However, every effort has been made to ensure that the most important sections of the work are described as fully as possible. The limits of such an introduction will be obvious – perhaps most significantly, that there is no way that such a brief introduction can *defend* the basic principles of the approach. That demands the spaciousness of the original three volumes, which enables a detailed engagement with its intellectual context and its alternatives. At best, this introduction can only summarize this project. Scholars wishing to engage with my ideas should do so on the basis of the full discussion of the issues in the original three volumes, not the simplified and truncated summary offered in this volume. Yet such summaries have their value, despite their obvious shortcomings.

Bringing the trilogy to an end has turned out to be both a relief and a matter of some frustration. The process of unfolding what seemed like a bright idea back in 1976 has proved to be far more difficult than I had imagined, and its execution less satisfactory than I had hoped. Initially, it seemed to me that the vast spaciousness afforded by these three volumes would be more than adequate to deal with the issues I knew had to be addressed in articulating a coherent and plausible vision of 'a scientific theology'. My frustration is partly due to the obvious fact that this has turned out to be signally less than adequate for my purposes. What I had hoped might be extensive discussions of central methodological questions have ended up being rather shallow; what I had hoped to be close readings of seminal texts seem to have turned out to be little more than superficial engagements. To use an image which may be familiar to readers of sixteenth-century Spanish spiritual writers, I have carried out some explorations in the foothills of Mount Carmel, but have yet to ascend it. It is my hope that this introduction will help with the process of understanding and assessing a scientific theology, and – hopefully! – to move on to the greater challenges to which theology is called.

Alister McGrath, Oxford, September 2003

Introduction

The Background to a Scientific Theology

This opening chapter begins to lay the groundwork for encountering a scientific theology, and beginning to interact with its approach and distinctive themes. It opens with an explanation of how I developed the approach, from its origins in 1976 to the final crystallization of its themes in 1998. This is followed by an essay on the vision that lies behind the scientific theology project, in which I set out some of the possibilities offered by a scientific theology. Some of these are addressed within the three volumes of the original project; others remain future projects. And finally, the structure of the three volumes is introduced and explained, before moving on to a more detailed summary of its themes in the remainder of the book.

The Historical Origins of the Project

My own background lies in the natural sciences. I have always been fascinated by the natural world. When I was about ten years old, I built a small refracting telescope out of some old camera lenses so that I could begin to explore the heavens. I learned the names of the constellations and brighter stars, observed the moons of Jupiter, and studied the mountains and seas of the moon. A new world was opened up to me. I can still recall the shivers of excitement I felt on a cold winter's night, when I first saw the rings of the planet Saturn.

Yet my interest in the sciences was by no means limited to astronomy. An old microscope, originally belonging to a great-uncle who was a pathologist at the Royal Victoria Hospital, Belfast, allowed me to begin the serious study of biology around the same time. I would regularly collect local pond-water, and found myself intrigued by the structure of its microscopic plant and animal life. It seemed obvious to me that I would end up in a scientific career, possibly related to medicine.

While I was a school student at the Methodist College, Belfast (1966–71), I immersed myself in the study of the natural sciences, specializing in mathematics, physics and chemistry. While all these subjects excited me, none was quite so stimulating as chemistry. Above all, I developed an interest in some aspects of inorganic chemistry, especially the theoretical analysis of what are known as 'inorganic ligands'. One of my favourite books while studying chemistry during my final years at school was *Inorganic Chemistry*, by C. S. G. Phillips and R. J. P. Williams. When I discovered that Williams was a chemistry don at Wadham College, Oxford, an idea began to crystallize in my mind. I wanted to go to Oxford University to read chemistry, and be taught by R. J. P. Williams.

In early December 1971, I went to Oxford for interview. I had never been to the city before, and got completely lost on trying to find my way from the railway station to Wadham College. My initial impressions were not especially encouraging. The city was enveloped in fog for much of my visit, and power blackouts meant that the college was plunged into darkness for hours at a time. I braced myself for the interview with the college's three chemistry dons: J. R. Knowles, C. J. S. M. Simpson and Williams. In the end, it was Williams who subjected me to close questioning for twenty minutes about the theoretical basis of the nephelauxetic effect – a particularly interesting aspect of inorganic chemistry, which examined the impact of various ligands on the behaviour of inorganic ions in solutions. I emerged from the interview convinced that I had not given particularly good answers to his probing questions. They obviously thought otherwise. A few days later, Knowles send me a handwritten note, telling me that I was to be offered a major scholarship at the college, hoping that I would accept. So in October 1971, I made my way from Belfast to Oxford, travelling by ship to the port of Liverpool, and then by rail to Oxford.

Then events took what I can only describe as a rather unexpected turn. I had never had the slightest interest in religion, let alone Christian theology, while at school. In fact, I regarded Christianity and the natural sciences as mutually incompatible on the basis of the incorrigible certainties about life widely entertained by teenagers. For, like many back in the 1960s, I had bought into Marxism in quite a big way. I was completely convinced that the future lay with atheism, and that religion would either die of exhaustion or be eliminated by a resentful humanity within my lifetime. I had read popular works such as A. J. Ayer's *Language, Truth and Logic*, and was persuaded that atheism was the only worldview that had any intellectual integrity. Some doubts began to creep into my mind when studying the history and philosophy of science during my final months at school, when I realized that the 'science proves things, religion demands blind obedience' school of thought was talking educated nonsense. But I was able to repress those doubts without undue difficulty.

In my first term at Oxford University, late in 1971, I began to discover that Christianity was much more exciting than I had realized. While I had been severely critical of Christianity as a young man, I had never extended that same critical evaluation to atheism, tending to assume that it was self-evidently correct, and was hence exempt from being assessed in this way. During October and November 1971, I began to discover that the intellectual case for atheism was rather insubstantial. Christianity, on the other hand, seemed rather more interesting. As I talked to friends, my doubts about atheism's credibility began to coalesce into a realization that atheism was a belief system, where I had assumed it to be a factual statement about reality. I also discovered that I knew far less about Christianity than I had assumed. It gradually became clear to me that I had rejected a religious stereotype. I had some major rethinking to do. By the end of November 1971, I had made my decision: I turned my back on my schoolboy faith, and embraced another. I left atheism behind, and committed myself to Christianity.[1]

To my parents' surprise, I took home some college library books dealing with aspects of Christian theology for my Christmas vacation reading in December 1971. Having now discovered that Christianity was decidely more resilient and intrinsically fulfilling than I could ever have imagined, I began to wonder what to do next. Should I abandon my study of chemistry, and switch to theology? The conclusion that I came to was quite simple. I would complete my studies in chemistry. In fact, I would do more than that: I would undertake research in some aspect of the natural sciences. And then I would switch to theology, and try to establish the connection between them. So after completing my undergraduate studies in chemistry in 1975, having specialized in aspects of quantum theory, I began a research programme in molecular biophysics, which would allow me to develop new physical techniques for measuring diffusion rates in biological membranes and their models – in other words, to measure how quickly components of natural or artificial membranes moved about. It was a fascinating topic, which allowed me to branch out into some aspects of the vast field of molecular biology, as well as keep up my reading of the physical and chemical literature.

However, I was not prepared to wait to begin the formal study of theology. Although few students studied theology at Wadham College back in the 1970s, the college library was reasonably well stocked with theological books. I found myself working through them, taking notes which might one day come in useful (although, to tell the truth, they never did). I became an amateur theologian, at this stage distinguished far more by enthusiasm than wisdom. Yet that enthusiasm was compelling. I knew that I would not be satisfied until I had wrestled with the classical questions of theology. I explained my situation to J. R. Knowles, my chemistry tutor at this time, who subsequently went on to become Dean of the Faculty of Arts and Sciences at Harvard University. He urged me to 'stoke the intellectual fires' that burned within me. But how, I wondered, could I keep up my interest in the sciences, while at the same time studying theology properly? There was a limit to what I could teach myself; I would need help.

By this stage, I was deeply involved in doctoral research in the Department of Biochemistry at Oxford, focusing on aspects of molecular biophysics, with a particular interest in the biophysical properties of biological membranes and their models. A major concern was the manner in which artificial models of complex biological membranes could be designed, validated and deployed. I won an E. P. A. Cephalosporin Research Studentship to allow me to undertake this work, on the basis of a research paper prepared during my final year as an undergraduate. Although my work largely took the form of practical empirical research, I also found time to work systematically on aspects of the history and philosophy of the natural sciences. The research went well, and led to some rewards. I was awarded a Fellowship by the European Molecular Biology Organization to work for several months at the University of Utrecht in the Netherlands, and a Senior Scholarship at Merton College, Oxford.

It was while I was working at Utrecht during the long, dry summer of 1976 that the idea came to me – an idea which would captivate my imagination, and bring about the redirection of my life. While working on my research, I had time to reflect on the more philosophical and theological issues which were raised by molecular biophysics in general. As I wrote in *Scientific Theology* (1:xi):

> I cannot recall quite how the idea came into my mind; it was as if a mental bolt of lightning flashed across my consciousness, eclipsing my thoughts on how best to apply Fourier Transforms to study the time-resolved anisotropy of a fluorescent probe that I had developed for studying lipid viscosity in biological membranes and their models. The idea that shot through my mind was simple: explore the relation between Christian theology and the natural sciences, using philosophy and history as dialogue partners. It would be grounded in and faithful to the Christian tradition, yet open to the insights of the sciences. This would be more than a mere exploration of a working relationship; it would be a proposal for a synergy, a working together, a mutal cross-fertilization of ideas and approaches – in short, a scientific theology.

But how could I realize this vision, when I had yet to begin the formal study of theology? As I returned home to Oxford late that summer, it seemed to me that I had little hope of achieving the goals I had set myself. I moved my belongings to my new rooms at Merton College late in August, and prepared to enjoy my time at this ancient college, which had been kind enough to elect me to a Senior Scholarship. In September, it occurred to me to check the small print, and see exactly what the scholarship entitled me to. And there I found my answer. As well as promising free lodging, financial support and dining rights at high table, I found that the scholarship allowed its holder either to undertake advanced research, or to study for a second undergraduate degree. And funding was guaranteed for the lifetime of the scholarship – two years.

Having dabbled in theology in a very amateurish manner for five years or so, I decided that the time had come to treat the subject with the seriousness it deserved. I therefore asked permission to continue my research in molecular biology, while at the same time beginning the formal study of theology at Oxford. This would mean completing a three-year undergraduate course in two years, a privilege Oxford University allowed to graduates, who were presumably assumed to be capable of the additional pressures this created. My request caused a degree of consternation and bewilderment among the fellows of the college, not least because Merton did not take undergraduates to read theology; nevertheless, they gave me the permission I needed. And so, from October 1976, I spent part of the day working in the Oxford University Department of Biochemistry, and the remainder of my time trying to master the basics of Christian theology. I benefited considerably here from Oxford's commitment to the tutorial system, in that I was able to study the subject at the feet of some of the finest scholars in the field. I also encountered the ideas of Karl Barth, which I continue to find an invaluable stimulus to my own thinking, no matter how much I may disagree with him.

In 1978 I was awarded my doctorate in molecular biology, while at the same time gaining first class honours in theology, and winning the Denyer and Johnson Prize in theology for the best examination performance that year. As a result, I was invited to lunch shortly afterwards by a senior editor at Oxford University Press, who asked me to consider writing a book on the theme of Christianity and the natural sciences, in particular to respond to Richard Dawkin's book *The Selfish Gene*. I gave this proposal very serious consideration. However, I came to the conclusion that I would need to immerse myself in the further study of religion, and especially the history of Christian theology, before I could make a positive and informed contribution to this field.

After this, I transferred to Cambridge University, taking up an award at St John's College, Cambridge. The 'Naden Studentship in Divinity', which I held for the period 1978–80, was established in the eighteenth century to encourage the study of serious theology. I benefited significantly from this new intellectual environment. My initial hope had been to study the Copernican controversy as a means of opening up the interaction between Christian theology and the natural sciences through a single case study. However, I was persuaded to study Martin Luther instead, and this led me to a detailed study of historical theology, focusing on three interrelated themes: the theology of one individual (Martin Luther), the general theological development of a specific period (the sixteenth-century Reformation), and the historical development of one specific doctrine (the doctrine of justification, which was of critical importance to Luther in particular, and to the Reformation in general).[2]

My research continued thereafter, focusing on mastering the complexities of the development of Christian doctrine, and the specifics of leading individuals and controversies which I regarded as being of central importance to the development of a scientific theology. Three landmarks may be noted along the way to the production of a scientific theology.

The first of these landmarks, *The Genesis of Doctrine* (1990),[3] dealt with the pressures which lead to the formulation of

Christian doctrines in the first place, and the factors which account for at least some aspects of their subsequent development. This allowed me to begin a critical engagement with the theories of George Lindbeck, which is consolidated in the second volume of *A Scientific Theology*.

The second, *The Foundations of Dialogue in Science and Religion* (1998),[4] signalled my readiness to begin publishing on themes related to a scientific theology. This work takes the form of a considerably expanded version of a lecture I was invited to deliver at the Faculty of Theology of the University of Utrecht in January 1997 on 'The Relation of the Natural Sciences and Christian Theology', and sets out – although in a rather tentative manner – some of the themes that would be more fully and confidently developed in the three volumes of *A Scientific Theology*. It was a particular pleasure to be able to return to the University of Utrecht to speak on this theme more than twenty years after conceiving the project there in the first place, and an even greater pleasure to be able to speak again at Utrecht in April 2003, on the completion of the project.

The third landmark represents my growing interest in, and appreciation of, Thomas F. Torrance, whose 1969 work *Theological Science* seemed to me to open up a new way of approaching the theological appropriation of the methods of the natural sciences. In investigating his ideas, I found myself researching the human being behind these ideas, leading to the publication of his biography in 1999.[5] Torrance's careful and perceptive engagement with Barth's views on natural theology seemed to me to represent a major advance. I also found myself agreeing strongly, for both theological and scientific reasons, with his emphasis on theological science engaging with reality according to its own distinctive nature. I engage with Torrance extensively in the first and second volumes of *A Scientific Theology* (indeed, I dedicate the first to him).

So what is the vision lying behind a scientific theology? In what follows, I shall set out the major themes that lay behind my work in this field.

The Vision of a Scientific Theology

The critical thing to appreciate is that a scientific theology is a *system*, not a single idea or cluster of ideas. A technological analogy will clarify the point I need to make here. In the fifteenth century, Johann Gutenberg developed the printing press to the point at which the large-scale commercial production of printed books could begin. Although it is often suggested that Gutenberg's breakthrough was the invention of moveable type, this is an inadequate account of his development. This new invention was placed within a system of components, each of which was brought together to create a new way of producing books. A number of existing technologies were combined with a major innovation – moveable metal type – to allow a new technology to emerge, which was greater than the sum of its individual parts. Put together, these made a coherent system, in which these developments were integrated. Each successive stage in the process depended upon that which preceded it.

Gutenberg's printing system included the following components:

1. The kind of wooden screw-press traditionally used to crush grapes for wine or olives for oil, or to compress bales of cloth. A similar press was already used in paper production, to squeeze water out of newly made paper. Gutenberg appears to have realized that the process which removed water from paper might also be used to print ink onto that same medium. An existing idea was thus adapted to a new purpose.

2. A new type of ink, made from lampblack – the soot deposited by candle flames on cold surfaces – and varnish. The older printing technology used a water-soluble brown ink, which faded over time; the new process used a dark black ink, which was permanent.
3. Moveable type – that is, letters which could be reused after printing one book.

The essential point here is that Gutenberg brought these elements together in such a way that they were integrated into an entire system which was capable of achievements which transcended the capacities of any one element.

A scientific theology is also to be seen as an integrated system, which brings together in a functional manner a number of important ideas, some of which find their first significant theological application. The accumulated significance of these is greater than any of the individual contributions. These interlocking elements include a number of complex ideas which will be explained throughout the course of this introductory volume, and are mentioned here without any explanation or comment, simply to indicate the broad scope of this systemic approach.

1. The development and thorough examination of the concept of the working methods and assumptions as a helpmate and comparator for Christian theology.
2. The insistence that Christian orthodoxy possesses in itself adequate intellectual resources to undertake a direct and fruitful engagement with the natural sciences.
3. The identification of the scientific and theological consequences of the postmodern deconstruction of nature.
4. The reappropriation of the Christian doctrine of creation as a means of revalidating an engagement with the natural world.

5. The retrieval and reconstruction of a responsible and authentically Christian natural theology.

6. The reaffirmation of theological realism, especially in a non-foundationalist context.

7. The important concept of a 'tradition-mediated' rationality, developed in response to the failures of both the Enlightenment project and its antithetically conceived postmodern alternatives.

8. The theological application of Roy Bhaskar's 'critical realism', especially the highly significant notion of the 'stratification of reality'. This represents the first such theological application of this important philosophical development.

9. A reaffirmation of the legitimate place and purpose of doctrine in the Christian life.

10. The development of new models of doctrinal development.

11. The revalidation of the traditional notions of 'heresy' and 'orthodoxy'.

12. The reaffirmation of the legitimate place of metaphysics in Christian theology.

These elements of a scientific theology are not disparate and disconnected ideas, linked together at a purely verbal level. They are seamlessly integrated to yield a coherent vision of the theological enterprise, and a justification of its existence and methods in the face of modern and postmodern criticisms and anxieties.

The distinctive feature of a scientific theology is its critical yet positive use of the natural sciences as both comparator and helpmate for the theological task, seen against the backdrop of the intellectual engagement with reality as a whole. While a scientific theology is positioned somewhere on a delicate and at times somewhat fuzzy borderline between a treatise on the relation of Christian theology and the natural sciences and a full-blown work on theological methodology, there is a third way in which my three volumes might be read – perhaps the most significant, even if it has not been uppermost in my mind as I wrote them – namely, as an apologia for the entire theological enterprise itself. Christian theology is here conceived and presented as a legitimate coherent intellectual discipline, with its own sense of identity, place and purpose. A unitary understanding of reality, such as that I believe to be mandated by a Christian doctrine of creation, thus does not demand that each human intellectual discipline should adopt identical methods for their tasks, but that they should accommodate themselves to the distinctive natures of those aspects of reality which they attempt to represent and depict.

This leads to one of the major themes of the vision that lies behind a scientific theology – my deep longing to develop a *public* theology, capable of interacting with other disciplines on its own terms. A public theology is able to stand its own ground, while engaging in dialogue with others. I have intense misgivings concerning the insular approaches to theology that I discern in some theological quarters, which prevents theology from dialoguing, debating and learning. The project for theology set out by John Milbank and others in the 'radical orthodoxy' school[6] seems to me merely to drive Christian theology into a self-imposed and intellectually sterile isolation, refusing to talk to anyone in case their theological purity gets contaminated. The approach I set out, having placed the theological enterprise on a secure footing, encourages public debate and dialogue.

The roots of a scientific theology are thoroughly evangelical, resting on a deep and passionate conviction that 'theology must be nourished and governed at all points by Holy Scripture, and that it seeks to offer a faithful and coherent account of what it finds there'.[7] This task of rendering Scripture faithfully is, in my view, best carried out in dialogue with the 'great tradition' of Christian theology and in response to the challenges to the Christian faith which are raised by other disciplines – such as the natural sciences. Yet I know that many Christian theologians who would not wish to identify or style themselves as 'evangelical' find much in *Scientific Theology* that they can welcome and appropriate; indeed, my correspondence since these volumes began to appear in print demonstrates that it is being widely and appreciatively read in mainline Protestant and Roman Catholic theological circles, as well as among natural scientists.

Yet in writing these volumes, I have had in mind a specific concern about evangelicalism, which was explored most thoroughly in 1994 by the historian Mark Noll. In his *Scandal of the Evangelical Mind*,[8] Noll argued that evangelicalism, although having developed a robust theological base since the Second World War, had yet to establish connections between its theological vision and other aspects of human intellectual and cultural activity. Evangelicalism's theological development had outstripped its capacity and will to make its appropriate intellectual applications. In developing the scientific theology project, I have been deeply mindful of this consideration. Noll may have brought this problem into sharp focus; it existed, however, before he pointed it out. A scientific theology attempts to stimulate further development, by laying a foundation which encourages academic engagement and the forging of intellectual connections.

The approach I adopt throughout these volumes is designed to safeguard the distinct place and space of Christian theology, while at the same time accentuating its intrinsic capacity to connect up with other disciplines. Theology is conceived as an intellectually robust discipline, offering Christians a vantage point from which they may explore and engage the world around them, making sense of what they observe, and offering points of contact for significant conversations and interactions. Intellectual timidity, modesty or sheer laziness must be set to one side, in order to bring Christian perspectives to bear on the many facets of the human situation. Although my approach focuses on the natural sciences, it has the capacity to relate to other disciplines. Although my approach is resolutely evangelical in orientation, I suspect that most orthodox Christians will find themselves able to relate to and identify with much of what I propose, even if they may feel the need to develop it in certain directions for their own purposes.

The approach set out, then, offers theology the opportunity to engage with the world, without being obligated to capitulate to that world as a precondition of such an engagement. Although rigorously grounded in the Christian tradition, it possesses a capacity to address issues far beyond the community of faith. A scientific theology offers an integrationist worldview, which allows faith to be brought to bear on other activities – such as the teaching and practice of the natural sciences. It remains to be seen how useful and productive this aspect of a scientific theology might be. Nevertheless, it is a characteristic feature of its approach, which distinguishes it from many of its rivals in the contemporary theological marketplace.

I

Prolegomena

1. The Legitimacy of a Scientific Theology

Many writers in the past have seen the natural sciences as an obvious dialogue partner for their own thinking. The great Marxist writer Friedrich Engels argued that Marxism represented a 'scientific' account of the world, which used basically the same methods as the natural sciences themselves. This rather naive view proved impossible to sustain, not least because Engels gave little thought to the very different issues facing the natural and social sciences. The result of his rather rhetorical appeal to the natural sciences was an allegedly 'universal' method which simply could not be applied, and was discreetly abandoned by his embarrassed successors, such as the noted Hungarian Marxist theorist Georg Lukács (1885–1971).

Yet the vision of engaging in a critical yet appreciative dialogue with the natural sciences retains a powerful appeal, not least for theologians. The real difficulty is clarifying how this dialogue can take place without destroying the distinctive character of theology.

Wrestling with this issue has been one of the central themes of the entire 'scientific theology' project, and the solution I offer rests heavily on the recognition that each scientific discipline demands an approach to its subject area which is determined by its own distinctive features – a notion which is encapsulated in the Greek phrase *kata physin*, 'according to its own nature'.

Science as the 'handmaid of theology' (ancilla theologiae)

There is a long tradition within Christian theology of drawing on intellectual resources outside the Christian tradition as a means of developing a theological vision. This approach is often referred to by the Latin phrase *ancilla theologiae*, 'a handmaid of theology'. The basic idea is that philosophical systems can be a very helpful way of stimulating theological development, and enabling a dialogue to be opened up between Christian thinkers and their cultural environment. The two most important examples of this approach to theology are the dialogues with Platonism and Aristotelianism.

The dialogue with Platonism was of immense importance during the first five centuries of the Christian Church, especially in the Greek-speaking world of the eastern Mediterranean. As Christianity expanded in that region, it encountered rival worldviews. Platonism – the immensely influential worldview resting on the dialogues of the great classical philosopher Plato and his later disciples – was easily the most important of these. Such worldviews could be seen positively or negatively: they were both an opportunity for dialogue and intellectual development, and also a threat to the existence of Christianity. The task faced by writers such as Justin Martyr or Clement of Alexandria was how to make use of the obvious intellectual merits of Platonism in constructing a Christian worldview, without compromising the integrity of Christianity itself. After all, when all is said and done, Christianity is not Platonism.

A new debate opened up in the thirteenth century, during the golden age of scholastic theology. The rediscovery of Aristotle by medieval writers seemed to offer new resources to help in every aspect of intellectual life, including physics, philosophy and ethics. It was inevitable that theologians should also want to see what use they could make of Aristotelian ideas and methods in constructing a systematic theology – such as Thomas Aquinas's massive *Summa Theologiae*, widely regarded as one of the greatest works of theology ever written.

In both these cases, using another intellectual discipline as the *ancilla theologiae* offers opportunities and risks in about equal measure. As a scientific theology argues that the working methods and assumptions of the natural sciences represent the best – indeed, we might say, the *natural* – dialogue partner for Christian theology, it is important to appreciate what these opportunities and risks are.

The two major *opportunities* offered to theology by the critical appropriation of another discipline can be summarized as follows.

1. It allows for a much more rigorous exploration of ideas than would otherwise be possible. Problems that Christian theology encounters in trying to develop its ideas often have their parallels in other disciplines. Thomas Aquinas, for example, found Aristotle's notion of an 'unmoved mover' helpful in setting out some reasons for defending the existence of God.
2. It allows Christian theology to engage in a dialogue with another worldview – a major element of the Church's witness to its secular context. Justin Martyr clearly believed that many Platonists would be so impressed by the parallels between Platonism and Christianity that they might consider

conversion. Similarly, in his 'Areopagus address' (Acts 17:22–31), Paul draws on some themes from Stoic philosophy in attempting to communicate the Christian message to Athenian culture.

Yet alongside these positive aspects of such an engagement, an obvious risk must also be noted. Ideas which are not distinctively Christian come to play a significant role in Christian theology. For example, Aristotelian ideas about how ideas were logically correlated to one another, or Cartesian ideas about the proper starting-point for any intellectual discipline, might find their way into Christian theology. On some occasions, this might turn out to be a neutral development; on others, it may eventually be recognized to have negative implications, undermining the integrity of Christian theology, and ultimately causing it to be distorted. Martin Luther, the great German reformer, argued that medieval theology had allowed a number of such distortions to arise through an excessive, and partially uncritical, use of Aristotelian ideas in the Middle Ages. A good example is the theological use of the secular Aristotelian idea that justice involves the reward of a person according to his or her achievements, which Luther regarded as a serious distortion to the doctrine of grace. For Luther, God's saving actions towards us are not based on our achievements, but upon God's graciousness.

So what 'handmaid' or 'helpmate' should be adopted? No philosophy has ever gained global acceptance. Yet the working methods of the natural sciences come very close to representing a globally valid and acceptable means of encountering reality, not least because those methods seem independent of culture, race and gender. Indeed, many natural scientists would argue that the scientific method is the nearest thing to a universally accepted and valid way of thinking that has ever been known. The natural

Saved by grace but rewarded for works.

sciences, when rightly understood, thus represent an obvious and credible dialogue partner for Christian theology. The task facing a scientific theology is thus to encourage and facilitate a respectful and positive dialogue between Christian theology and the natural sciences, without the latter overwhelming the former.

But is this dialogue arbitrary, or a matter of pure convenience? Is it theologically opportunistic? Or are there deeper reasons for seeing this dialogue as a natural element of the theological method?

The ontological imperative for theological engagement with the natural sciences

The basic argument of the 'scientific theology' project is that a positive working relationship between Christian theology and the natural sciences is demanded by the Christian understanding of reality itself. At this point, we encounter a theme of major importance to the project: the critical role of a Christian doctrine of creation. If the world is indeed the creation of God, then there is an ontological ground for a theological engagement with the natural sciences.[1] Far from being an *arbitrary* engagement – like the suggestion that we explore the interaction of stamp-collecting and Indonesian village crafts – it is a *natural* dialogue, grounded in the fundamental belief that the God about whom Christian theology speaks is the same God who created the world that the natural sciences investigate.

To speak of ontology is to introduce the idea that creation possesses a special character or nature, precisely because it has been created by God. While many twentieth-century theologians have been resistant to the idea of ontology, often seeing it as an outmoded idea of classical Greek metaphysics, a scientific theology welcomes the notion, arguing that one of the most fundamental tasks of both the natural sciences and Christian theology is to engage with the nature of reality – not deciding this in advance, but exploring and establishing it through a process of discovery and encounter.

A fundamental assumption of a scientific theology is that, since the ontology of the natural world is determined by and reflects its status as God's creation, the working methods and assumptions of the natural sciences can stimulate and inform the working methods and assumptions of a responsible Christian theology. The basic theme of 'encountering reality' runs throughout both these natural sciences and a scientific theology, and is rooted in the Christian doctrine of creation. This is not to say that the natural sciences and Christian theology are identical, either in substance or in method; the notion of an 'engagement with reality' contains within itself the related notion of engaging with each stratum of that reality *according to its distinct nature*.

Yet the Christian understanding of creation is not limited to the idea that God created the totality of reality, so that every aspect of reality, to a greater or lesser extent, mirrors the divine nature. The New Testament sees Jesus Christ as the agent of creation – the one through whom the world was made. This leads to the recognition that the same divine rationality that is *embedded* in creation is *embodied* in Jesus Christ, as God incarnate. This theme, which is found in some of the writings of the leading Scottish theologian Thomas F. Torrance, plays a major role in a scientific theology, and recurs frequently throughout these volumes.

The meanings of 'science'

The word 'science' is open to misunderstanding. In an English-language context, it has come to mean specifically 'natural science'. In other languages, however, the word has a broader sense. For example, the German term *Wissenschaft* has the more general sense of 'discipline' or 'area of study', and does not imply the specific type of approach that is associated with the human sciences such as hermeneutics, rhetoric, and so forth. The key point is that a 'scientific theology' designates a style of theology which arises out of an engagement with the *natural sciences* rather than a more generalized approach, taking into account the arts and humanities. Although the scientific theology project interacts with these at many points – for example, the exploration of the theological potential of the literary notion of 'defamiliarization' (see pp. 181–4) – the primary emphasis is always on the interaction of theology with the working methods and assumptions of the *natural* sciences.

The fragmentation of intellectual discourse

One of the underlying concerns of a scientific theology is to lay a foundation for bringing together the various aspects of the long human quest for wisdom and authenticity within the framework set out by the Christian tradition. The twentieth century witnessed a massive fragmentation of intellectual discourse. Many writers were fearful of the agenda of the Enlightenment, which they held to be disrespectful of the distinctive identities of the different areas of human thought. The Enlightenment demand that one single method could be used for – and hence imposed upon – all intellectual disciplines was fiercely resisted by writers such as Giambattista Vico (1688–1744) and Johann Gottfried Herder (1744–1803). They stressed the individuality of each discipline and, in particular, drew attention to the very different working methods of the humanities and the natural sciences.

Perhaps the most famous statement of this fragmentation of human wisdom is found in C. P. Snow's 1959 Rede Lecture at

Cambridge University. Snow argued that 'two cultures' had emerged in the West, which failed to speak to, let alone understand, each other.[2]

> The intellectual life of the whole of western society is increasingly being split into two polar groups . . . Literary intellectuals at one pole . . . at the other scientists, and as the most representative, the physical scientists. Between the two a gulf of mutual incomprehension.

So how can any such reconnection take place, without falling victim to the naive and unrealistic belief of the Enlightenment – that there exists a single method, which can be applied consistently to every discipline? That is one of the major themes to be explored by a scientific theology. Although focusing on the critical relationship between theology and the natural sciences, its methods are capable of being extended to other areas as well. The two central ideas which underlie the reformulation of method which a scientific theology demands are:

1. The notion of a *stratified reality*,[3] with reference to the writings of Roy Bhaskar. This 'critical realist' approach recognizes that reality is multi-levelled, and that a working method appropriate for one level (such as the physical) may not work at another (such as the biological or psychological). A unitary conception of reality does not entail the completely unrealistic Enlightenment dogma that every intellectual discipline must use precisely the same method of investigation.

2. The recognition that each aspect of reality demands its own distinctive method of investigation, not determined in advance by philosophers, but as a result of an engagement with reality. In other words, it is to be *a posteriori* rather than *a priori*, and is conducted *kata physin*, according to the distinctive nature of the aspect of reality under investigation.

Each of these aspects of a scientific theology will be explored in much greater detail in later chapters.

2. The Approach to be Adopted

A scientific theology is based on traditional Christian orthodoxy, rather than any of the situation-specific theologies that have emerged – and then faded away – in recent theological history. Two reasons may be given for this:

1. From a *theological* perspective, Christian orthodoxy must be considered to be the most authentic form of Christian theology, representing the consensus of the Christian communities of faith over an extended period of time.
2. From a *historical* perspective, alternatives to Christian orthodoxy generally tend to be transient developments, often linked to specific historical situations. When these circumstances pass away, their passing leads to a severe weakening of the situation-specific theology itself.

The problem of transient theological trends

Anyone who has studied the history of Christian theology soon becomes aware of the rapid rise and fall of some styles of theology. An approach to theology which was highly influential in 1920 has become useless by 1960, just as a style of theology which seemed highly promising in 1960 seems hopelessly dated by 2000. As the works of leading twentieth-century writers such as Hans Urs von Balthasar (1905–88), Karl Barth, Eberhard Jüngel (born 1934), Jürgen Moltmann and Wolfhart Pannenberg demonstrate, the most relevant and permanent contributions to theology are those which are firmly grounded in the Christian tradition as a whole. To be anchored in the past does not for one moment prevent an engagement with the present; it simply provides the stability and resources necessary for this engagement.

In the case of the scientific theology project, the theologian who exemplifies the capacity of Christian orthodoxy as a foundation for a major engagement with the natural sciences is Thomas F. Torrance (born 1914), formerly Professor of Christian Dogmatics at the University of Edinburgh, Scotland. Torrance's massive theological legacy is firmly anchored to the 'great tradition' of Christian theology, including a substantial engagement with and appropriation of the ideas of writers such as Athanasius, John Calvin and Karl Barth. From about 1969, Torrance developed a highly significant approach to the relation and interaction of Christian theology and the natural sciences.

Having thoroughly researched Torrance's theological development prior to writing the 'scientific theology' project,[4] I found him an invaluable role model for the construction of my own approach.[5] Yet my own approach to the matter was informed, not only by the intellectual resiliency of the 'great tradition' of Christian theology, but also by the vulnerability and transience of contemporary theological trends. In particular, I found myself puzzled by the way in which one clearly transient theological trend – process thought – had become so influential within the 'science and religion' field. Process thought, based primarily on the philosophy of Alfred North Whitehead (1861–1947), interprets doctrines in Christianity and other world religions in terms of Whitehead's view of the world as a 'process'. The approach was developed theologically in the writings of Charles Hartshorne (1897–2000), distancing it significantly from the approach of classical Christian theology. For an influential group of theologians, especially in North America, process thought had become the only acceptable intermediary in the dialogue between Christian theology and the natural sciences. Perhaps because I initially specialized in the natural sciences, I could easily relate to those natural scientists who found process thought totally implausible.

The approach to a scientific theology which I adopt is based on the assumption that there is no *specific* intermediary necessary for a dialogue between Christian theology and the natural sciences, let alone one so unconvincing and outdated as process thought. A direct, rather than a mediated dialogue is clearly called for, and can easily be grounded in the basic notions of Christian orthodoxy, such as a doctrine of creation. For this reason, I insist that it is the 'great tradition' of Christian theology which offers the best approach to a constructive engagement with the natural sciences, both in terms of its *resilience* (it will not become outdated, unlike some of its proposed alternatives) and its *fecundity* (as the writings of Torrance and others make clear, such a basis is immensely productive and helpful).

This might seem to suggest that this is an essentially pragmatic approach, in that I have selected the approach to Christian theology which seems best suited for the task in terms of its permanency and utility. In fact, the real reason is that I believe that this is the *right* approach, in that it is grounded in the ontology of the created world, as disclosed by the Christian revelation, and that its double merits arise directly from its theological reliability.

However, it is not only Christian theology which undergoes changes. The natural sciences themselves have undergone radical change over the last centuries, and will do so in the future. So how can this be accommodated within a scientific theology?

The provisionality of scientific conclusions

Neither Christian theology nor the natural sciences are static disciplines. We have already noted how Christian theology undergoes periodic revision, often in response to particular situations within the culture at large, even if it could be argued that it nevertheless keeps certain core ideas at the centre of its vision. The same is also true of the natural sciences. Each generation within the scientific community finds itself overturning the judgements of earlier generations, even though these were firmly believed to be correct at the time.

Many examples can be given to illustrate this point. Isaac Newton's theory of light was widely regarded as the best available by scientists of the eighteenth century. It was displaced by Fresnel's rival theory in the nineteenth, before both were overtaken by the quantum theory of light, developed in the early twentieth century. The development of scientific theories is a relatively well understood aspect of the history and philosophy of the natural sciences, and has important implications for a 'scientific theology'. The most important of these is the recognition that today's scientific theories may give way to something quite different in the future.

A theology which thus grounds itself in 'the secure findings of the natural sciences' will find itself shifting with every scientific advance, as old theories are abandoned, and new ones adopted. As the philosopher Karl Popper has pointed out, the paradox of the scientific method is that while science is the most criticially tested and evaluated form of knowledge available, it is nevertheless tentative and provisional. Indeed, the history of science shows a steady progression from one theory which was believed to be right in its day to another which replaces it – for example, the ether theory of light. As Michael Polanyi (1891–1976), a chemist and noted philosopher of science, pointed out, natural scientists find themselves having to believe some things that they know will later be shown to be wrong – but not being sure *which* of their present beliefs will subsequently turn out to be erroneous.

One of the most dramatic changes in recent scientific culture has been Albert Einstein's theory of relativity, which called into question some of the settled assumptions of Newton's physics. Yet many theologians were unwise enough to assume that Newton's ideas were permanent features of the intellectual landscape, and based their theologies upon them. What was regarded as thoroughly up-to-date by the standards of 1730 now seems hopeless outdated. The same issue arises in connection with William Paley's celebrated *Natural Theology*, the credibility of which was unassailable in 1830, yet fatally compromised by 1870 through the rise of Charles Darwin's theory of natural selection. Yet this is the inevitable consequence of rapid scientific advance: any theology which is based on contemporary scientific theories will find itself outdated with embarrassing speed.

So what can be done? How can a scientific theology be developed, when the natural sciences themselves are undergoing such rapid change, through the accumulation of experimental observations, and the development of new theoretical approaches?

The procedure adopted here bases a scientific theology on the working methods and assumptions of the natural sciences, not any specific theories which result at any given time from the application of those theories – supremely a belief in the regularity of the natural world, and the ability of the human mind to uncover and represent this regularity in a mathematical manner. Both the Copernican and Ptolemaic theories of the solar system were based upon the same rigorous observations and the assumption of mathematical representation of the system; yet the two theories were quite different. This approach avoids locking a scientific theology into a theory which is acceptable today, but is discarded tomorrow. Instead, it grounds the interaction on something more fundamental than scientific theories – namely, the scientific method itself, which ultimately underlies them.

The importance of this conclusion will be obvious. The approach to a scientific theology I advocate in this project is not dependent upon current (provisional) scientific theorizing. Although I make an appeal to the Copenhagen school of quantum theory at several points, this is primarily to note issues of approach or representation that are encountered in the natural sciences. My approach would not be invalidated – or even disadvantaged – if it were to be shown in fifty years' time that this specific approach to quantum theory now had to be regarded as untenable.

Or, to take a more radical possibility. Suppose that, one hundred years from now, Darwin's theory of evolution was no longer accepted as the best explanation of the origins of our present biological system. Once more, my approach would not be invalidated. My appeal to Darwin has been primarily to the issues he faced in relation to explanatory issues and the complex set of questions that arise concerning abduction to the past in any scientific discipline – including, incidentally, a scientific theology itself. (The term 'abduction' is here used in the sense developed by the American philosopher Charles Sanders Peirce (1839–1914), meaning the way in which it is appropriate to argue backwards from observations to their presumed explanation – in other words, to the process by which a hypothesis is generated. Peirce contrasted this approach with induction and deduction.) Yet a new theoretical interpretation of the biological data would not invalidate any of the assumptions of my approach.

This might be seen as an attempt to evade difficult issues. In fact, I regard it as the only possible informed response to the historical inevitability of theoretical development. It is a simple matter of fact that scientific theories change, often quite radically – even though this must be seen as a legitimate aspect of the overall scientific quest for the best possible approximation to the truth. In his 1997–8 John Locke lectures at Oxford University, Lawrence Sklar noted the importance of the transience of scientific theories:[6]

> There have been periods in the history of physics when scientists may very well have believed, and believed with good reason, that they had finally found the stable, true theory of at least a portion of the world. Perhaps the first half of the eighteenth century constitutes such a period, at least as far as a portion of dynamics is concerned. But after the history of radical expansion, revision and revolution that has constituted theoretical physics over the last centuries, isn't it the case that the only reasonable belief to hold is that our current best theories are ultimately headed for the scrap-heap that has welcomed their predecessors?

In practice, Sklar does not draw this conclusion, and makes some important points about continuity within theory development. Yet the importance of his point to the project of a scientific theology can hardly be overlooked, nor its implications conveniently disregarded. The only legitimate means of coping with this is to affirm the priority of the scientific method itself over the outcomes of its applications – which is the approach adopted throughout the scientific theology project.

Engaging with Christian theology, not 'religions'

A scientific theology project deals specifically with the interaction between Christian theology and the natural sciences. This specific focus on Christian theology, rather than the more generalized and elusive category of 'religion', is of major importance. There are two main reasons for this.

First, no general theory of 'religion' commands universal assent. There have been a number of rather ambitious proposals set forward over the last two hundred years, including classic

accounts from Karl Marx and Sigmund Freud, and more recent
suggestions from writers such as John Hick and Wilfred Cantwell
Smith. Yet none seem capable of doing justice to the rich diversity of the religious landscape of humanity, just as none seem
entirely innocent of the particular purposes and prejudices of
those who develop them.

Second, it is quite clear that there are major divergences between
the religions on a number of themes of direct relevance to the
natural sciences. An obvious example is provided by Islam's intense
misgivings concerning any idea of a 'natural knowledge of God',
independent of the Qur'an. Although there was a period during
the Middle Ages in which Islamic philosophers were receptive to
the ideas of Greek philosophy, including the concept of 'natural
theology', these notions were generally viewed with intense suspicion by the more militant defenders of Islamic orthodoxy, such as
al-Ghazali (1058–1111). In the brief conclusion to his major work
On the Incoherence of the Philosophers, al-Ghazali argues that
'anyone who believes in them ought to be branded with infidelity,
and punished with death'. Other examples could easily be given.

A scientific theology is explicitly grounded on the distinctive
ideas of Christianity, some of which can be argued to have been
of importance to the historical development of the natural sciences. This is a position which may be maintained with integrity,
rather than attempting to identify a set of universal religious
beliefs, common to all faiths – an undertaking, it must be added,
which has failed to achieve its stated objectives with any degree of
conviction. This position cannot be finally refuted as wrong; yet
it is so flawed and contested that it cannot conceivably act as the
basis of a critical and systematic engagement of the relation of
Christianity – or, for that matter, any religion – and the natural
sciences. A scientific theology is thus fundamentally Christian in
its foundation and in its approach.

This is not to say that a scientific theology is unable or unwilling to enter into dialogue with other religious traditions. As I make clear later, one of the major advantages of this approach to theology is that it is able to offer a respectful account of why other traditions exist, as well as defending its own distinctive position and ideas. Instead of offering a 'view from nowhere', a scientific theology is firmly rooted in the realities and particularities of the Christian tradition, from which it is able to offer an account of the successes of the natural sciences, as well as the existence of alternatives to itself.

Finally, it is vital to adopt a realist perspective in theology. Commitment to such an approach immediately suggests that a scientific theology does not lay down in advance what God is like or how God may be encountered, but seeks to establish these by reflection on how God is actually known. In other words, knowledge of God and of the things of God is declared to be *a posteriori* rather than *a priori*. It also raises the question of how this reality may be represented and depicted – an issue discussed at considerable length in the third and final volume of the series – *Theory* (pp. 171–245).

This brief introduction to some of the themes of a scientific theology has laid the groundwork for the first major topic to be explored in depth – the status of nature as a theological resource.

2

Nature

3. The Construction of Nature

We now turn to one of the most important questions to confront any contemporary Christian theology: What is nature? The word is often used loosely, apparently on the assumption that its meaning is self-evident. In fact, it is an extremely elusive concept, which possesses different meanings for different interest groups. The clarification of what the word 'nature' means is therefore of considerable importance.

The first major issue to be considered is the difficult issue of the social construction of 'nature'. Many writers assume that 'nature' is easily defined, so that the morally and theologically important concept of 'the natural' can be clarified without any great difficulty. The family of philosophies known as 'naturalism' rather charmingly assume that there is an objective concept of nature which can be established by unbiased observation, and which is in some way philosophically and ethically normative. For some writers, moral behaviour is about *natural* behaviour. To define 'nature' is thus the first step in constructing a major philosophical or ethical system. The issue is also of considerable importance theologically, on account of the concept of 'natural theology'. Is there a theology implicit within nature itself, that might allow us access to God on our own terms, without reference to divine self-revelation? To gain such knowledge would, in the view of some early Enlightenment writers, be like stealing fire from the gods.

The many faces of nature

A close examination of writings on nature over the last two thousand years reveals a disturbing and immensely significant fact. Far from being an *autonomous* and self-sufficient notion, 'nature' turns out to be an *interpreted* concept. There is no single 'correct' notion of nature, but a multiplicity of competing notions. In his important work *The Abolition of Man*, C. S. Lewis argues that 'nature' is the term we use to describe what we have mastered.[1]

> We reduce things to mere Nature *in order that* we may conquer them. We are always conquering Nature, *because* 'Nature' is the name for what we have, to some extent, conquered. The price of conquest is to treat a thing as mere Nature.

Lewis's argument illustrates the difficulties in treating the notion of 'nature' as a self-evident category. For some, nature is what humanity has failed to control – such as the great wildernesses of North America; for others, Lewis suggests, it is the name applied to what humanity has conquered.

We are faced with the intensely troubling conclusion that definitions of nature do not depend upon some intrinsic property of the natural world, but are actually the construction of human agents. There is no self-evidently correct definition of 'nature' which has been accepted at all times, in all places, and by all people – or anything even approaching such a consensus. The history of the concept of nature demonstrates that a wide variety of concepts have been developed, discarded, invented and re-invented, throughout the long period of human reflection on the world around them.

The history of nature

Human understandings of nature have developed considerably over the last two thousand years, without any consensus emerging or being entailed by the natural order itself. This is evident from the classic period, in which the Greek word *physis* ('nature') is used by various writers in different senses, without any obvious consensus on how it is to be defined. While Aristotle offers what is perhaps the most developed classic account of how 'nature' is to be understood, it is immensely problematic.

While pre-Socratic Greek writers suggested that *physis* ('nature') was a blind force, operating by chance, Plato argued that three levels of agency or operation could be distinguished within the world – nature, art and chance. These ideas were developed further by Aristotle, who attempted to bring clarity to the distinction. 'Art' (*techne*) refers to those aspects of the world which are clearly the result of human agency, whether this refers to features of the landscape – such as temples or cities – or actions which clearly owe their origins to humans, such as a stone being thrown in the air. 'Nature' (*physis*) designated those remaining aspects of the world which happen on a regular basis, apparently as a result of the way things are, without any human agency being required – such as water flowing, or plants growing. Finally, Aristotle recognized a third category, 'chance' (*tyche*), to account for those events in the world which cannot be accounted for by human agency or natural processes.

There is no doubt that, at least at some points in history, nature was seen as something that was ontologically given – something that possessed a definite, objective character, which human reason could grasp and use as the basis of moral living. Yet in more recent times, this view has become increasingly difficult to sustain, precisely because it has become more and more obvious that nature is an interpreted notion. It is not a piece of 'raw data', but something which we choose to view in certain ways. In the twentieth century, those ways of 'viewing' nature have included:[2]

- nature as a mindless force, causing inconvenience to humanity, and demanding to be tamed;
- nature as an open-air gymnasium, offering leisure and sports facilities to affluent individuals who want to demonstrate their sporting prowess;
- nature as a wild kingdom, encouraging scuba-diving, hiking and hunting;
- nature as a supply depot – an ageing and increasingly reluctant provider which produces (although with growing difficulty) minerals, water, food and other services for humanity.

These views of nature are not simply different; they are inconsistent with each other.

The changing understandings of what 'nature' entails can also be seen in the imagery that is used to depict nature. Medieval writers regarded nature as a living organism, and often used the image of 'the female' as a means of emphasizing its living, productive aspects. Thus Geoffrey Chaucer saw nature as a nurturing mother, who sustained and supported humanity during its time on earth. Yet the rise of the mechanical worldview of the eighteenth century led to a new way of looking at nature, which stressed its regularities. Nature was now conceived primarily as a mechanism, with the image of a clock or watch being regarded as especially appropriate. Isaac Newton's immense scientific successes in explaining the motions of the planets led many to draw the conclusion that nature was a titanic self-regulating mechanism. This idea is also found in William Paley's *Natural Theology*, which uses the image of nature as a watch to affirm the importance of believing in a divine watchmaker.

Other images of nature can be set alongside these – for example, the great Renaissance images of nature as a mirror, theatre, or book, or the more recent suggestion that nature is again to be conceived as a living organism, found in the 'Gaia' hypothesis – that nature is essentially a living organism – set out by James Lovelock. In every case, the preferred image corresponds to the prejudices and settled convictions of a given social group at a given point in history. Yet this fluidity of imagery reflects a corresponding indeterminacy of the concept of nature itself. To define nature is thus not to respond to some objective aspect of the world, which must be normative for our thinking. It is to *impose* such a meaning upon it, choosing to view it in a certain way, which ultimately reflects the agendas of those wishing to define it in this highly prescriptive manner.

For this reason, many writers have argued that nature is a constructed notion, which must be deconstructed in order to expose and neutralize these hidden agendas of those who seek to define nature in such ways.

The deconstruction of nature

The rise of postmodernity in the last fifty years has been of enormous importance to the way in which the concept of nature is interpreted. A fundamental weariness with the pretensions of the Enlightenment has swept through western culture. There has been a widespread reaction against Marxism, Stalinism, imperialism, colonialism and many other aspects of the culture of the Enlightenment. 'It is the nature of men having escaped one extreme, which by force they were constrained long to endure, to run headlong into the other extreme, forgetting that virtue doth always consist in the mean' (Sir Walter Raleigh). In reacting against the intellectual totalitarianism of the Enlightenment, western culture has generally set its face against such ideas, and turned to embrace their antithesis. Instead of accepting that there is only one, objective, self-evidently correct way of seeing things, we must recognize that there are many equally valid ways of conceiving the world.

The Enlightenment's rigid approach to reality, which recognized only one valid way of thinking and representing reality, is now held to be inflexible by postmodern writers. Writers such as Michel Foucault argued that the philosophical systems of the Enlightenment encouraged oppression and totalitarianism. Jean-François Lyotard argued that all allegedly 'universal' systems, such as Marxism, were totalitarian in their outlook, and hence potentially capable of generating mindsets which were conducive to 'crimes against humanity'. If people are convinced of the rightness of their own position, there is inevitably a temptation to control or destroy those who disagree with them. The Enlightenment thus had a hidden agenda: the domination of others and nature. It was inevitable, according to Foucault, that the great totalitarian states of the twentieth century would rise. Only by rejecting the philosophy on which they were ultimately based could humanity avoid future catastrophes of this kind.

For postmodern writers, the dismantling of the dysfunctional Enlightenment project involved abandoning the notion that there is any 'right' way of reading a text, or seeing the world. The interpretations people offer of texts are constructions, reflecting their own agendas. They are free creations of the human mind, not con-clusions which are imposed upon humanity, by force of argument or evidence. Three elements can be discerned within this approach.

First, there is no objective reality outside the text which somehow determines the shape of the text, or the manner in which it is to be interpreted. This is often summarized in Jacques Derrida's famous slogan *il n'y a pas de hors-texte* ('there is no outside the text'). There is thus no controlling reality outside the text by which the meaning of that text can be determined.

Second, the identity and intentions of the author of a text are declared to be an irrelevance to its interpretation. It is the reader, not the author, of the text who has the right to determine its meaning. This idea is often referred to using Roland Barthes's famous phrase 'the death of the author'.

Third, having challenged the assumption that there exists some reality outside the text, postmodern writers argue for the legiti-macy of multiple readings of all texts. As there is no objective reality outside the text to control its interpretation, the text must either be recognized to have no intrinsic meaning or an indeter-minate meaning. As a result, any meanings that are attached to the text are the creation of its readers, not the necessary outcome of the text itself.

When taken together, these three factors lead to the recogni-tion that any meaning that is identified within a text is ultimately the creation of the reader. There is no means of validating that interpretation, because there is no objective criterion – such as authorial intention, or an extra-textual reality – by which such a reading may be challenged, and either found to be wanting, or corroborated. While I personally regard this as a considerable overstatement, and would wish to critique this position at several major points, the postmodern criticism of the Enlightenment raises fundamental questions about how nature is to be seen.

The relevance of postmodernism to the issue of the theological status of nature will be fairly obvious. Postmodernity argues that there is no single authoritative reading of the concept of 'nature'. Historical analysis demonstrates that there have been multiple readings of nature throughout human culture, just as philosophical analysis makes it clear that the notion that there is only one such reading is repressive and authoritarian. Nature has often been likened to a book. Galileo Galilei affirmed that 'philosophy is written in this grand book, the universe, which stands continually open to our gaze'. Similar thoughts can be found expressed in Sir Thomas Browne's 1643 classic *Religio Medici*:[3]

> There are two books from whence I collect my divinity. Besides that written one of God, another of his servant, nature, that universal and publick manuscript, that lies expansed unto the eyes of all. Those that never saw him in the one have discovered him in the other.

Writers such as Browne argued that their divinity was based on the reading of two texts – Scripture and nature. The image of nature as a book, however, has proved vulnerable to some of the core assumptions of the postmodern deconstruction of both texts and their authors, on the basis of the points noted above. There is thus no self-evidently correct way of 'reading the book of nature', no single objective concept of nature that may be regarded as normative, and no universal doctrine of the natural.

To make this point is most emphatically not to endorse the postmodern agenda. There are serious problems with the postmodern insinuation that the theories of the natural sciences are just as socially constructed as any other kinds of theory. This failure on the part of postmodern writers to engage properly with the working assumptions and methods of the natural sciences is deeply troubling. When added to the self-referentiality which plagues postmodern accounts of reality, these concerns severely undermine the plausibility of the entire postmodern project.

The postmodern agenda fails when dealing with the empirical investigation of – for example – the behaviour of alpha particles in an electric field, and its theoretical implications. Yet the postmodern critique is powerful and effective when dealing with notions which clearly are 'constructed' – such as the idea of 'nature'. This is not to deny the existence of trees, rivers, stars and wild animals. It is to reject the notion of the 'reification' of nature – that is, the idea that there is one coherent concept, arising naturally and objectively out of such things, which can be called 'nature', which is uninterpreted and can hence function in a philosophically, theologically or ethically *foundational* role.

This point is not new. In the seventeenth century, Robert Boyle protested against the reification of nature. 'Nature', he argued, is a fictitious entity, which exists to no greater extent than the 'astral beings' of some of the more exotic schools of philosophy of his day. 'Nature', for Boyle, is merely a conventional way of referring to an external reality consisting of an aggregate of individual entities. Trees, elephants and other such bodies can be considered to make up 'nature'; yet there is no substance or self-sufficient entity of 'nature', existing in and of itself. 'Nature is the aggregate of bodies, that make up the world.' Its individual members have real existence; but the inferred overall notion of 'nature' is questionable.

A theology which builds on an alleged 'natural' approach to ethics or philosophy (such as 'Naturalism') thus finds itself in serious difficulties. Its plausibility rests on the belief that there is something *objective* or *given* about nature, which can function as the basis of a philosophical or ethical system. Yet it is now widely recognized that there is no 'given' – only the 'constructed'. In the end, naturalism is one of many rival readings of nature, not the only one (as its supporters seem to believe). It is not the only

option, nor even the most plausible, in that the reasons for accepting it lie not so much in nature itself, as in the social situation of
those who construct it.

Some might regard this as a problem. A scientific theology,
however, regards this as opening the way to reclaiming the validity of a Christian reading of *nature as creation*. In a series of writings, the philosopher of science Norbert R. Hanson argues that
we always see the world as something. We view the world through
theoretical spectacles, whether we realize this or not. We do not
simply 'see' nature; we *see it as something*. So what is the best way
of viewing nature? Or, if this question cannot be answered – and
most would now say that it cannot – what is the most authentically *Christian* way of viewing nature? What does Christian tradition see nature as?

If there is no autonomous character to creation, which forces
humanity to see it in one way, to the exclusion of all others, then
Christianity is free to reassert its distinctive understanding of
nature. Nature, it must be agreed, is an *interpreted* concept; all
bring their own interpretations to the natural order, and none can
be regarded as authoritative or binding for all. There is, after all,
a distinctive Christian way of looking at nature – as creation.

For this reason, we may proceed immediately to explore the
contours of a Christian doctrine of creation, and the reading it
offers of the natural world.

4. The Christian Doctrine of Creation

If the concept of nature is not autonomous or free-standing, but
ultimately represents an *interpretation* of the world, there is no self-
evidently correct or 'objective' way of reading nature. The
Enlightenment view that there is only one reading of nature, forced
upon us by nature itself, is no longer regarded as convincing.

Nature does not demand to be interpreted in any particular way, but is capable of being 'read' (to use the textual metaphor of 'nature as a book') in a number of quite different ways. This has a vitally important corollary: *the Christian theologian is not under any obligation to accept as normative a definition of nature originating from outside the Christian tradition.* Instead, Christian theology may deploy and explore its own distinctive understanding of what others call nature, but which the Christian tradition prefers to name 'creation'. I thus criticize Wolfhart Pannenberg's somewhat hasty abandonment of the category of 'creation'. Pannenberg's insistence that we speak of a 'theology of nature' fails to take account of the problems in conceiving 'nature', and seems to suppose that 'nature' is an uncontested observable reality, firmly located in the public arena.

The Christian tradition is bilingual, using its own distinctive language and that of the world around it. For this reason, my emphasis on the importance of the language of 'creation' should not be seen as implying that the somewhat different language of 'nature' should be avoided. I can see a perfectly good case being made for using 'creation' (or related phrases, such as 'the created order') when speaking of the world from a specifically Christian perspective, and 'nature' (or related phrases, such as 'the natural world') when speaking of that same entity from a more secular perspective. Translation and interpretation of terminologies are an essential aspect of any constructive theology, especially one that is sensitive to the need to speak to an audience outside the Christian tradition.

Yet the fact remains that the most authentic Christian mode of conceiving and engaging with the natural order is framed in terms of *creation*. The Oxford philosopher Michael B. Foster (1903–59) highlights the critical role of the doctrine of creation, especially in relation to the development of the natural sciences.[4]

Foster argues that Christianity's doctrine of creation made it possible to study *the works of God* without being hamstrung by the unhelpful notion that nature *is God*.[5]

> On the Christian conception, on the other hand, nature is made by God, but *is not* God. There is an abrupt break between nature and God. Divine worship is to be paid to God alone, who is *wholly other than nature*. Nature is not divine.

Having established the importance of the doctrine of creation to the relation – both historical and intellectual – of Christian theology and the natural sciences, I now turn to a detailed engagement with the themes of the doctrine of creation, beginning by exploring its biblical foundations.

The biblical concept of creation

Although it is traditional to base an analysis of the biblical doctrine of creation primarily on the Genesis creation accounts, with which the Old Testament canon opens, it must be appreciated that the theme is deeply embedded throughout the historical, wisdom and prophetic literature – the three main types of writing found in the Old Testament. For example, Job 38:1–42:6 (usually regarded as a piece of wisdom literature) sets out what is unquestionably the most comprehensive understanding of God as creator to be found in the Old Testament, stressing the role of God as creator and sustainer of the world. A variety of Hebrew verbs is found, with slightly different overtones, embracing such notions as 'to make', 'to form', 'to establish', 'to create', and 'to found'.

It is possible to discern two distinct, though related, contexts in which the notion of 'God as creator' is encountered. First, in contexts which reflect the praise of God within Israel's worship, both individual and corporate. Reflection on the glories of the creation are understood to elicit praise of God as their creator. Second, in contexts which stress that the God who created the world is also the God who liberated Israel from bondage, and continues to sustain her in the present. This becomes of particular importance to Israel in moments of national distress – for example, during the period of exile in Babylon. The declaration that the Lord is creator of all the world is an assertion of the sovereignty of the Lord over all the nations, including those who temporarily oppress the people of Israel. This can be seen in texts such as Isaiah 40, addressed to the community in exile:

> To whom will you compare me? Or who is my equal? says the Holy One. Lift your eyes and look to the heavens: Who created all these? He who brings out the starry host one by one, and calls them each by name. Because of his great power and mighty strength, not one of them is missing. Why do you say, O Jacob, and complain, O Israel, 'My way is hidden from the LORD; my cause is disregarded by my God?' Do you not know? Have you not heard? The LORD is the everlasting God, the Creator of the ends of the earth. He will not grow tired or weary, and his understanding no one can fathom. He gives strength to the weary and increases the power of the weak. Even youths grow tired and weary, and young men stumble and fall; but those who hope in the LORD will renew their strength. They will soar on wings like eagles; they will run and not grow weary, they will walk and not be faint. (Isaiah 40:25–31)

Of particular interest for our purposes is the Old Testament theme of 'creation as ordering', and the manner in which the critically important theme of 'order' is established on and justified with reference to cosmological foundations. It has often been pointed out how the Old Testament portrays creation in terms of an engagement with and victory over forces of chaos. This 'establishment of order' is generally represented in two different ways:

1. Creation is an imposition of order on a formless chaos. This model is especially associated with the image of a potter working clay into a recognizably ordered structure (e.g. Genesis 2:7; Isaiah 29:16; 44:8; Jeremiah 18:1–6).

2. Creation concerns conflict with a series of chaotic forces, often depicted as a dragon or another monster (variously named 'Behemoth', 'Leviathan', 'Nahar', 'Rahab', 'Tannim', or 'Yam') who must be subdued (Job 3:8; 7:12; 9:13; 40:15–32; Psalms 74:13–15; 139:10–11; Isaiah 27:1; 41:9–10; Zechariah 10:11).

It is clear that there are parallels between the Old Testament account of God engaging with the forces of chaos and Ugaritic and Canaanite mythology. Nevertheless, there are significant differences at points of importance, not least in the Old Testament's insistence that the forces of chaos are not to be seen as divine. Creation is not be to understood in terms of different gods warring against each other for mastery of a (future) universe, but in terms of God's mastery of chaos and ordering of the world.

Old Testament writers sometimes appeal to God's victory over the primeval forces of chaos as a means of reassurance. Will not the God who battled and overwhelmed such enemies at the foundation of the world be able to protect his people from their enemies in the present?

> Awake, awake! Clothe yourself with strength, O arm of the LORD; awake, as in days gone by, as in generations of old. Was it not you who cut Rahab to pieces, who pierced that monster through? Was it not you who dried up the sea, the waters of the great deep, who made a road in the depths of the sea so that the redeemed might cross over? (Isaiah 51:9–10)

In the New Testament, we find a growing emphasis upon the Christological aspects of creation. Christ is to be seen as the agent of creation. The prologue to John's Gospel (John 1:1–18) offers a highly suggestive parallel to the first Genesis creation account, while making it clear that creation is to be seen as Christological. The Word, or *logos*, by whom God created all things is declared to have 'become flesh', and dwelt among humanity. We see here one of the most important themes to inform the distinctive approach of a scientific theology – the recognition that the *logos* through whom God created the world became incarnate in Christ. The same *logos* which is embedded in creation is embodied in Christ. The rationality reflected in the ordering of the world is thus incarnate in the redeemer, establishing a link between the divine acts of creation and redemption.

Creation out of nothing (ex nihilo): *the development of a doctrine*

The Old Testament places considerable emphasis on the idea of creation as *ordering*. Yet this could, some argue, be interpreted in terms of imposing order on existing material. Creation would thus be understood as the fashioning of building materials into an ordered construction, or the moulding of an existing plastic material into something more structured. In each case, the act of creation is understood to presuppose starting materials. The development of the doctrine of creation out of nothing (*ex nihilo*) is linked with the growing realization that the idea of 'creation as ordering pre-existent matter' was vulnerable to certain criticisms, and seemed inconsistent with some fundamental New Testament themes.

In one of his dialogues (*Timaeus*), Plato developed the idea that the world was made out of pre-existent matter, which was fashioned into the present form of the world. This idea was taken up by most Gnostic writers, who professed a belief in pre-existent matter, which was shaped into the world in the act of creation.

Creation was not *ex nihilo*; rather, it was to be seen as an act of construction, on the basis of material which was already to hand, as one might construct an igloo out of snow, or a house from stone. The existence of evil in the world was thus to be explained on the basis of the intractability of this pre-existent matter. God's options in creating the world were limited by the poor quality of the material available. The presence of evil or defects within the world are thus not to be ascribed to God, but to deficiencies in the material from which the world was constructed.

However, the conflict with Gnosticism forced reconsideration of this issue. In part, the idea of creation from pre-existent matter was discredited by its Gnostic associations; in part, it was called into question by an increasingly sophisticated reading of the Old Testament creation narratives. Writers such as Theophilus of Antioch insisted upon the doctrine of creation *ex nihilo*, which may be regarded as gaining the ascendency from the end of the second century onwards. From that point onwards, it became the received doctrine within the Church.

In the long process of seeking the best interpretation of the biblical witness to the divine act of creation, especially in the face of the threat from Gnosticism, Christian theologians gradually came to the conclusion that creation was best understood as an action *ex nihilo* ('out of nothing'). For Gnosticism, in most of its significant forms, a sharp distinction was to be drawn between the God who redeemed humanity from the world, and a somewhat inferior deity (often termed 'the demiurge') who created that world in the first place. The Old Testament was regarded by the Gnostics as dealing with this lesser deity, whereas the New Testament was concerned with the redeemer God. As such, belief in God as creator and in the authority of the Old Testament came to be interlinked at an early stage.

The importance of the decisive rejection of Gnosticism by the early Church for the development of the natural sciences has been explored by Thomas F. Torrance, who points out that the affirmation of the fundamental goodness of creation 'established the reality of the empirical, contingent world, and thus destroyed the age-old Hellenistic and Oriental assumption that the real is reached only by transcending the contingent'. Against any idea that the natural order was chaotic, irrational or inherently evil (three concepts which were often regarded as interlocking), the early Christian tradition affirmed that the natural order possessed a goodness, rationality and orderedness which derived directly from its creation by God.

A radical dualism between God and creation was thus eliminated, in favour of the view that the truth, goodness and beauty of God (to use the three famous concepts usually known as 'the Platonic triad', which so influenced many writers of the period) could be discerned within the natural order, in consequence of that order having been established by God. For example, Origen argued that it was God's creation of the world which structured the natural order in such a manner that it could be comprehended by the human mind, by conferring upon that order an intrinsic rationality and order which derived from and reflected the divine nature itself.

The doctrine of creation *ex nihilo* has a double significance for a scientific theology:

1. The doctrine of creation *ex nihilo* is primarily concerned with the ontological dependence of the cosmos upon its creator.
2. The doctrine affirms that God, in creating the universe, was not constrained by the limitations of the already existing stuff from which that universe was to be fashioned, but was free to bring into existence a universe in which the divine

will was recognizably embodied and enacted. This has particular importance for the positive statement of a 'natural theology', as we shall note later.

Christian formulations of the doctrine of creation

In most classic formulations of Christian dogmatics, the doctrine of creation is given a very high profile, often being the first major doctrine to be explored within the system as a whole. Two factors are of particular importance in relation to this development:

1. The doctrine of creation is the first major theological statement to be encountered by the reader of the Bible, as set out in the canonical form.
2. The two most influential communal statements of Christian faith to be recognized by the Church – the Nicene Creed, and the Apostles' Creed – both open with an affirmation of God as creator. In that many classic Christian discussions of systematic theology tend broadly to follow the credal ordering of doctrinal affirmations (see, for example, John Calvin's *Institutes of the Christian Religion*), the doctrine of creation is thus frequently to the fore in theological analysis.

The doctrine is of especial consequence for a scientific theology, which accentuates this doctrine on account of its obvious importance to an engagement with the world, especially through the natural sciences.

The rich theological potential of this doctrine for a scientific theology is illustrated in the doctrines of creation found in Thomas Aquinas, John Calvin and Karl Barth. These different yet representative writers can be seen as exploring some of the major themes of the doctrine. Aquinas, for example, stresses the analogi-

cal implications of creation; Calvin notes the distorting impact of
sin upon both the created order and the human ability to perceive
the creator through the creation; Barth raises concerns as to
whether creation can be said to possess an intrinsic capacity to
reveal its creator, or whether this ought to be regarded as
grounded in the covenant between God and humanity.

An emphasis on creation: a Deist strategy?

A scientific theology places considerable emphasis upon a
Christian doctrine of creation, regarding this as the most appropriate and most truthful lens through which to view and interpret
the world. Yet even a modest knowledge of the history of
Christian doctrine flags up a potential problem at this point.
Surely this sounds like Deism, a discredited and impoverished
account of Christian theology which flourished in the eighteenth
century, and is now regarded as philosophically and theologically
untenable? It is an important point, and merits close discussion.
First, we may clarify what Deism is.

The rise of Deism is to be traced back to the late seventeenth
and early eighteenth centuries, and is particularly associated with
the rise of the Newtonian worldview. Isaac Newton (1642–1727)
was able to demonstrate that a single physical principle could be
seen as lying behind the complexities of 'celestial mechanics' – the
motions of the planets. Newton was able to demonstrate that a vast
range of observational data could be explained on the basis of a set
of universal principles. Newton's successes in explaining terrestrial
and celestial mechanics led to the rapid development of the idea
that the universe could be thought of as a great machine, acting
according to fixed laws. This is often referred to as a 'mechanistic
worldview', in that the operation of nature is explained on the
assumption that it is a machine operating according to fixed rules.

The religious implications of this will be clear. The idea of the world as a machine immediately suggested the idea of *design*. Newton himself was supportive of this interpretation. Although later writers tended to suggest that the mechanism in question was totally self-contained and self-sustaining – and therefore did not require the existence of a God – this view was not widely held in the 1690s. Perhaps the most famous application of Newton's approach is found in the writings of William Paley, who compared the complexity of the natural world with the design of a watch. Both implied design and purpose, and thus pointed to a creator.

Newton's emphasis on the regularity of nature also encouraged the rise of 'Deism'. The term 'deism' (from the Latin *deus*, 'god') is often used in a general sense to refer to that view of God which maintains God's creatorship, but denies a continuing divine involvement with, or special presence within, that creation. It is thus often contrasted with 'theism' (from the Greek *theos*, 'god'), which allows for continuing divine involvement within the world. Deism can be regarded as a form of Christianity which placed particular emphasis on the regularity of the world, yet which was widely regarded by its critics as having reduced God to a mere clockmaker.

The term 'Deism' is used to refer to the views of a group of English thinkers during the 'Age of Reason', in the late seventeenth and early eighteenth centuries. In his influential study *The Principal Deistic Writers* (1757), John Leland grouped together a number of writers – including Lord Herbert of Cherbury, Thomas Hobbes and David Hume – under the broad and newly coined term 'deist'. Whether these writers would have approved of this designation is questionable. Close examination of their religious views shows that they have relatively little in common, apart from a general scepticism concerning several specifically Christian ideas, most notably concerning aspects of the traditional views of the nature of revelation and salvation. The Newtonian worldview offered Deism a highly sophisticated way of defending and developing their views, by allowing them to focus on the wisdom of God in creating the world.

The nature of Deism can be grasped to some extent from John Locke's *Essay concerning Human Understanding* (1690). This developed an idea of God which became characteristic of much later Deism. Indeed, Locke's *Essay* can be said to lay much of the intellectual foundations of Deism. Locke argued that 'reason leads us to the knowledge of this certain and evident truth, that there is an eternal, most powerful and most knowing Being'. The attributes of this being are those which human reason recognizes as appropriate for God. Having considered which moral and rational qualities are suited to the deity, Locke argues that 'we enlarge every one of these with our idea of infinity, and so, putting them together, make our complex idea of God'. In other words, the idea of God is made up of human rational and moral qualities, projected to infinity.

Matthew Tindal's *Christianity as Old as Creation* (1730) argued that Christianity was nothing other than the 'republication of the religion of nature'. God is understood as the extension of accepted human ideas of justice, rationality and wisdom. This universal religion is available at all times and in every place, whereas traditional Christianity rested upon the idea of a divine revelation which was not accessible to those who lived before Christ. Tindal's views were propagated before the modern discipline of the sociology of knowledge created scepticism concerning the idea of 'universal reason', and are an excellent model of the rationalism that characterized the movement and that later became influential within the Enlightenment.

The ideas of English Deism percolated through to the continent of Europe through translations (especially in Germany), and through the writings of individuals familiar with and sympathetic to them, such as Voltaire's *Philosophical Letters*. Enlightenment rationalism is often considered to be the final flowering of the bud of English Deism. For our purposes, however, it is especially important to note the obvious consonance between Deism and the Newtonian worldview; indeed, it is possible to argue that Deism owed its growing intellectual acceptance in part to the successes of the Newtonian mechanical view of the world. God created an ordered and regular world, which could now be allowed to function by itself. Once the watch was wound up, it needed no further attention from its creator. This concept of an absentee God of a clockwork universe is widely regarded as characteristic of Deism.

If valid, this would be an important criticism. However, I am clear that there is substantial clear blue theological water between my approach and that of Deism.

1. Deist writers were severely critical of substantial sections of traditional Christian belief, such as the possibility and necessity of divine revelation, the continuing involvement of God with the creation, the Trinity, and the divinity of Christ. Their emphasis upon God as creator reflected their unhappiness with most other fundamental aspects of Christian theology. A scientific theology places an emphasis upon the doctrine of creation on account of its obvious importance: it offers a framework for seeing the world as God's creation. Yet this emphasis reflects the specific concerns of a scientific theology; it does not rest upon any fundamental difficulty or disagreement with the core doctrinal statements of the Christian faith, as set out, for example, in the Nicene creed.
2. Historically, one of Deism's particular concerns was to develop a 'natural religion', which can be known through reason or solely through the reading of the 'book of nature'.

The characteristic Deist rejection of divine revelation in favour of a 'republication of the religion of nature' (Matthew Tindal) leads to an emphasis being placed upon God as creator as a result of a rejection of the legitimacy of divine revelation. A scientific theology is fully committed to the notion of divine revelation. Its emphasis on the doctrine of creation does not arise from any difficulties with the notion of revelation – or, indeed, any aspect of traditional Christian orthodoxy, which is affirmed rather than questioned – but from a concern to develop those aspects of this belief system that have particular relevance to an engagement with the natural world.

3. Where Deism regards the doctrine of creation as isolated from other Christian beliefs (which it tends to regard as problematic), a scientific theology recognizes that Christian orthodoxy sees the doctrine of creation as existing within a web of interconnecting doctrines. In particular, there are vital connections that must be recognized between creation and the doctrines of providence and redemption, and Christology.

The connection between the doctrine of creation and the person of Christ is of particular concern to a scientific theology, and is developed more substantially later in the work (for example, see 2:297–313). I attempt to summarize the importance of this connection as follows (1:188):

In recent theological discussion, there has been a welcome and somewhat overdue realization of the need to return to a trinitarian understanding of creation, which recognizes the Christological dimensions of that doctrine and explores their implications. One such implication, which will be justified and unfolded in this present study, is that the divine rationality – whether we choose to refer to this as *logos* or *ratio* – must be thought of as *being embedded in creation and embodied in Christ.*

While I have the work of Karl Barth particularly in mind at this point, it is important to appreciate that very similar insights are articulated by Colin Gunton and Thomas F. Torrance. The intimate link between these areas of theology is affirmed by a scientific theology, and identified as an important element of the quest for a unitary approach to knowledge and wisdom (1:188–9):

> The same divine rationality or wisdom which the natural sciences discern within the created order is to be identified within the *logos* incarnate, Jesus Christ. If indeed Christian theology is concerned, in part, with the unfolding of the significance of Jesus Christ – as traditional Christian orthodoxy has suggested that it is – there is a direct continuity between the study of the creator and of the redeemer. The *duplex cognitio Domini* – which Calvin found so useful a theological device – can be put to fresh use. The study of the creation and of Jesus Christ are contiguous, not unrelated activities. Both creation and Christ bear witness to the one God, and the one divine rationality. As will become clear during this study, this kind of consideration leads to the possibility of seeing theology as a science in its own right, yet related to other sciences, each of which has their own distinctive subject-matters and means of investigation appropriate to that subject.

To explore the potential of this approach, I conclude this chapter by noting some aspects of Torrance's scientific theology, noting in particular the way in which he uses the classical patristic notion of the *homoousion* (that is, that Christ is 'of the same substance' with the Father) in his approach to the engagement with reality. The doctrine of creation declares that God's free creation of the universe *ex nihilo* means that there were no impediments preventing the distinctive character or imprint of God from being embedded in that creation. That divine imprint is found in the *logos*. The contingency of creation means that nothing happened necessarily – that is to say, nothing that exists is the outcome of a decision in which God was coerced to behave in any way other than his own will dictated. As such, creation bears his imprint, not the image or likeness of any other divinity or force.

The full concept of contingency of the creation carries with it the idea that God is related to the universe, neither arbitrarily or necessarily, but through the freedom of his grace and will, when out of sheer love he created the universe and grounded it in his own transcendent Logos or Rationality.

Having explored some aspects of the Christian doctrine of creation, we may now turn to consider some of its implications for the project of a scientific theology.

5. Implications of a Christian Doctrine of Creation

The significance of a Christian doctrine of creation for the scientific theology project lies in its implications. We may begin our discussion of this point by turning to consider some comments of John Polkinghorne. In his useful study *Science and Creation: The Search for Understanding* (1988), Polkinghorne comments:[6]

> We are so familiar with the fact that we can understand the world that most of the time we take it for granted. It is what makes science possible. Yet it could have been otherwise. The universe might have been a disorderly chaos rather than an orderly cosmos. Or it might have had a rationality which was inaccessible to us. . . . There is a congruence between our minds and the universe, between the rationality experienced within and the rationality observed without. This extends not only to the mathematical articulation of fundamental theory but also to all those tacit acts of judgement, exercised with intuitive skill, which are equally indispensable to the scientific endeavour.

The point that Polkinghorne makes is fundamental: there seems to be some kind of 'resonance' or 'harmonization' between the ordering of the world and the capacity of the human mind to discern and represent it. Polkinghorne himself sets out the common Christian interpretation of this congruence as follows:[7]

> If the deep-seated congruence of the rationality present in our minds with the rationality present in the world is to find a true explanation, it must surely lie in some more profound reason which is the ground of both. Such a reason would be provided by the Rationality of the Creator.

This appeal to the 'rationality' of the creation can be rephrased in terms of the *logos* – the divine 'rationality' through which God created the world, and which was incarnate in Christ. The entire possibility of a scientific theology rests upon this created rationality.

The doctrine of creation *ex nihilo* is important to the notion of the 'rendering' of God in creation, and the idea of creation as ordering of pre-existing matter places ontological distance between God and the world. A similar issue arises if creation is conceived as the work of an intermediary – as, for example, in some Gnostic creation myths. The traditional Christian idea of creation through the divine *logos* allows us to infer that the created order stands in a direct relationship to its creator. While it must be conceded immediately that the distorting impact of sin upon any knowledge of God must be fully recognized, the doctrine of creation lays the foundations for a 'natural theology', which we shall explore in more detail presently.

Created rationality and the possibility of theological reflection

A scientific theology makes a particular appeal to the intrinsic reso-nance between the structures of the world and human reasoning, which it grounds in the doctrine that humanity is created in the 'image of God' (*imago Dei*). This concept has been interpreted in a number of ways within the Christian tradition. One of the most important is the approach which interprets the 'image of God' in terms of human reason. On this approach, the 'image of God' is understood to be the human rational faculty, which mirrors the wisdom of God. This approach is set out with particular clarity in Augustine's *De Trinitate* ('On the Trinity'):[8]

> The image of the creator is to be found in the rational or intellectual soul of humanity . . . Although reason and intellect may at times be dormant, or may appear to be weak at some times, and strong at others, the human soul cannot be anything other than rational and intellectual. It has been created according to the image of God in order that it may use reason and intellect in order to apprehend and behold God.

Such ideas are developed by Aquinas and Calvin, with the latter placing considerably more emphasis than the former on the distorting impact of sin upon human cognition. In more recent years, the Swiss theologian Emil Brunner sought to clarify and develop the idea by distinguishing its material and formal aspects.

For the purposes of a scientific theology, the most theologically significant analysis of the *imago Dei* is found in the writings of Athanasius, who forges a connection between divine and human rationality in the concept of the *logos*. We find this idea developed throughout the treatise *de incarnatione Verbi* ('On the Incarnation of the Word'), as in the following extract:[9]

> God knew the limitations of humanity; and though the grace of being made in the image of God was sufficient to give them knowledge of the Word, and through Him of the Father, as a safeguard against their neglect of this grace, God also provided the works of creation as a means by which the Maker might be known. . . . Humanity could thus look up into the immensity of heaven, and by pondering the

harmony of creation, come to know its Ruler, the Word of the Father,
whose sovereign providence makes the Father known to all.

Throughout this work, Athanasius insists that there is an intricate
network of connections between the rationality (*logos*) of God, the
created rationality of humanity, who bears the image of that God,
and the incarnation itself, in which the divine *logos* – who, for
Athanasius is the *agent* of creation – assumed human nature, and
dwelt among us.

To help explain the importance of this idea of 'created rationality' to understanding how humanity is able to engage with the
world, I explore three areas in which the notion plays a particularly interesting role – Feuerbach's views on the origins of the
notion of God, the 'unreasonable effectiveness of mathematics' in
representing reality, and the moral issues raised by the Euthyphro
dilemma. In each case, a Christian doctrine of creation has a
significant role to play.

Ludwig Feuerbach (1818–83) argued that the concept of God
arose from the 'projection' or 'objectification' of human longing for
significance. Beginning from an essentially materialist assumption,
Feuerbach argued that, since there was no objective basis in reality
for the human concept of God, its origins had to be explained as
lying within humanity itself. The notion of God is thus constructed in response to the internal needs of humanity. Feuerbach
offers an account, based on the ideas of the leading German philosopher G. W. F. Hegel, of how this process of 'objectification'
takes place. A related account was developed by Karl Marx, who
argued that the construction of the concept of God was determined by social and economic factors, laying the groundwork for
its elimination through radical social transformation.

A Christian doctrine of creation, however, offers a radically
different perspective. If humanity has been created to relate to

God – in effect, so that there is an absence within humanity which can only be satisfied through the presence of God – then a sense of *longing* for God arises precisely on account of our created status. This point has long been recognized within the Christian tradition. It is perhaps best stated in the writings of Augustine, as in the opening section of his *Confessions*:[10]

> To praise you is the desire of humanity, a small piece of your creation. You stir humanity to take pleasure in praising you, because you have made us for yourself and our heart is restless until it rests in you.

Similar points can be made from other Christian writers to explore this theme, such as Anselm of Canterbury, George Herbert, and C. S. Lewis. On the basis of such considerations, I suggest that the doctrine of creation offers an entirely acceptable alternative to Feuerbach's account of the origins of the notion of God (1:209):

> The human sense of longing is therefore not to be interpreted – as in Feuerbach – as a misdirection of purely natural human feelings, hopes or fears, which leads to the illegitimate construction of the notion of God when there is, in fact, no such God. Rather, it is to be seen as an integral aspect of a coherent Christian doctrine of creation, set within the economy of salvation. The rationality of faith thus offers a very different interpretation of the same phenomenon, observed yet interpreted in a very different manner by Feuerbach.

The second area to be explored is what Eugene Wigner once referred to as the 'unreasonable effectiveness of mathematics'. By this, Wigner wished to draw attention to the remarkable ability of mathematics to mirror the world of nature. An excellent example is Johann Balmer's discovery that the wavelengths of certain solar spectral lines could be represented precisely by a rather elegant mathematical formula. Other examples could easily be given. Yet why is this so? Why does mathematics possess such a capacity?

We shall return to a more detailed engagement with this question later. The answer to be given, however, is entirely consistent with the doctrine of creation just outlined: 'Mathematics offers a puzzling degree of correlation with the natural world – puzzling, that is, unless one operates with a Platonic notion of "recollection" or a Christian doctrine of creation, which postulates a direct connection of the mind of God with the rationalities of the created order and the human mind, as created in the image of God.'

The third area to be touched on relates to moral philosophy. In a famous epigram, Pindar (*c*.518–438 BC) spoke of law as 'king of all, mortals and immortals', implying that the gods ought to be subject to law, just like everyone else. All too often, Homer and Hesiod seemed to believe that events in the world rested on the outcome of power politics on Mount Olympus, without any perceptible moral foundation. Can justice or holiness really be defined in terms of the occasionally highly dubious activities and judgements from Olympus? Or is there not some law to which even the gods of Olympus are subject and by which their actions and decisions may be judged?

Precisely this question is dealt with in one of Plato's early dialogues. The 'Euthyphro dilemma' – which takes its name from the dialogue in which the issue is raised – is framed by Socrates' killer question:[11]

> Is that which is holy loved by the gods because it is holy, or is it holy because it is loved by the gods?

In other words, do the gods endorse a previously existing standard of morality? Or do those same gods independently create the standards of morality by their own actions, which we are meant to imitate?

The force of the question is immediately obvious, when set against the background of Homer's epics. If something is intrinsically good, righteous or holy, who needs the gods to tell us that it is so? The judgement of the gods is an irrelevance if goodness or holiness is determined by standards that are independent of them. They might as well not exist. This line of argument leads to a 'practical atheism', which in effect argues that the existence of the gods has no real relevance to life.

But suppose that holiness or goodness are determined by the gods themselves. On the basis of Homer's accounts, the gods indulge in behaviour which cultured people now find offensive – such as deception, adultery and a shameless jostling for power. Are these things to be defined as 'good' or 'holy', simply because the gods do them? If the gods determine what is right and wrong, they are liberated from any accountability, and free to act as they please. Do we say that deception is 'holy', because Homer's gods behave in this manner? This second line of argument sets out Plato's basic criticism of the Homeric gods – namely, that they fall short of what human reason determines to constitute moral excellence.

For Plato, metaphysics was the true basis of morality – a recognition that the universe was rationally constructed, and that it could therefore be understood through the right use of human reason and argument. Philosophy identified a direct link between the way the universe was constructed and the best way for human beings to live. To reflect on the nature of the universe was to gain insights into the nature of the 'good life' – the best and most authentic way of living. If, on the other hand, the gods are under obligation to respect a prior or higher notion of justice, then there is no need to invoke the behaviour of the gods in any account of human morality – providing, of course, that this standard of justice can be known by humans. Who could take the antics of Hesiod's gods with moral seriousness when human beings themselves possessed the means of uncovering what was right? The end result is the celebrated view of Protagoras (*c.*490–420 BC) that 'man is the measure of all things'.

Yet a Christian doctrine of creation allows an alternative response to Plato's dilemma. The Euthyphro dilemma gains its force precisely because we are asked to consider the relationship between two allegedly independent entities: what *human beings* recognize as good, and what *God* recognizes as good. The dilemma forces us, through the terms in which it is posited, to choose between human and divine conceptions of goodness or justice. But if these can be shown to be related to each other in any way, the force of the dilemma is lost. The choice we are forced to make is then seen as false. And a Christian doctrine of creation affirms precisely such a connection. As I argued earlier, one of the implications of the idea of the *imago Dei* is that there is a congruence between divine notions of truth, beauty and goodness and proper human notions of the same through the creaturely status of humanity. A Christian doctrine of creation affirms a correspondence between the moral ordering of creation – including humanity as the height of that creation – and the mind of God.

The ordering of creation

The theme of 'regularity within nature' is widely regarded as an essential theme of the natural sciences. Indeed, one modern physicist has suggested that 'the God of the physicists is cosmic order' (Heinz Pagels). It could be argued that the natural sciences are founded on the *perception of explicable regularity to the world*. In other words, there is something about the world – and the nature of the human mind – which allows us to discern patterns within nature, for which explanations may be advanced and evaluated. One of the most significant parallels between the natural sciences and religion is this fundamental conviction that the world is characterized by regularity and intelligibility. This perception of ordering and intelligibility is of immense significance, at both the scientific and religious levels. As Paul Davies points out in his *Mind of God* (1983), 'in Renaissance Europe, the justification for what we today call the scientific approach to inquiry was the belief in a rational God whose created order could be discerned from a careful study of nature'.[12]

This insight is directly derived from the Christian doctrine of creation, and reflects the deeply religious worldview of the medieval and Renaissance periods, which ensured that even the most 'secular' of activities – whether economic, political or scientific – were saturated with the themes of Christian theology. This foundational assumption of the natural sciences – that God has created an ordered world, whose ordering could be discerned by humanity, which had in turn been created 'in the image and likeness of God' – permeates the writings of the period, whether it is implicitly assumed or explicitly stated.

We have already noted how the theme of 'order' is of major importance within the Old Testament, and noted briefly how it was incorporated into subsequent theological reflection. In view of its importance to our theme, we shall consider it in more detail. One of the most sophisticated explorations of the centrality of the concept of ordering for Christian theology and moral reasoning is to be found in Oliver O'Donovan's *Resurrection and Moral Order* (1986), now firmly established as a classic work in the field. In this work, O'Donovan establishes the close connection between the theological notions of 'creation' and 'order':[13]

> We must understand 'creation' not merely as the raw material out of which the world as we know it is composed, but as the order and coherence *in* which it is composed. . . . To speak of this world as 'created' is already to speak of an order. In the first words of the creed, before we have tried to sketch an outline of created order with the

phrase 'heaven and earth', simply as we say 'I believe in God the Creator', we are stating that the world is an ordered totality. By virtue of the fact that there is a Creator, there is also a creation that is ordered to its Creator, a world which exists as his creation and in no other way, so that by its existence it points to God.

Three highly significant themes of major relevance to our theme can be discerned as emerging from O'Donovan's analysis.

1. The concept of creation is understood to be focused on the establishment of ordering and coherence within the world.
2. The ordering or coherence within the world can be regarded as expressing or reflecting the nature of God himself.
3. The creation can thus be seen as pointing to God, in that the exploration of its ordering or coherence leads to an understanding of the one who ordered it in this manner.

O'Donovan rejects the idea – especially associated with the Scottish philosopher David Hume – that any such discernment of 'ordering' is nothing more than a creation of the human mind, rather than an objective reality in itself. For Hume, 'ordering' was the creation of an order-loving human mind, and was not itself objectively present in nature. It was a human construct, rather than an intrinsic feature of the natural world itself. As O'Donovan argues:[14]

> In speaking of the order which God the Creator and Redeemer has established in the universe, we are not speaking merely of our own capacities to impose order upon what we see there. Of course, we can and do impose order on what we see, for we are free agents and capable of creative interpretation of the world we confront. But our ordering depends upon God's to provide the condition for its freedom. It is free because it has a given order to respond to in attention or disregard, in conformity or disconformity, with obedience or rebellion.

A Christian understanding of the concept of creation is, as we have seen, closely linked with the concept of ordering. One of the most theologically productive means of exploring this idea is found in Thomas F. Torrance's distinctive idea of the 'contingent ordering of creation'. In a series of works, Torrance argued that the ordering observed within creation is not the consequence of God being under an obligation to respond to external necessities, but expresses his own sovereign decision to create the world in a specific manner, expressing his own will and nature. In an important essay, 'Divine and Contingent Order' (1981), he developed this idea as follows:[15]

> [The notion of contingent order] is the direct product of the Christian understanding of the constitutive relation between God and the universe, which he freely created out of nothing, yet not without reason, conferring upon what he has made and continues to sustain a created rationality of its own dependent on his uncreated transcendent reality. . . . [This doctrine of creation] liberated nature conceived as the timeless embodiment of eternal forms from a necessary relation to God, which made it impossible to distinguish nature from God; and it destroyed the bifurcation of form and matter, affirming each as equally created out of nothing and equally real in their indissoluble unity with one another in the pervasive rational order of the contingent universe under God.

A similar idea is developed by Eric L. Mascall in his *Christian Theology and Natural Science* (1956). For Mascall, the contingent order of the creation is such that it cannot be identified in advance, but must be uncovered by empirical investigation. What God is like cannot be determined *a priori*, but must be established *a posteriori*.[16]

> [The created order] will embody regularities and patterns, since its Creator is rational, but the particular regularities and patterns which

it embodies cannot be predicted *a priori*, since he is free; they can only be discovered by examination. The world of Christian theism will thus be one whose investigation requires the empirical method, that is to say, the method of modern natural science, with its twin techniques of observation and experiment.

As Stephen Hawking, among many others, has pointed out, the existence of God is easily and naturally correlated with the regularity and ordering of the world. 'It would be completely consistent with all we know to say that there was a Being who is responsible for the laws of physics.' The noted theoretical physicist Charles A. Coulson pointed out the importance of 'religious conviction' in explaining the 'unprovable assumption that there is an order and constancy in Nature'. This is expressed in the idea of the 'laws of nature', a highly significant way of depicting (and interpreting) the order found within the world.

The theme of cosmic order is of major importance within the writings of Isaac Newton, who argued that the regularity and predictability of the world were a direct consequence of its created origins. Pope's celebrated epitaph for Newton captures aspects of this point well:

> Nature and Nature's Law lay hid in Night
> God said, let Newton be, and all was Light.

The universe is not 'random', but behaves in a regular manner which is capable of observation and explanation. This led to the widespread belief that systems which satisfied Newton's laws of motion behaved in manners which were predetermined, and which could therefore be predicted with considerable accuracy – a view which is often represented at a popular level in terms of the (actually somewhat unhelpful) image of a 'clockwork universe'.

I conclude this chapter by noting the importance of beauty in relation to a doctrine of creation, tracing the by now familiar theological trajectory from the beauty of the creator to the beauty of the creation. Beauty is here identified as being an important aspect of nature itself, as well as the theoretical representation of nature. This is especially clear from the writings of Paul Dirac, who managed to establish a connection between quantum theory and general relativity at a time when everyone else had failed to do so. Dirac's approach appears to have been based on the concept of 'beauty', in that an explicitly aesthetic criterion is laid down as a means of evaluating scientific theories.

So if we can speak of nature displaying such attributes as 'beauty', what follows for a Christian understanding of the ultimate ground of nature, when this is seen as God's creation? We have already seen how important it is to make secure connections between God's creation and God as creator. Such a theological strategy is integral to the development of a responsible natural theology – to which we now turn.

6. The Purpose and Place of Natural Theology

Starting from the revealed insight that the divine rationality created both the world and the human rationality which reflects upon it, Christian theology is able to argue the case for a 'natural theology'. This approach is to be found in writers as diverse as Thomas Aquinas and John Calvin, and can reasonably be argued to be the common wisdom of the Christian tradition.

In his *Summa contra Gentiles*, Thomas Aquinas argues that, since God created the world, something of the divine character may be seen within nature. To put it another way, the doctrine of creation posits that a divine 'signature' may be found within the created order. Aquinas puts this point as follows:[17]

> Meditation on [God's] works enables us, at least to some extent, to admire and reflect on God's wisdom . . . We are thus able to infer

> God's wisdom from reflection upon God's works . . . This considera-
> tion of God's works leads to an admiration of God's sublime power,
> and consequently inspires reverence for God in human hearts . . . This
> consideration also incites human souls to the love of God's goodness
> . . . If the goodness, beauty and wonder of creatures are so delightful
> to the human mind, the fountainhead of God's own goodness (com-
> pared with the trickles of goodness found in creatures) will draw
> excited human minds entirely to itself.

Something of God's beauty can thus be known through the
beauty of the creation. Note that Aquinas is not grounding this
approach to a 'natural theology' on human reason's capacity to
uncover God, but upon God's creation of the natural order – itself
a revealed truth.

Calvin develops a related approach, arguing that the created
order is a 'theatre' or a 'mirror' for the displaying of the divine
presence, nature, and attributes. (Note how Calvin takes two
Renaissance metaphors of nature, and reworks them to reassert
the divine origins of the world.) Although invisible and incom-
prehensible, God wills to be known under the form of created and
visible things, by donning the garment of creation.[18]

> There is within the human mind, and that by natural instinct, a sense
> of divinity. This we take to be beyond controversy. So that no-one
> might take refuge in the pretext of ignorance, God frequently renews
> and sometimes increases this awareness, so that all people, recogniz-
> ing that there is a God and that he is their creator, are condemned by
> their own testimony because they have failed to worship him and to
> give their lives to his service.

Once more, the doctrine of creation plays a major role. The ability
of creation to display the creator is a direct consequence of its
created status.

This concept of natural theology received a particularly

significant development within the confessional element of the Reformed tradition. The *Gallic Confession of Faith* (1559) argues that God reveals himself to humanity in two manners:[19]

> First, in his works, both in their creation and their preservation and control. Second, and more clearly, in his Word, which was revealed through oracles in the beginning, and which was subsequently committed to writing in the books which we call the Holy Scriptures.

A related idea is found in the *Belgic Confession* (1561), which expanded the brief statement on natural theology found in the *Gallic Confession*. Once more, knowledge of God is affirmed to come about by two means:[20]

> First, by the creation, preservation and government of the universe, which is before our eyes as a most beautiful book, in which all creatures, great and small, are like so many characters leading us to contemplate the invisible things of God, namely, his eternal power and Godhead, as the Apostle Paul declares (Romans 1:20). All of these things are sufficient to convince humanity, and leave them without excuse. Second, he makes himself known more clearly and fully to us by his holy and divine Word; that is to say, as far as is necessary for us to know in this life, to his glory and our salvation.

The two themes which emerge clearly from these Reformed confessional statements can be summarized as follows:

1. There are two modes of knowing God: one through the natural order, and the second through Scripture.
2. The second mode is clearer and fuller than the first.

This basic framework is of considerable importance in relation to the development of the 'two books' tradition within Reformed theology, especially in England, which regarded nature and Scripture as two complementary sources of our knowledge of God. Thus Francis Bacon commended the study of 'the book of

God's word' and the 'book of God's works' in his *Advancment of Learning* (1605). This metaphor of the 'two books' with the one divine author was of considerable importance in holding together Christian theology and piety and the emerging interest and knowledge of the natural world in the seventeenth and early eighteenth centuries. It may be regarded as an integral element of the Reformed tradition prior to Barth.

This idea of 'natural theology', however, is not to be understood in the sense of 'access to knowledge of God without recourse to revelation' – an idea implicit in William Alston's definition of 'natural theology' as 'the enterprise of providing support for religious beliefs by starting from premises that neither are nor presuppose any religious beliefs'.[21] Rather, the assumption is that natural theology must begin from premises which are founded on revelation – namely, that the natural order is to be seen as God's creation. Without this insight, there is no way in which *nature* can lead to a *theology*. A viable 'natural theology' thus rests upon foundations which themselves lie beyond the scope of such a natural theology – namely, the insight that the natural order and the human mind that reflects upon it are shaped by the divine *logos*.

Karl Barth and his followers make a sustained and formidable critique of 'natural theology'. He mounts a theologically informed and responsible critique of certain approaches, which he regards as perpetuating the human quest for autonomy, which reached its high water mark in the culture of the Enlightenment. For Barth, 'natural theology' represents a concerted human attempt to subvert revelation, by declaring that what needs to be known about God can be determined without recourse to divine self-disclosure. I believe that his concerns can be met fully and fairly by a refocusing of the category of 'natural theology', which grounds it in divine revelation rather than autonomous human reflection on the natural order. This lays a foundation for the development of a responsible natural theology as a means for offering the Christian tradition a significant means of justifying its own claims to universality, while affirming that it is anchored in a series of particularities. First, I turn to consider the historical origins of the type of natural theology which Karl Barth so thoroughly detested.

The historical origins of modern natural theology

History offers us the possibility of understanding why certain developments took place. Natural theology – as this notion would now be understood – is actually a recent invention, and is best seen as a response to upheavals in the intellectual world in England during the seventeenth and eighteenth centuries. Four major factors may be seen as leading to the emergence of this 'new style' of natural theology, which reached its culmination in the eighteenth century.

1. The rise of biblical criticism, which called into question the reliability or intelligibility of Scripture, and hence generated interest in the identification and exploitation of alternative routes to a knowledge of God. The metaphor of the 'two books' (nature and Scripture) was here pressed far beyond its original limits, and taken to imply that the 'book of nature' was just as capable of illuminating the divine as Scripture itself.

2. A growing impatience with and dislike of ecclesiastical authority, which caused more libertarian individuals to seek for sources of knowledge which were seen to be independent of ecclesiastical control. The Church might have control of the Bible; nobody could control the natural order.

3. A dislike of the pomposity of organized religion and the apparent complexity of Christian doctrines caused many to

seek for a simpler form of religion, free of complications and distortions. A highly idealized quest for an original 'religion of nature' thus began to take place, in which nature was given priority as the source of revelation and object of worship over the Christian equivalents.

4. The continuing successes of the mechanical worldview prompted many to wish to gain a deeper knowledge of God through the intricacies of creation. The invisible God could be studied through God's visible works. As we have stressed, this is a theologically valid line of argument. However, at the hands of Deist writers, the divine creation of the world was increasingly proposed as a truth of reason, not of revelation. There was no need, it was argued, to presuppose any notion of revelation in safeguarding the insight that nature was a divinely constructed machine.

By the end of the eighteenth century, an approach to natural theology had developed which saw a rational appeal to the natural order, without reference to revelation, as a means of defending the Christian faith at a time of intellectual ferment. Yet paradoxically, precisely this appeal led to the undermining of the category of revelation. An appeal to nature increasingly turned out to be at the expense of, rather than in support of, revelation.

We have already seen that the term 'nature' is remarkably vague, capable of being remoulded and recast to suit various agendas. A careful analysis of Christian approaches to natural theology suggests that three major uses of the concept have shaped Christian thinking about 'natural theology' in recent years:

1. nature as the natural world of plants, animals and mountains;
2. nature as human rationality;
3. nature as human culture.

Once more, this diversity serves to remind us of the intrinsically indeterminate character of the concept of 'nature'. The approach adopted throughout this work is to stress that 'nature' is to be seen as God's creation, while recognizing that it is a multi-layered reality – a matter which we shall consider in greater detail when exploring the concept of 'critical realism', and its understanding of a stratified reality.

The biblical foundations of a natural theology

Both the Old and New Testaments maintain the notion of a revelation which is mediated through the natural world. The classic formulation of such a doctrine is found at Psalm 19:1:

> The heavens declare the glory of the Lord.

Yet while it is fair to point out that such a knowledge of God from the natural order is assumed at many points throughout the Old Testament, this idea is not subjected to any systematic development. Anyone looking for a concept of 'natural theology' as advocated by William Alston, for example, will find nothing even approaching this in the pages of the Old Testament (or New, for that matter). As we noted earlier, for Alston, natural theology is 'the enterprise of providing support for religious beliefs by starting from premises that neither are nor presuppose any religious beliefs'. Biblical writers see no need to offer proofs for God's existence, being more concerned with exploring the intellectual, ethical and social implications of the character of the God whose nature and will is disclosed through revelation.

In the New Testament, we encounter a number of passages which point towards some kind of natural knowledge of God. In Paul's letter to the Romans – which is specifically directed towards a *Christian* readership – the concept of a natural knowledge of

God is used to underscore human responsibility for sin. Since all humanity has the capacity to know God, their failure to do so is 'without excuse', as is their refusal to respond appropriately to what they know of God. For Paul, God's anger is revealed against those who refuse to respond to 'what can be known of God which is manifest among them', in that God has revealed this to them (Romans 1:18). From the creation of the world onwards, Paul continues, the 'invisible things of God have been plainly made known'; the context makes it clear that Paul specifically has God's eternal power and divine nature in mind. The general line of argument is that God's nature and will has been revealed to a sufficient extent within the created order for humanity to have no excuse for any failure to respond to God.

Yet elsewhere in the New Testament, we find another approach being taken, this time with a non-Christian audience in mind. According to Luke, Paul opens his address to the Athenians with a gradual introduction of the theme of the living God, appealing to the religious and philosophical curiosity of the Athenians in giving his theological exposition. The 'sense of divinity' present in each individual is here used as an apologetic device, by which Paul is able to base himself upon acceptable Greek theistic assumptions, while at the same time demonstrating that the Christian gospel goes beyond them. Paul shows a clear appreciation of the apologetic potential of Stoic philosophy, portraying the gospel as resonating with central Stoic concerns, while extending the limits of what might be known. What the Greeks held to be unknown, possibly unknowable, Paul proclaims to have been made known through the resurrection of Christ. The entire episode illustrates the manner in which Paul is able to exploit the situation of his audience, without compromising the integrity of faith.

At this point, we need to pause and consider the inscription on an altar to which Paul refers: 'to an unknown god' (Acts 17:23).

There are certainly classical precedents for this, especially according to the writings of Diogenes Laertius. Numerous Christian writers of the early patristic period explained Paul's meaning at this point by appealing to the 'anonymous altars' which were scattered throughout the region at that time. Several (including Didymus of Alexandria) suggested that Paul may have altered the inscription from the plural ('to unknown gods') at this point. However, there is no reason to suppose that Paul made any such change.

The fundamental point being made is that a deity of whom the Greeks had some implicit or intuitive awareness is being made known to them by name and in full. The god who is known indirectly through his creation can be known fully in redemption. Paul explicitly appeals to the idea of creation as a basis for his apologetic approach, apparently using the theme of creation as a way of introducing the theme of redemption in Christ. While the precise apologetic strategy deployed by Paul at Athens is the subject of some dispute, it is clear that the address presupposes some form of natural theology. The notion of the created order corresponding to the mind of a god who may be known plays a critical role in Paul's preaching on this occasion. The passage indicates that an apologetic, based in part on a natural theology, was a recognized option within the early Christian church.

On the basis of a detailed survey of the biblical material, it seems that a knowledge of God, however limited, is indeed presupposed. Yet there is no sign of any endorsement of the view that God can be known, fully and authentically, by any mode other than revelation. As James Barr concluded in his magisterial work *Biblical Faith and Natural Theology* (1993):[22]

> The elements which we have detected, which we may call a 'biblical' natural theology, seem very limited in character. They do not amount to the fuller natural theology with which we have been familiar. They do not offer philosophical proofs of the existence of God, they do not

work by means of pure reason, they do not appear to amount to the total system of classical theism or anything like it.

Yet while the biblical material does not in any way endorse the form of 'natural theology' which Karl Barth so heavily criticized, neither does it entirely support his own position. We shall shortly turn to assess Barth's position. First, however, it is important to consider some philosophical misgivings over the notion of 'natural theology'.

The philosophical debate over natural theology

In recent years, philosophers of religion working within a Reformed theological perspective – such as Alvin Plantinga – have made highly significant contributions to the philosophy of religion. Plantinga understands 'natural theology' to be an attempt to prove or demonstrate the existence of God, and vigorously rejects it on the basis of his belief that it depends on a fallacious understanding of the nature of religious belief. The roots of this objection are complex, and can be summarized in terms of two foundational considerations:

1. Natural theology supposes that belief in God must rest upon an evidential basis. Belief in God is thus not, strictly speaking, a basic belief – that is, something which is self-evident, incorrigible or evident to the senses. It is therefore a belief which requires to be itself grounded in some more basic belief. However, to ground a belief in God upon some other belief is, in effect, to depict that latter belief as endowed with a greater epistemic status than belief in God. For Plantinga, a properly Christian approach is to affirm that belief in God is itself basic, and does not require justification with reference to other beliefs.

2. Natural theology is not justified with reference to the Reformed tradition, including Calvin and his later followers.

As we shall see, the latter point is inaccurate historically, and need not detain us. However, the first line of argument has met with growing interest.

Plantinga clearly regards Aquinas as the 'natural theologian *par excellence*', and directs considerable attention to his methods. For Plantinga, Aquinas is a foundationalist in matters of theology and philosophy, in that '*scientia*, properly speaking, consists in a body of propositions deduced syllogistically from self-evident first principles'. The *Summa contra Gentiles* shows, according to Plantinga, that Aquinas proceeds from evidential foundations to argue for a belief in God, which clearly makes such belief dependent upon appropriate evidential foundations. Plantinga thus conceives of natural theology as an attempt to *prove* the existence of God.

Now this is certainly the approach to the nature and scope of a natural theology which became dominant in the eighteenth century. It is, however, clearly not necessary that a natural theology should make any such assumption. In fact, there are excellent reasons for suggesting that Aquinas regards natural theology as a demonstration, from the standpoint of faith, of the consonance between that faith and the structures of the world. In other words, natural theology is not intended to prove the existence of God, but presupposes that existence; it then asks, 'What should we expect the natural world to be like if it has indeed been created by such a God?' The search for order in nature is therefore intended not to demonstrate that God exists, but to reinforce the plausibility of an already existing belief.

We may now turn to consider the origins and foundations of Karl Barth's critique of natural theology, before examining the reworking of this critique found in the writings of Thomas F. Torrance.

The Barthian objection to natural theology: an evaluation

For Barth, natural theology is a human attempt to subvert the necessity of divine revelation. It is an attempt to know God in a manner and under conditions which are determined by humanity, not by God. The great Scottish theologian Hugh Ross Mackintosh once summarized the questions centring on revelation as follows: 'A religious knowledge of God, wherever existing, comes by revelation; otherwise we should be committed to the incredible position that a man can know God without His willing to be known.' Barth's polemic against natural theology can be seen as a principled attempt to safeguard the integrity of divine revelation against human attempts to construct their own notions of God, or undermine the necessity of revelation.

Although Barth's earlier polemic against human attempts to subvert revelation were framed in terms of a critique of the category of *religion*, from II/2 of the *Church Dogmatics* onwards this is directed specifically against the category of natural theology. Barth offers an extended and systematic critique of natural theology, arguing that this represents a theology 'which comes to humanity from nature', expressing humanity's 'self-preservation and self-affirmation' in the face of God. Barth treats natural theology as the supreme expression of the human longing for self-justification and intellectual autonomy.

Barth's hostility towards natural theology thus rests on his fundamental belief that it undermines the necessity and uniqueness of God's self-revelation. If knowledge of God can be achieved independently of God's self-revelation in Christ, then it follows that humanity can dictate the place, time and means of its knowledge of God. For Barth, there is a close link between natural theology and the theme of human autonomy. As Barth understands the concept, natural theology affirms and expresses the human desire to find God on our own terms. Natural theology thus appears to posit a second source of revelation alongside Jesus Christ. For Barth, revelation is only to be had through the revelation of God, as a consequence of God's gracious decision that he is to be known. There is no manner in which God can be known outside and apart from God's self-revelation.

The central question arising from Barth's concerns is this: While conceding these points, is it thereby necessary to reject totally the concept of natural theology? There is a growing feeling within the theological community that Barth's theology marks an over-correction of the Reformed theological position, and that an informed recovery of an older position is overdue. A scientific theology offers such a reappropriation.

Three major criticisms are increasingly being directed against Barth's stridently negative views on natural theology.

1. It rests on inadequate biblical foundations. Barth's engagement with the biblical texts are increasingly being seen in terms of the imposition of Barth's views upon those texts, rather than a faithful attempt to expound them. Writers such as James Barr have argued that Barth's rejection of natural theology was never really based on biblical exegesis, but rather reflected trends and developments in modern theology, philosophy and society.
2. Barth's views on natural theology clearly represent a significant departure from the Reformed tradition which he clearly regards himself as representing. We have already noted Calvin's views on natural theology – views, incidentally, which Barth rather misrepresents in the pages of his *Church Dogmatics*, in which Calvin is presented as an *opponent* of natural theology!
3. Barth's negative attitude towards natural theology appears

to be linked to an indifferent attitude towards the natural sciences, stifling what potentially could be a significant theological exploration and engagement – such as the 'scientific theology' developed in these volumes.

The second of these merits close attention. It is a simple fact of historical theology that the Reformed theological tradition has not, on the whole, opposed natural theology. The majority of thinkers who might be considered to be representative of the Reformed tradition have affirmed some natural knowledge of God. Although some influential Reformed theologians have criticized natural theology, such criticisms are often directed toward natural theology construed in a particular sort of way, and thus their criticisms should not be regarded as representing a wholesale rejection of natural theology.

This can be seen by considering the views of writers of the 'Old Genevan School' – in other words, the founders of the Reformed theological tradition which Barth himself represents. John Calvin's defence of a natural knowledge of God is well known. While stressing the reality of such knowledge, Calvin argues that such a natural knowledge of God is imperfect and confused on account of sin, even to the point of contradiction on occasion. A natural knowledge of God serves to deprive humanity of any excuse for ignoring the divine will; nevertheless, it is inadequate as the basis of a fully fledged portrayal of the nature, character and purposes of God.

Having stressed this point, Calvin then introduces the notion of revelation; Scripture reiterates what may be known of God through nature, while simultaneously clarifying this general revelation and enhancing it. 'The knowledge of God, which is clearly shown in the ordering of the world and in all creatures, is still more clearly and familiarly explained in the Word.' It is only through Scripture that the believer has access to knowledge of the redeeming actions of God in history, culminating in the life, death and resurrection of Jesus Christ. For Calvin, revelation is focused upon the person of Jesus Christ; our knowledge of God is mediated through him. God may thus be fully known only through Jesus Christ, who may in turn be known only through Scripture; the created order, however, provides an important point of contact for this revelation.

Theodore Beza (or de Bèze), Calvin's successor at Geneva, developed a more sophisticated approach to the matter than Calvin, but retained its general features. While not conceding any notion of a source of saving knowledge of God apart from divine revelation, Beza is clear that nature possesses a created capacity to mirror its creator.[23]

> God has engraved, as if with gigantic letters, his eternity and existence as creator above the creation onto even the smallest things. God shows his omnipotence, without which the world could not be created or governed; his omniscience, which is manifest in the arrangement and direction of so many creatures; and his absolute goodness.

Beza's cautious and responsible account of the nature and scope of natural theology renders him invulnerable to the criticisms directed by Barth against natural theology. Beza's construal of the notion is clearly not that which Barth had in mind when making these criticisms.

So what notion of natural theology did Barth have in mind? If we turn to consider the later Genevan school of theology, we find more or less the approach that caused Barth such pain. The writings of Jean-Alphonse Turrettini (1671–1737) are a particularly good illustration of this point. In his *Theses de theologia naturali* ('Theses on Natural Theology'), Turrettini sets out the case for a knowledge of God which may be gained from nature, without the need for any revelational groundwork. Yet such an idea is not found with Calvin or Beza. To reject Turrettini's approach to natural theology is not to reject that of Calvin or Beza.

Thomas F. Torrance on natural theology

One of Barth's most influential English-language interpreters offers a significant redirection of the concept of natural theology, both responding to Barth's concerns while reappropriating older insights. Thomas F. Torrance offers a reconstrual of natural theology which is essentially that of the early Genevan school, tightened up as necessary in response to Barthian concerns. On Torrance's reading of Barth, set out in a 1970 study 'The Problem of Natural Theology in the Thought of Karl Barth', the fundamental concern is with the human quest for autonomy.[24]

> The claim to a natural knowledge of God, as Barth understands it, cannot be separated out from a whole movement of man in which he seeks to justify himself over against the grace of God, and which can only develop into a natural theology that is antithetical to knowledge of God as he really is in his acts of revelation and grace. From this point of view, the danger of natural theology lies in the fact that once its ground has been conceded it becomes the ground on which everything else is absorbed and naturalized, so that even the knowledge of God mediated through his self-revelation in Christ is domesticated and adapted to it until it becomes a form of natural theology.

Torrance concedes this danger, but believes it arises only from one particular way of conceiving natural theology. What, he asks, would be the implications of seeing natural theology as existing within revealed theology, rather than being its rival? Where Barth tends to see natural and revealed theology as two rival contenders for knowledge of God, Torrance argues that natural theology must be reconceived as an account of nature, undertaken from within the sphere of a revealed knowledge of God. To undertake natural theology, some revealed notions of God are required – above all, a doctrine of creation.

Torrance follows Barth in arguing that a natural theology which is understood as being *independent* of God's self-revelation must be regarded as a serious challenge to authentic and responsible Christian theology. But in Torrance's construal of the notion, natural theology has its place *under the aegis of revelation*, not outside it – and certainly not opposed to it. In its improper form, natural theology represents an approach to theology which is grounded on concepts which lie outside the Christian revelation, thus subverting or distorting it.

Torrance's view of natural theology thus rigorously grounds it in God's self-revelation, and views it as located within and subordinate to that revelation. The doctrine of creation plays an especially important role in Torrance's reflections on the place of such a reconstructed natural theology. The doctrine of creation *ex nihilo* is, for Torrance, the foundation of the idea that the world is contingent, and dependent upon God for its being and order. Torrance therefore insists that creation can only be held to reveal God from the standpoint of faith. Knowledge of God is presupposed, not established or determined, by a responsible natural theology. From the standpoint of revelation – which establishes nature as God's creation, rather than an autonomous and self-created entity – the creation now has potential to point to its creator.

Torrance's most developed statement of this revitalized notion of a natural theology is to be found in his 1978 Richards Lectures at the University of Virginia, published as *The Ground and Grammar of Theology*. Here, he identified the doctrine of the triune God as essential to a responsible natural theology. To fail to lay the trinitarian foundations for a reconstituted natural theology is to open the door to Deism.[25]

Natural theology by its very operation abtracts the existence of God from his act, so that if it does not begin with deism, it imposes deism upon theology. If really to know God through his saving activity in our world is to know him as Triune, then the doctrine of the Trinity belongs to the very groundwork of knowledge of God from the very start, which calls into question any doctrine of God as the One God gained apart from his trinitarian activity – but that is the kind of knowledge of God that is yielded in natural theology of the traditional kind.

Against this 'traditional' natural theology – by which he really means 'natural theology as developed in the eighteenth century' – Torrance sets an understanding of nature as created by the triune God. It is thus not merely the doctrine of creation, but an explicitly *trinitarian* reading of the doctrine of creation, that underlies the form of natural theology that Torrance wishes to commend.

It is such a trinitarian natural theology which underlies a scientific theology.

The place of natural theology within a scientific theology

Given the importance of definitions, we must be clear what form of natural theology is being endorsed, and which excluded. I reject any approach which holds that 'nature provides a foundational resource for Christian theology'. I endorse the following approach (1:295):

A legitimate Christian natural theology interprets nature in a Christian manner – namely, as God's creation. This involves construing natural theology in line with the foundational insights of the Christian tradition.

For this reason, natural theology cannot be conceived as an autonomous theological discipline, precisely because its foundational and legitimating insight – namely, that nature is to be viewed and recognized as God's creation – is derived from divine revelation. 'Nature' is not a self-sufficient category, capable of bearing the philosophical weight which an autonomous natural theology demands. In its legitimate and defensible form, natural theology is to be viewed as a legitimate and proper theological exercise to be conducted *within* the scope of a revealed knowledge of God, rather than as an autonomous discipline outside its bounds.

Such a natural theology cannot conceivably be regarded as a 'proof' of the Christian revelation, not least on account of the intrinsically circular and self-referential modes of argument that this entails. Instead, such a natural theology offers a resonance – a realization that what is being proclaimed makes sense of things, even if this resonance fails to even approach the status of 'proof'. There is thus a fundamental resonance – but nothing more – between nature and theology, with the latter offering a prism through which the former may be viewed and understood.

There are three converging factors which are necessary for a viable conception of natural theology:

That the created order is held to be the work of the Christian God, not any other entity, whether divine or otherwise.

That the act of creation was not determined or significantly influenced by the quality of the material which was ordered through this act.

That the human mind possesses the capacity to recognize this work of creation as such, and to draw at least some reliable conclusions concerning the nature and character of God from the created order.

None of these can be regarded as 'necessary truths of reason', which demonstrates once more that a viable natural theology depends upon a revelational foundation. It cannot be regarded as self-evidently true, or as resting upon the common notions of our culture.

Perhaps most significantly, natural theology enables the Christian tradition to engage in discourse in the public arena. For example, Wolfhart Pannenberg's programme of engaging with publicly observable realities – evident both in his early works dealing with the interpretation of the publicly accessible history of Jesus of Nazareth, and his later works focusing on the publicly accessible reality of the natural order – is important here.

While endorsing Pannenberg's call for a public engagement with the natural world, it is important to note that Pannenberg's approach is vulnerable on account of its failure to explicitly acknowledge the tradition-embedded character of the intellectual frameworks through which the natural order is viewed, and on the basis of which it is interpreted. The natural world which is to be interpreted may indeed be regarded as a publicly observable entity (although to far less an extent than Pannenberg seems to appreciate); nevertheless, the process of *observation* entails '*seeing nature as God's creation*'. A publicly accessible entity is thus to be observed and interpreted on the basis of a way of viewing reality which is specific to the Christian tradition.

I have shown that the Enlightenment demanded a single, universal rationality for the investigation of the world, including the 'reading' of nature. Modernity insisted that there was only one way of seeing things. There was only one way of viewing the world, determined by a universal and omnicompetent human reason. Those who took their stand on particularities – such as the notion of divine revelation – were excoriated as 'irrational', and charged with 'the scandal of particularity'.

Yet with the collapse of the Enlightenment and the rise of post-modernity, such ideas seem implausible and seriously outdated. The allegedly 'universal' rationality of the Enlightenment is now recognized as being strongly ethnocentric, and hence as an example of – not the sole exception to! – precisely the same 'scandal of particularity' which it so deplored. As the plausibility of the Enlightenment vision of a single, universal and necessary way of thinking eroded to the point at which it could no longer be taken seriously, alternatives began to emerge. The most significant of these is the notion of 'tradition-mediated rationalities', developed by Alasdair MacIntyre and his followers. The second volume in the scientific theology project, entitled *Reality* (pp. 93–169), therefore moves on to deal with this new development, and demonstrate how it enhances the appeal and intellectual credibility of the approach to theology set out in this work.

Yet a broader issue must also be addressed – that of *realism*. Is there an external world, and how may it be accessed and represented? Can transcendent ideas be developed by an appeal to the natural order – or is the naturalist position correct? How does a scientific theology offer an account of reality? And how does such a rendering relate to rival accounts, such as those of the natural sciences? Or the cultural and intellectual enterprises loosely gathered together as 'postmodernity'? To these questions we now turn.

3

Reality

I have indicated that a scientific theology is realist in its outlook, and noted the explicit commitment of writers such as Thomas F. Torrance to this approach. However, this brief statement of theological realism is completely inadequate. In the first place, it fails to offer a defence of realism, indicating why this position is to be preferred over its alternatives. In the second, it leaves open the precise kind of realism which is to be adopted. In the case of a scientific theology, I advocate the view that the form of realism best adapted for theological engagement is the 'critical realism' of Roy Bhaskar. This is one of the most innovative and distinct features of the Scientific Theology project, which represents the first major theological application of this philosophy. But what is this form of realism, and what specific advantages does it confer? The first major issue to be considered is the question of how reliable knowledge is acquired.

7. Rationality and Knowledge in Theology and the Natural Sciences

Theology is concerned with knowledge of God and the world. It is therefore important to give careful consideration to the question of how such knowledge is acquired. The debate goes back to Plato, who attempted to distinguish between 'opinion' and 'knowledge' – in other words, between a weaker and stronger form of knowledge. My basic position is that knowledge arises through a sustained and passionate attempt to engage with a reality that is encountered or made known.

Yet this insistence that theology is a response to reality must be qualified. It is not enough simply to assert that knowledge arises as a response to reality: the question of how that reality is represented must be given consideration as well. At times, the process of the investigation of reality will give rise to hypotheses arising from reality – for example, proposing that our available evidence requires us to postulate the existence of entities that presently cannot be proved, even though we may believe that their existence is fully warranted. For this reason, a scientific theology must extend to include both knowledge that arises through engaging with a reality that is encountered or made known, as well as the postulation of hypothetical entities or the formulation of such constructs as seem appropriate in attempting to represent that reality, however provisionally.

One approach to the failure of the Enlightenment is to argue for a communitarian approach to knowledge. This is exemplified by Richard Rorty, in works such as *The Consequences of Pragmatism* (1982). In an earlier work, *Philosophy and the Mirror of Nature* (1979), Rorty argued for the failure of the Enlightenment project, which he traces back to the classical Greek period. Its leading features, he argues, can be summarized as follows:[1]

To know is to represent accurately what is outside the mind; so to understand the possibility and nature of knowledge is to understand the way in which the mind is able to construct such representations. Philosophy's central concern is to be a general theory of representation.

We must reject any idea that there is some objective reality, standing above history and culture, which the human mind is able to grasp and represents – as in the classical image of philosophy as a 'mirror' of the natural order itself. In place of this outmoded approach, Rorty argues for a communitarian approach to knowledge.[2]

Our identification with our community – our society, our political tradition, our intellectual heritage – is heightened when we see this community as ours rather than nature's, shaped rather than found, one among many which men have made. In the end, the pragmatists tell us, what matters is our loyalty to other human beings clinging together against the dark, not our hope of getting things right.

Rorty's solution to the philosophical crisis of postmodernity is to argue that human communities create their own values and ideas, without any need to refer to, engage with or feel accountable to an alleged 'external reality'. Truth and morality are both the creations of communities, which define themselves with reference to such ideas or values. As he insists in *The Consequences of Pragmatism*:[3]

There is nothing deep down inside us except what we have put there ourselves, no criterion that we have not created in the course of creating a practice, no standard of rationality that is not an appeal to such a criterion, no rigorous argumentation that is not obedience to our own conventions.

There are a number of difficulties with this approach, not least the arguments of the Italian Marxist writer Antonio Gramsci, who pointed out that such communitarian consensus was the product of social engineering on the part of people with definite agendas, and access to power. Furthermore, the reception of certain scientific theories – such as Darwinism – clearly rests upon the community's perception that they are true and hence demand respect on account of their correspondence with reality.

A significant theological variant of this 'communitarian' approach is found in the post-liberal or 'Yale' school of theology, perhaps most significantly in George Lindbeck's 1984 work *The Nature of Doctrine*. This approach gives priority to the existing beliefs and practices of the Church, considered as a socio-linguistic community. A scientific theology, in contrast, argues that the central task of theology is to respond coherently to reality – in other words, insisting that theological formulations should be grounded in an external reality, and should be internally consistent. This could be summarized like this:

1. Scientific theories are grounded in the real world.
2. They are regarded as being 'accountable' to the reality they purport to represent.
3. Ontological finality is thus firmly understood to rest with nature itself.
4. Scientific theories are not merely understood to be grounded in an external reality; the ideas which arise from such an engagement with reality should ultimately be consistent with each other.

This can be summarized by proposing external and internal – or, to put this more formally, extrasystemic and intrasystemic – criteria for the validation of scientific theorizing. Scientific theories should be grounded in the bedrock of an engagement with the real world, and the theories resulting from this engagement should be internally consistent.

In recent years, a number of theological approaches have been

developed which stress the importance of internal consistency –
for example, George Lindbeck's proposal that doctrine regulates
the language of the Christian community. Yet coherentism – the
idea that the internal consistency of a system is itself good enough
as a marker or guarantor of truth – is inadequate, and needs sup-
plementation. The coherentist position, taken on its own, is perfectly capable of validating an internally consistent worldview
which makes no significant point of contact with the real world,
or which evades such contact altogether. Coherency does not guarantee truth – merely logical consistency. A belief can be consistent
with all other beliefs within a system, and yet have no independent
supporting evidence. A scientific theology affirms the critical
importance of both extrasystemic reference and intrasystemic
consistency, holding that a proper grasp of spiritual reality will
ensure both.

We now have to engage with some of the issues arising from the
collapse of foundationalism, especially the view, expressed by
some writers, that this development entails the rise of a non-realist
or anti-realist philosophy. Foundationalism is an integral aspect
of the philosophical project of modernity, resting on foundations
laid by René Descartes. For Descartes, true knowledge would be
infallible, incorrigible and indubitable. Its axioms would be generated by the human mind, and shown to be immune from error,
refutation and doubt. Other propositions could then be derived
from these basic axioms of reason, which served as a foundation
(hence 'foundationalism') of all knowledge.

The polemical aspects of this programme can hardly be overlooked. For the Enlightenment, a foundationalist philosophy
opened the way to neutralizing – possibly even eliminating – the
authority of divine revelation, whether through Scripture or the
teaching office of the Church. There was no need to acknowledge
either authority; what was true could be established and known

through human reason. Rationalism was thus proposed as the intellectual and cultural liberator of humanity.

A favourite comparison at the time was between a rationalist philosophy and geometry. Benedict (or Baruch) Spinoza, for example, wrote an influential treatise in which he argued that ethics could be treated in essentially the same manner as geometry. Euclid's five principles of geometry – from which an entire geometrical system could be deduced – were often appealed to by rationalist writers as demonstrating that a great secure edifice of philosophy and ethics could be deduced from a foundational set of indubitable assumptions. But the dream turned sour. The discovery of non-Euclidian geometry during the nineteenth century destroyed the appeal of this analogy. It turned out that there were other ways of doing geometry, each just as internally consistent as Euclid's.

There are three fundamental assumptions underlying such a foundationalist approach to philosophy, such as that of Descartes:

1. That there are 'foundational' or 'basic' beliefs which guarantee their own truth, which are accessible to any rational person, irrespective of their historical or cultural context. In other words, human reason, unimpeded by its historical or cultural location, is capable of deducing certain fundamental truths, which can act as the foundation of a system of knowledge.

2. That the human mind may use these 'foundational' or 'basic' beliefs to construct other beliefs, which are based upon them. A series of 'mediate' or 'non-basic' beliefs may thus be derived from these 'foundational' or 'basic' beliefs by the use of right reason.

3. That the truth of these 'foundational' or 'basic' beliefs is maintained when deriving such 'mediate' or 'non-basic' beliefs from them.

It used to be held that mathematics was a classic example of such foundationalist beliefs. For Gottlob Frege, arithmetic was founded on logical principles which were available to any rational being, irrespective of their historical or cultural location. The laws of logic were thus foundational, the 'laws of the laws of nature', as Frege put it. They could act as the foundation of other beliefs derived from them. However, Bertrand Russell pointed out that there was a fallacy in Frege's argument, which undermined the credibility of the foundationalist approach. As the philosopher of mathematics Reuben Hersch commented:[4]

> We are still in the aftermath of the great foundationist controversies of the early twentieth century. Formalism, intuitionism and logicism each left its trace in the form of a certain mathematical research program that ultimately made its own contribution to the corpus of mathematics itself. As *philosophical* programs, as attempts to establish a secure foundation for mathematical knowledge, all have run their course and petered out or dried up.

While the failure of mathematical foundationalism prompted some philosophers to seek certainty elsewhere, others yielded to what seemed the inevitable outcome of such explorations – namely, that the search for such indubitable foundations of knowledge had failed. As has often been pointed out, foundationalism has now been rejected by virtually every major epistemologist and philosopher of science of the last half of the century, from the later writings of Ludwig Wittgenstein through Karl Popper, W. F. Sellars and W. V. O. Quine. The belief that foundationalism is philosophically indefensible is the closest thing to a philosophical consensus there has been for a very long time.

But what are the implications of this? From the standpoint of the natural sciences, the death of foundationalism has little impact. Knowledge is grounded in a rigorous engagement with

reality, and does not depend on deducing 'first principles'.
Knowledge is inferred from observation (and its extended variant,
experimentation), not deduced from allegedly self-evident truths.
Foundationalism is the form of philosophy required for the
Enlightenment project, which rests on the assumption that the
human mind is capable of generating and validating its own ideas.
This kind of approach is found in the writings of Spinoza.
Spinoza's philosophy is essentially deductive, rational and monist
– that is, Spinoza holds that all things, no matter how many or of
what variety, can be reduced to one unified thing or quality in time
and space. Like Descartes, he has an intensely mathematical appreciation of the universe. Things make sense when understood in
relation to a total structure; truth, like geometry, follows from first
principles with a logic accessible and evident to the human mind.

Neither the natural sciences nor Christian theology depend
upon such a philosophy; indeed, both can be argued to develop
approaches which avoid the pitfalls of the Enlightenment. In the
case of the natural sciences, the starting-point is not allegedly
certain beliefs about the world, deduced by reason, but the empirical observation of the world, and such resulting theories as are
held to be entailed by those observations.

Natural scientists thus do not need to make (and, indeed,
cannot make) *any* foundational assumptions about the world *a
priori*. Rather, what knowledge of the world they come to regard
as reliable is based upon experimental investigation of the world,
and reflection on what this investigation appears to disclose,
which itself may be subject to further experimental investigation.
Arguing that scientific theories offer some degree of correspondence with reality does not depend upon *a priori* beliefs, but upon
a posteriori conclusions resulting from an empirical engagement
with the real world. To abandon foundationalism is not to
become reliant solely upon a coherentist account of truth – a line

of argument which can be found, for example, in the philosophy of Richard Rorty, or the theology of George Lindbeck.

In the case of Christian theology, it is possible to argue for an *extrasystemic* accountability to a set of realities which are held to be 'foundational' to the Christian tradition (meaning that they underlie its distinctive claims), without falling into the discredited and outmoded Enlightenment belief that they are 'foundational' in the sense of being purely rational axioms, independent of the contingencies of history and culture. Yet alongside this, there is a clear need for an *intrasystemic* accountability, framed in terms of the internal consistency of Christian doctrine. A scientific theology seeks to respond coherently to reality.

Yet some within the theological world appear to have drawn the somewhat premature conclusion that the demise of foundationalism forces theology to adopt a purely coherentist account of Christian doctrine. In light of the influence of the views of George Lindbeck and the 'Yale' school of theology, this position must be critiqued.

A critique of post-liberal coherentism: George Lindbeck

George Lindbeck's *Nature of Doctrine* (1984) set out an approach to Christian doctrine which gained much critical attention throughout the 1990s. What can now be seen as unrealistically high hopes for its potential were entertained by many writers, who were attracted by its stripped-down and thoroughly functionalist account of Christian doctrine as the grammatical regulator of the Christian language.

Lindbeck argues that theories of doctrine can be broken down into three broad categories. He defines these as:

1. A *cognitive-propositionalist* model, which regards doctrines as making cognitive truth-claims. Doctrines are here

understood to make objective statements concerning reality. Lindbeck regards this as the position of classic and recent scholastic writers, such as Thomas Aquinas.

2. An *experiential-expressive* model, which holds that doctrines are outward expressions of an identifiable core experience common to all Christian traditions, and possibly all world religions. Lindbeck sees this as characteristic of liberal Protestant writers, beginning with the great Berlin theologian F. D. E. Schleiermacher.

3. A *cultural-linguistic* model, which is basically a form of coherentism. This is Lindbeck's own position.

In view of the weight which I place on 'critical realism', it is important to note that Lindbeck adopts a reductionist strategy which improperly holds that only one level of reality – namely, the present-day beliefs of the ecclesial community – need be engaged in theological analysis. On a critical realist reading of things, each of these three models of doctrine can be accommodated as engaging with a distinct level of a greater reality.

Lindbeck argues that the concept of *intrasystemic consistency* is of critical importance. Doctrines regulate religions, in much the same way that grammar regulates language, with the objective of ensuring coherence and consistency within a cultural or linguistic system. Lindbeck thus de-emphasizes the intellectual content of a doctrinal statement in order to stress its formal function. It is not what a doctrine appears to say that matters, but its place and function within the overall fabric of the Christian faith. Lindbeck illustrates this point with reference to Shakespeare's *Hamlet*: the statement 'Denmark is the land where Hamlet lived' makes no claim to ontological truth or falsity, but is to be viewed as a statement concerning the internal ordering of the elements of Shakespeare's narrative.

Doctrines thus regulate the language of a religious community. On the basis of this coherentist approach to doctrine in general, as well as individual doctrines, Lindbeck seems to hold that there is no need to believe that they have anything to do with God, or even with reality in general. This is perhaps one of the most troubling aspects of Lindbeck's approach to doctrine. For example, consider his views on the role of creeds:[5]

> A creed may function regulatively (doctrinally) and yet not propositionally. It seems odd to suggest that the Nicaenum in its role as a communal doctrine does not make first-order truth claims, and yet this is what I shall contend. Doctrines regulate truth claims by excluding some and permitting others, but the logic of their communally authoritative use hinders or prevents them from specifying positively what is affirmed.

From a historical point of view, it may be noted at this point that the church fathers who formulated the Nicene position would not have concurred with Lindbeck's account of their goals. Lindbeck is quite right when he suggests that it 'seems odd' to suggest that doctrine merely regulates truth-claims, rather than making such truth-claims in the first place. The reason that it 'seems odd' is that it is not what the Christian tradition has understood itself to be doing, despite Lindbeck's attempts to redirect it or reinterpret it on this point. Applied consistently, Lindbeck's approach renders doctrine incapable of making any cognitive, propositional or even intelligible statements about God.

Lindbeck seems to believe that conceiving doctrine as the grammar of the Christian language entails the abandonment of any talk about God as an independent reality and any suggestion that it is possible to make truth-claims (in an ontological, rather than intra-systemic, sense) concerning him. Lindbeck thus argues that theology is a 'second-order' activity which does not make truth-claims.[6]

Just as grammar by itself affirms nothing either true or false regarding the world in which language is used, but only about language, so theology and doctrine, to the extent that they are second-order activities, assert nothing either true or false about God and his relation to creatures, but only speak about such assertions.

On the basis of this severely limited conception of theology, it can only be thought of as 'talk about talk about God', not 'talk about God'. Theology addresses the language and conventions of the community, not the subject it believes itself to be representing in, through or under that language.

There are two fundamental difficulties with Lindbeck's approach, both of which are resolved through the type of approach I wish to offer in its place.

First, as David Tracy pointed out in a penetrating review of *The Nature of Doctrine*,[7] Lindbeck suffers all the weaknesses of 'Barthian confessionalism' in that theology 'has to be done purely from within the confessing community'. This seems to mark a retreat from any significant cultural or intellectual engagement. This serious problem – both for Barth and for Lindbeck – can be countered by an approach to natural theology which recognizes and emphasizes its role as an explanatory tool by which the Christian tradition may engage in faithful yet productive dialogue with other traditions. This is, however, not a move that Barth or Lindbeck regard as legitimate.

Second, Lindbeck does not explain how doctrines are grounded in, or related to, reality. They are just there. Historically, this is simply unacceptable. Lindbeck is unable to account for the phenomenon of doctrinal development, or respond to the need for theological reformulation and revision – such as the entire theological project of the Reformation. He is trapped by his pragmatism, in that his vision of the contents of Christian theology is determined by what the community currently happens to believe, without any means of probing whether such beliefs are authentic or not. This weakness can be countered by proposing that Christian theology aims to offer a coherent account of a reality to which it ultimately refers – the approach adopted throughout the scientific theology project.

What seemed to some in the 1980s to be George Lindbeck's theological superhighway has turned out to be something of a dead end, snarled up with all kinds of problems and shortcomings that can no longer be ignored. In its place, a scientific theology proposes an approach based on a new appreciation of the role played by a Christian natural theology. When properly interpreted along the lines set out in the first volume of *A Scientific Theology*, this offers a tool for the interpretation of a publicly accessible entity – namely, the natural world – which is located within a specific tradition, yet capable of extending far beyond that original tradition in terms of its explanatory power. We shall turn to consider this in what follows.

8. Natural Theology and the Trans-Traditional Rationality of the Christian Tradition

One of the most distinctive features of recent discussions of the foundations of knowledge has been the collapse of the Enlightenment dogma of the universality of human rationality. Based on the assumption that there is a 'universal human reason', independent of the exigencies of space, time and culture, Enlightenment writers insisted that there was one single, universal set of criteria by which all beliefs could be established and confirmed. It was a powerful vision. If it was correct, then it followed that humanity had in its possession a universally valid means of adjudicating on every issue of importance, without the need to appeal to the authority of God, church or tradition. It was possible, such writers believed, to identify criteria of judgement, valid for all minds and across all cultures and traditions at all times.

Yet the vision failed. The empirical study of cultural rationalities disclosed a very different pattern – namely, that people possessed (and still possess) different and at times contradictory notions both of what is 'rational', 'true' and 'right', and how those qualities might be defended. The Enlightenment turned out to be just as ethnocentric as any of its rivals. As Nicholas Wolterstorff and other recent philosophers have pointed out, what seemed 'obvious' or 'basic' were actually person-specific and situation-specific. What was once thought to be globally valid was gradually realized to be historically situated and socially constructed. The Enlightenment assumption that there was only one 'rationality', independent of time, space and culture, has given way to the recognition that there are – and always have been – many different 'rationalities'.

So, given the failure of the Enlightenment, what are its alternatives? One reaction to the failure of the Enlightenment project has been the systematic postmodern inversion of many of its foundational judgements. Perhaps most importantly for our purposes, the alleged 'objectivity' of knowledge has been called into question, and displaced by an increasing emphasis upon the social construction of reality. Postmodern writers have argued that our intellectual worlds are free constructs of the autonomous individual, who is unrestricted in that process of construction by external limitations or pressures. Postmodernity countered the Enlightenment pretensions to universality with an emphasis upon the local. Since there is no globally valid rationality or ethic, the solution lies in local options. There is no universal, overarching metanarrative; just lots of local ones, with chastened and modest claims to validity.

Paul Feyerabend took the consequences of the collapse of the defining Enlightenment belief in a single, universal rationality to its obvious conclusion in a famous comparison between a primitive tribe and the rationalists of the Enlightenment: 'There is hardly any difference between the members of a primitive tribe who defend their laws because they are the laws of the gods . . . and a rationalist who appeals to objective standards, except that the former know what they are doing while the latter does not.'[8]

Yet the postmodern position is equally vulnerable. Indeed, the natural sciences and mathematics are the two most awkward stumbling-blocks to the advancement of the postmodern agenda. The natural sciences offer no support for the relativism of the postmodern project. In its place they recognize an objectivity, tempered by a degree of social construction appropriate to the distinctive nature of the scientific discipline in question. The development of such social constructs as are appropriate to any given intellectual discipline is nothing other than a principled exercise in attempting to understand the world as best as possible, and to develop for this purpose whatever tools or conceptualities are demanded by any given natural science and the strata of reality it engages.

These differing modes of interplay and representation are governed by the nature of the strata of reality under investigation, each of which demands its own distinctive mode of engagement. To set up a principle that is of decisive importance throughout this project: *ontology (the way things are) determines epistemology (the ways things are known)*. The nature of reality is such that certain things can only be known to a certain extent, and in a certain way – and that is the reality of the situation. We are not in a position to determine whether and how things may be known; that is decided by the things themselves. The recognition of some degree of social construction in some of the natural sciences, such as psychology, does not entail that we are free to invent ideas, just as the individual thinker or community of discourse

pleases. The natural sciences do not see themselves as representing a free construction of the human mind, but as attempts to
respond coherently and responsibly to the external reality of the
world. I consider some particular concerns about the postmodern
enterprise later in the work.

So what is the alternative to the dead ends of modernism and
postmodernism? Is there a third way, which avoids the sterility of
both of these discredited and intensely problematic approaches?
The modernist vision of one, universal rationality has been
exposed as an illusion; the postmodern alternative is widely recognized to be an over-reaction against modernism, insensitive to
issues of evidence and truth. In recent years, considerable interest
has developed in the notion of tradition-mediated rationality,
which has been especially associated with the name of Alasdair
MacIntyre. In what follows, we shall consider this philosophy,
and its relevance to the scientific theology project.

Alasdair MacIntyre and the role of tradition

Since about 1990, Alasdair MacIntyre has come to be recognized
as one of the most significant moral philosophers of the twentieth century, whose work has implications far beyond the
rather limited field of morality, and extends to the entire intellectual enterprise. As MacIntyre may be unfamililar to some
readers, some introductory comments will be useful. Before
1971, MacIntyre's work was somewhat fragmented, involving
interesting yet not always fruitful explorations in areas such as
the relation of Christianity to Marxism. Around that time, he
left his native England, and settled in North America, where he
worked until 1977. This was a period of critical self-reflection,
which eventually led him to chart a new and coherent philosophical path.

MacIntyre had given careful thought to how a moral system might be constructed and defended, often focusing his thinking on some of the ethical dilemmas which arose within Marxism – for example, the failure of many within the movement to mount a viable critique of Stalinism. The research lying behind his 1966 work *A Short History of Ethics* persuaded him that there was no 'universal morality'; instead, history disclosed that different moral systems were adopted by different groups of people, situated at different locations in history, for different reasons. The Enlightenment dream of a universal ethics, grounded as securely as Euclidian geometry, simply could not be maintained. It was an illusion, quite inconsistent with the brute facts of history.

His influential and important solution to this dilemma was developed in a series of works published over the ten-year period 1981–1990,[9] whose volumes set out his critique of existing positions, and his formulation of a tradition-based rationality and morality.

Alasdair MacIntyre's relentless exposure of the inconsistencies and failings of the Enlightenment project has itself played a significant role in the abandonment of the myth of a 'universal reason' and a rediscovery of the importance of the community and its traditions in rational discourse. In *Whose Justice? Which Rationality?*, MacIntyre points out the inconsistencies and failures which plagued the Enlightenment attempt to identify universal moral and rational principles.[10]

> Both the thinkers of the Enlightenment and their successors proved unable to agree as to precisely what those principles were which would be found undeniable by all rational persons. One kind of answer was given by the authors of the *Encyclopédie*, a second by Rousseau, a third by Bentham, a fourth by Kant, a fifth by the Scottish philosophers of common sense and their French and American disciples. Nor has subsequent history diminished the extent of such disagreement. Consequently, the legacy of the Enlightenment has been the provision

of an ideal of rational justification which it has proved impossible to attain.

For MacIntyre, the only conclusion that can be drawn from this obvious failure is that there is no universal rationality. Intead, we must accept that there are competing tradition-mediated ration-alities, which are in conflict, and which cannot be totally detached from the traditions which mediate them. They may have preten-sions to universality; nevertheless, the historical fact remains that they are specific to traditions.

MacIntyre argues that we are driven to accept the concept of a tradition-mediated rationality for a number of reasons, chief among which is the verdict of history. Historical analysis – such as that which he set out in his 1966 work *A Short History of Ethics* – demonstrates that there is no universal rationality, no privileged vantage point or mode of thought which allows these competing traditions to be judged. We are confronted with a series of different traditions, which both *constitute* and *mediate* rival visions of reason and justice. As he puts it in *Whose Justice? Which Rationality?*[11]

> The history of attempts to construct a morality for tradition-free individuals . . . has in its outcome . . . been a history of continuously contested disputes, so that there emerges no uncontested and incon-testable account of what tradition-independent morality consists in and consequently no neutral set of criteria by means of which the claims of rival and contending traditions could be adjudicated.

The Enlightenment held that it occupied a privileged position from which it could adjudicate between traditions; in fact, the Enlightenment is simply another tradition, not something which stands over and against them. Modernity believed that it was somehow excused from the specifics of history and culture, when it was, in reality, simply another strand of the historical web. It was just as entangled in the contingencies of history as those worldviews that it critiqued, and sought to displace.

A similar line of argument is developed in his work *Three Rival Versions of Moral Inquiry*. MacIntyre here argues once more that philosophy in general and ethics in particular cannot proceed by means of reasoning from neutral, self-evident facts accepted by all rational persons. He concedes that many intellectuals of the late Victorian period believed exactly that, confusing the customs of their time with universal truths. However, this view simply cannot be sustained. After setting out the views of what he terms the 'genealogists' and the 'encyclopedists' and subjecting them to a withering criticism, MacIntyre turns to set out a third option, which alone he regarded to be viable – the rediscovery of tradition.

So how does this approach work? For MacIntyre, the solution to moral problems does not, and cannot, lie in an appeal to an allegedly universal conception of moral judgement, but in working within the tradition that supplies the framework of judgement for those posing that moral problem. Both conceptions of rationality and morality are shaped and transmitted by traditions, which act like the *polis* of ancient Greece. Perhaps MacIntyre's greatest achievement, from the perspective of a scientific theology, is to rehabilitate the notion that Christianity possesses a distinct yet rational understanding of reality – a coupling which the Enlightenment regarded as impossible. Christianity is once more free to reassert its distinctiveness, instead of submitting itself to the Enlightenment insistence on a universal human reason which determined all things, seeing divergence from its judgements as 'irrationality'.

MacIntyre fully realizes that his approach raises some important questions, not least whether these traditions merely transmit unstable and ultimately untenable ideas. Yet he points out that history suggests that traditions have a capacity to reform and renew themselves, through a constant process of re-examination

and restatement. MacIntyre points to traditions developing in
new directions, abandoning previous approaches in the light of
the recognition of tensions and inconsistencies within the tradition. Thus a tradition might be abandoned or reconstituted 'when
the discrepancy between the beliefs of an earlier stage of a tradition of enquiry are contrasted with the world of things as they
have come to be understood at a later stage'.[12]

MacIntyre is clear that a rationality, although specific to a tradition, is often capable of offering a universal perspective on things,
despite not being universally accepted. In other words, a tradition-
specific way of thinking or explaining may, despite being specific
to a tradition, offer a way of making sense of the entire vista of the
world, rather than the bounds of its own tradition. A tradition-
mediated rationality may thus be *universal* in the scope of its application, while being *particular* in the extent to which it is accepted.
Two issues then emerge as being of especial importance.

> First, how does a tradition account for its own existence?
> Second, how does a given tradition account for the existence of
>   rival traditions?

The plausibility of the answers given will be of major importance
to determining the reliability of a tradition.

MacIntyre offers answers to each of these. First, he argues that
each tradition is to be analysed on its own internal terms, to establish whether it is internally coherent, and whether it is able to
address the questions that the tradition itself generates.

It is MacIntyre's second criterion which is of especial interest.
Can questions which cannot be answered by tradition *A* be
answered by tradition *B*? In other words, can tradition *A* recognize
that tradition *B* is able to answer a question that tradition *A* has been
unable to answer satisfactorily in its own history? It is this second
question which is of major importance. MacIntyre argues that it is

perfectly possible to compare one tradition with another, and conclude that one is to be preferred, *without* needing to bring in a third arbitrating tradition – which would, of course, be in the same epistemological position as the other two. (The Enlightenment, remember, thought it stood above traditions, in a privileged transhistorical position.) Nevertheless, raising this question forces us to look more closely at how any given tradition is able to account for both the existence and at least something of the character of competing traditions. In effect, we are called upon to account for the commonalities which unquestionably exist between traditions, despite their radical divergences at other points, while at the same time confronting the critical question which cannot be evaded – namely, *which tradition is to be preferred, and on what grounds?*

It is at this point that a natural theology, in the sense in which we have been using this term, becomes of major explanatory importance. For a scientific theology, natural theology is to be understood as 'the enterprise of seeing nature as creation, which both presupposes and reinforces fundamental Christian theological affirmations'. This natural theology is able to offer important insights as to why rival traditions exist, especially in offering a coherent explanation of why certain themes are common to most traditions. The Christian doctrine of creation can thus be said to be of meta-traditional significance – in other words, although specific to the Christian tradition, the doctrine is able to explain aspects of other traditions. The scientific tradition, for example, finds itself having to presuppose the uniformity and ordering of creation; Christian theology offers an account of this. The scientific tradition recognizes that the natural world has a rationality which human rationality can discern and systematize; Christian theology, however, offers an explanation of why this is the case. On both of MacIntyre's criteria, the Christian tradition is able to set forth a plausible claim to represent a robust and resilient account of reality.

The capacity of a natural theology – which, it must be stressed, is specific to the Christian tradition – to deal with MacIntyre's second question is then explored in detail. The essential point here is that this natural theology posits that something of God may be known outside the Christian tradition. The possibility of truth is grounded, not merely in the existence of a God, but in the existence of the *Christian* God – that is, the God who is specifically revealed, known and worshipped within the Christian tradition – who is held to have created the world and humanity, and has not left us 'without witness' to the divine presence and activity (Acts 14:16). The impetus to quest for God is, according to Paul's Areopagus sermon, itself grounded in the creative action of God (Acts 17:26–7).

Other traditions, without necessarily realizing that they have done so, may thus base their conceptions of rationality upon an attenuated yet real perception of the nature and character of God, based upon a predisposition of the created mind to quest for such a God, and the proclivity of nature in bearing witness to that same God, in however nuanced and indirect a fashion. The doctrine of creation is thus a tradition-mediated notion which offers a framework by which the publicly accessible natural order may be interpreted and assessed.

A Christian natural theology, speaking from within the Christian tradition and from a Christian perspective, offers a specific vantage point from which the intellectual landscape may be charted and explained. Though tradition-specific, it has aspirations to universality precisely because the story which it relates offers an ultimate and coherent organizing logic which accounts for its own existence, as well as that of its rivals. In short: natural theology offers and accounts for a trans-traditional rationality, which is grounded in the particularities of the Christian tradition alone. It offers insights into both the existence of the Christian tradition (MacIntyre's first concern) and that of its rivals

(MacIntyre's second concern). Christians believe these claims to be true and warranted, while recognizing that there is no means of *proving* these claims by universally accepted criteria – precisely because there *are* no universally accepted criteria. Once more, the importance of the failure of the Enlightenment dream of universal criteria of rationality and judgement must be noted.

So how does such a natural theology actually work? The long history of Christian theological reflection has thrown up at least three ways of conceiving how the Christian tradition offers what is in effect a meta-traditional 'reading' of the world:

1. The idea, particularly associated with patristic theologians (such as Justin Martyr) dialoguing with the Platonic tradition, that seeds of the divine wisdom or nature were planted within the fabric of the created order, and were capable of being discerned as such by the human mind.

2. The Thomist doctrine of the 'analogy of being' (*analogia entis*), which holds that the created order is able to offer an accommodated or refracted vision of God, particularly through analogies which ultimately rest upon the creative action of God, coupled with the faithful discernment of this analogy on the part of the observer.

3. The Barthian concept of the 'analogy of faith' (*analogia fidei*), which affirms the radical dependence of the created world order upon God, so that any correspondence between creation and God is established by God in the act of revelation, not by his creatures through the act of theological reflection.

Having established this general principle, I now examine a number of areas in which a natural theology offers a coherent and illuminating account of commonalities which exist with other traditions, while at the same time offering a plausible account of how those rival traditions might arise. I shall note these briefly, and summarize their importance.

Mathematics and trans-traditional rationality

Mathematics has a remarkable ability to represent the world – as Galileo famously remarked, the 'book of the universe' is 'written in the language of mathematics'. In a series of important writings, the Oxford mathematician Roger Penrose reflected on this capacity, and its theological implications. In his *Shadows of the Mind* (1995), widely regarded as one of the most important books on the philosophy of mathematics to appear in recent years, Penrose argued that the most satisfactory explanation of the beauty and structure of mathematics was that they were somehow given by God.[13] Mathematicians therefore do not invent equations and formulas *a priori*; they discover God's antecedent creations *a posteriori*.

The importance of a natural theology in explaining this development will be obvious. Penrose concludes that three worlds exist, which must somehow be correlated in the human quest for knowledge and understanding. These are the world of 'our conscious perceptions', the physical world outside us, and the 'Platonic world of mathematical forms'. This is completely consistent with the Christian notion of the world as God's creation, being interpreted by the human mind, created 'in the image of God'. We could summarize the situation in tabular form like this:

Penrose	Christianity
The Platonic world	The mind of God as creator
The physical world	The world as God's creation
The mental world	Humanity as God's creation

The Christian doctrine of creation establishes a continuity between these three worlds, whose relation for Penrose, while real, is nonetheless something of an enigma. Penrose himself argued that the most satisfactory explanation of the beauty and structure of mathematics is that they are somehow given by God. Mathematicians therefore do not invent equations and formulas; they discover God's antecedent creations. On the basis of this doctrine of creation, a fundamental harmony is to be expected between the 'laws of the mind' and the 'laws of nature'.

Natural theology and the trans-traditional religious quest

I now turn to consider perhaps one of the most important applications of natural theology – its role in accounting for other religious traditions. Again, we find the same line of thought: a Christian natural theology affirms the existence of partial and fragmentary – yet *real* – insights into the world outside the Christian tradition, while holding that this tradition itself represents their full disclosure, to the extent that they may be known at all. The Christian tradition possesses two advantages over its rivals:

1. It offers an explanation of the world which is internally coherent, and an explanation of the externally observable fact that related insights may be held, at least to some extent, outside the Christian tradition.

2. It holds that what may be known of God through nature, although in a fragmentary and potentially inconsistent manner, may be had in full through the Christian revelation, which is *specific* to the Christian tradition. Thus John Calvin explores the relation of a natural and revealed knowledge of God through a dialogue with Cicero, representing a comparison of two great traditions – classical pagan religion and the Christian faith.

The apologetic implications of this are considerable. Three points may be noted briefly.

1. In his Leslie Stephen Memorial Lecture at the University of Cambridge in November 1985, Georg Steiner pointed out how a natural theology, grounded in a Christian doctrine of creation, provided the basis of a meta-traditional appeal to beauty: 'there is aesthetic creation because there is *creation*'.

2. A similar point is made by Robert Jenson in exploring the way in which the eighteenth-century American theologian Jonathan Edwards finds a close correlation, if not outright identity, between God's holiness and beauty, with highly significant implications for Edwards's encounter with (and reading of) the 'book of nature'.

3. One of the more significant achievements of Hans Urs von Balthasar is to have demonstrated that such an approach can be extended far beyond an encounter with the purely natural world to embrace the world of human culture.

Balthasar's line of thought naturally leads us to move on, and consider the implications of a natural theology as a trans-traditional explanation of the human quest for wonder.

Natural theology and the trans-traditional sense of wonder

A natural theology offers an explanation of the sense of wonder often experienced by human beings on encountering the beauty of nature. On the basis of a Christian doctrine of creation, this sense of wonder is to be directly correlated with the dual origination of both the natural world and the human imaginative faculty in the mind of God.

The sense of wonder which is evoked before any rational reflection takes place must be seen both in terms of the natural resonance of the human imagination with the mind of God as expressed in creation, and in terms of a symbolic role as a pointer to the God who created both nature and humanity, and who will bring all things together in the final consummation. This point recurs throughout the writings of Augustine, particularly his *Confessions*.

The point is made by considering the criticisms made of the poet John Keats by Richard Dawkins in his 1998 work *Unweaving the Rainbow*. For Dawkins, Keats's expressions of concern about the reductionist tendencies of scientific theory were of no significance. Dawkins clearly believes that Keats argues that knowing how the rainbow works will destroy its beauty and our resulting sense of wonder. Yet this, he argues, is unacceptable. The rainbow remains just as beautiful if we know how it works. In fact, we can appreciate its beauty even more than before.

Dawkins's reading of the natural order is determined by a strongly anti-metaphysical and anti-religious scientific positivism, which clearly still lingers in at least some sections of the community of natural scientists. Keats wishes to read nature in the light of a transcendentalist framework, clearly derived from a Christian natural theology, which sees nature as possessed of a capacity to signify a transcendent dimension of reality. The recognition of the beauty of nature is thus for Keats an indirect acknowledgement of some grander yet veiled reason and power which lies behind it.

Natural law and the trans-traditional quest for goodness

Finally, we come to consider the role of a natural theology in relation to the great human quest for goodness. There has been a growing resurgence of interest in 'natural justice' in the closing years of the twentieth century, and all three elements of the famous Platonic triad – truth, beauty and goodness – can easily be accommodated by a Christian natural theology. The fundamental human conviction, shared far beyond the Christian tradition, that truth, beauty and goodness are things that are discovered – not invented – can best be grounded in a notion of the dual creation of the world we explore and the minds which we deploy in this process of exploration. A natural theology thus offers an important bridge between traditions, firmly grounded in the specifics of the Christian tradition, but finding a common grace in others.

A Christian doctrine of creation can be argued to set out an understanding of the relation of God, the natural order and human nature which lays the foundation for some trans-traditional understanding of 'goodness' or 'justice' – whether this is understood to be intuited or inferred or from the ordering of the world. Oliver O'Donovan's important work *Resurrection and Moral Ordering* (1986) is a good example of an approach of this kind.[14]

> The order of things that God has made is *there*. It is objective, and mankind has a place within it. Christian ethics, therefore, has an objective reference because it is concerned with man's life in accordance with this order. . . . Thus Christian moral judgements . . . are founded on reality as God has given it. In this assertion, we may find a point of agreement with the classical ethics of Plato, Aristotle and the Stoics which treated ethics as a close correlate of metaphysics. The way the universe *is* determines how man *ought* to behave himself in it.

O'Donovan thus sets out how creation and redemption have both epistemological and ontological relevance to both the nature of this order and the manner of how it may be known.

John Milbank and the critique of secular reason: an assessment

John Milbank is unquestionably one of the most interesting theological writers of the moment, with a particular concern to explore the intellectual autonomy and robustness of the Christian tradition. Firmly rejecting the Enlightenment view of knowledge, Milbank offers a highly significant reworking of an Augustinian vision of theology, linked with a tradition-specific understanding of its tasks. After a period teaching at various universities in England, Milbank moved to Charlottesville to take up the post of Francis Ball Professor of Philosophical Theology at the University of Virginia. His most important work was published in 1989, entitled *Theology and Social Theory: Beyond Secular Reason*. It was originally part of a series of rather introductory books entitled 'Signposts in Theology', which aimed to introduce students to some basic themes and debates in contemporary theology. Milbank's book was different: for a start, it was twice as long as any of its companion volumes.

More significantly, the work, far from being an introduction to social theory and theology, set out a bold original thesis, involving a sustained and highly energetic engagement with just about every luminary in the field of social theory. Milbank set out to demonstrate that secular social theory is characterized by a methodological atheism, which makes it an inappropriate dialogue partner for Christian theology. Milbank insists that this 'secular reason' has been allowed to assume an improper and quite unmerited position within theological discourse. Theology, he argues, should not allow itself to be placed from outside by philosophy and by secular thought generally. Rather, theologians should learn to get over their 'false humility' in the face of modern secular reason. He argues, therefore, for the need for a rediscovery of an authentically Christian and *theological* way of reasoning, which breaks free from the self-incurred bondage of theology to social theory.

In many ways, Milbank builds upon the work of MacIntyre, concurring with him on the importance of traditions in relation to both rationality and morality. Yet Milbank is no passive admirer of MacIntyre; he has some significant criticisms to direct against him, most notably in connection with his demand to purge what he discerns as continuing, yet unacknowledged, vestiges of the Enlightenment within MacIntyre's method. Yet for Milbank, the greatest difference between himself and MacIntyre is 'the role that must be accorded to Christianity and to Christian theology'. The Christian community is constituted by, and proclaims, a 'true Christian metanarrative realism', which is capable of embracing all of human life and activity. It does not need to rely on other narratives, being – at least in its own eyes – the 'grand narrative'.

There are many affinities between Milbank and myself. Indeed, in an important review of the first volume of *A Scientific Theology* in the *Times Literary Supplement* (2002), Richard Roberts suggested that our approaches represented different, yet clearly related, attempts to revision the grand enterprise of Christian theology. Natural theology, as I set out this notion, plays a role within a scientific theology similar to that played by Augustine's epistemology and ontology for John Milbank. We both affirm that a robust doctrine of creation offers a persuasive account of the nature and shape of the world, allowing the Christian worldview to be seen as something which *intentionally* seeks to embrace all human life and activity. Milbank focuses on issues of church, society and culture where I tend to focus on the natural sciences. Nevertheless, the continuity is there. My emphasis on the theological retrieval of nature as creation, and the ontological foundations of the dialogue between theology and the natural sciences can be seen as a transposition of Milbank's approach, rather than as its rival.

Yet there are very significant differences, reflecting the very different orientations of our programmes. I set out three particular divergences, which I consider represent difficulties for Milbank, rather than for myself.

1. Milbank refuses to engage with other traditions, precisely because they do not, and cannot, share common premises. I, on the other hand, cannot see how we can evade the fact that a Christian natural theology both undergirds and encourages a critical engagement with other traditions. Milbank seems to share the exclusivism of writers such as Karl Barth and Cornelius van Til who insist that there is no common ground between faith and unbelief. If I have understood Milbank correctly, he sees no possible point of connection between natural wisdom and the Christian tradition. Yet I see a very different scenario envisaged in the prototypical encounter of pagan wisdom and the Christian proclamation in Athens, as we find it recorded in the 'Areopagus Address' of Acts 17. Surely Paul here attempts to find common ground between the gospel and pagan culture, as a means of embedding the former in the conceptualities of the latter, eventually to transform them?

2. Milbank has a worrying tendency to marginalize the role of Scripture in theology. He does this in two ways. First, by maintaining what I can only describe as a curious silence about the role Scripture has to play in the Christian theological enterprise, despite the crucial role that Scripture has so obviously played in shaping the ideas of the patristic and medieval writers who he so values – such as Augustine and Aquinas. But, second, Milbank seems to assume that Augustine's theology just appeared, without giving careful thought to the long and complex process of doctrinal development within the Christian tradition, in which engagement with the Bible was often of central importance. Like George Lindbeck, Milbank seems to assume that the Christian tradition is just *there*, without being attentive to the complex story of how this complex tradition *emerged*

through historical development. Inevitably, this historically
shallow approach leads him to marginalize both the historical and contemporary role of the Bible in theological
reflection.

3. Milbank objects strongly to dialogue between traditions
(which he regards as somewhat pointless); more particularly, he has serious misgivings concerning the appropriation of ideas from outside the Christian tradition. I have
great sympathy with Milbank's agenda here, and have
myself argued against the uncritical importing of theologically normative ideas and values from outside the Christian
tradition. Milbank commends writers such as Augustine as
models of how theology ought to be done in this respect.
Yet I have serious unease about the reliability of both this
historical judgement and *theological* proposal.

Augustine himself entered into dialogue with non-Christian traditions, and commended others who had done so – such as
Cyprian of Carthage – not least for making the intellectual riches
of these traditions available to the Church. This can be seen from
a famous passage in his great treatise *de doctrina Christiana* ('on
Christian doctrine'):[15]

> Pagan learning is not entirely made up of false teachings and supersti-
> tions. It contains also some excellent teachings, well suited to be used
> by truth, and excellent moral values. Indeed, some truths are even
> found among them which relate to the worship of the one God. Now
> these are, so to speak, their gold and their silver, which they did not
> invent themselves, but which they dug out of the mines of the provi-
> dence of God, which are scattered throughout the world, yet which
> are improperly and unlawfully prostituted to the worship of demons.
> The Christian, therefore, can separate these truths from their unfor-
> tunate associations, take them away, and put them to their proper use
> for the proclamation of the gospel.

Augustine here decisively sets his face *against* the theological isolationism commended by early patristic writers such as Tertullian,
and now apparently endorsed by Milbank. Augustine clearly advocates the *critical appropriation of ideas*, whatever their origins
outside the Church, seeing this as the intellectual equivalent of
claiming the treasures of the Egyptians. Milbank thus finds himself
in the difficult position of endorsing engagement with other traditions *by surrogate*, in that he commends the ideas of others who
themselves adopted this practice and benefited from doing so.

Yet Milbank is unquestionably right in his concern to reaffirm
the importance of the Christian tradition in the theological enterprise. I reaffirm this principle, once again contextualizing this
within the failure of the Enlightenment project, and the new
awareness of the importance of communities and traditions in
relation to the quest for truth, beauty and goodness.

9. The Foundations of Realism in the Natural Sciences

The remarkable explanatory and predictive successes of the
natural sciences are widely held to point to the independent existence of what it describes in its theories. Aeroplanes fly; and the
reason that they fly, at least in part, is the relation between pressure and kinetic energy first set out by Daniel Bernouilli in 1738.
Television and radio work; and the reason that they work, at least
in part, is the implications of James Clerk Maxwell's 1864 theory
of electromagnetic radiation. A long list of technological developments, widely regarded as essential to modern western existence,
can be argued to rest upon the ability of the natural sciences to
develop theories which may initially explain the world, but subsequently allow us to transform it.

And what, many natural scientists ask, more effective explanation may be offered for this success than the simple assertion that

what scientific theories describe is really present? John Polkinghorne is one such scientist; he sets out the situation, as he sees it, in his 1986 work *One World: The Interaction of Science and Theology.*[16]

> The naturally convincing explanation of the success of science is that it is gaining a tightening grasp of an actual reality. The true goal of scientific endeavour is understanding the structure of the physical world, an understanding which is never complete but ever capable of further improvement. The terms of that understanding are dictated by the way things are.

The simplest explanation of what makes theories work is that they relate to the way things really are. If the theoretical claims of the natural sciences were not correct, their massive empirical success would appear to be totally coincidental. 'If scientific realism, and the theories it draws on, were not correct, there would be no explanation of why the observed world is as if they were correct; that fact would be brute, if not miraculous' (Michael Devitt).

For reasons such as these, natural scientists tend to be realists, at least in the broad sense of that term. It seems to many that the success of the natural sciences shows that they have somehow managed to uncover the way things really are, or to lock into something which is fundamental to the structure of the universe. The importance of this point is considerable, on account of the insight, validated by a Christian doctrine of creation, of the ontological grounding of the natural sciences in the divine creation. If a realist approach applies to the study of the works of God, how much more so must it apply to their ultimate ground?

Realism as the working philosophy of the physical sciences

Realism is by far the predominant working philosophy of the natural sciences. There is little difficulty in documenting this trend on the part of working natural scientists; the example of the Cambridge philosopher and physicist Michael Redhead will serve very well as an illustration:[17]

> Physicists, in their unreflective and intuitive attitude to their work, the way they talk and think among themselves, tend to be realists about the entities they deal with, and while being tentative as to what they say about these entities and their exact properties and interrelations, they generally feel that what they are trying to do, and to some degree successfully, is to get a 'handle on reality'.

We see here a commitment to the 'ontological finality of the natural order' (Nicholas Rescher) which insists that it is the engagement with reality itself, rather than any *a priori* reflections on the nature of knowledge, which is of critical importance. Scientific realism is an *empirical* notion, in that it is grounded in an actual encounter with reality. Its justification is not to be found in *a priori* philosophical reflections, but in *a posteriori* engagement with the natural world itself. Its plausibility and confirmations arise from direct engagement with the real world, through repeated observation and experiment.

While most natural scientists espouse a range of opinions which are recognizably 'realist' in their core affirmations, it is important to appreciate that there are various types of what might reasonably be called 'scientific realism'. Richard Boyd, one of the most important writers in the field, sets out a widely accepted four-point typology of what the term might reasonably mean:[18]

1. 'Theoretical terms' (or 'non-observational terms') in scientific theories are to be thought of as putatively referring expressions. Scientific theories should thus be interpreted 'realistically'. What Boyd means by this is that it is often necessary to infer the existence of entities that cannot actually be seen or otherwise observed, because of

the force of evidence pointing in this direction – for example, J. J. Thomson's arguments for the existence of the electron.

2. Scientific theories, interpreted in this realistic manner, are confirmable and are in fact often confirmed as approximately true by ordinary scientific evidence interpreted in accordance with ordinary methodological norms.

3. The historical development of the mature sciences is largely a matter of successively more accurate approximations to the truth concerning both observable and unobserved phenomena. Later theories tend to build on the observational and theoretical knowledge embodied in earlier theories.

4. The reality which scientific theories describe is largely independent of thoughts or theoretical commitments.

Boyd's particular approach to scientific realism rests largely on evidential considerations, and makes a particular appeal to the explanatory successes of the sciences.

Other writers have stressed different aspects of the matter. The Greek philosopher of science Stathis Psillos argues that three distinct themes are brought together in scientific realism:[19]

1. The *metaphysical* belief that the world has a definite and mind-independent structure – in other words, that there exists an objective reality, whose structures may be exposed and analysed intentionally by the working methods and assumptions of the natural sciences.

2. The *semantic* belief that scientific theories should be taken at face value – in other words, that they are to be seen as truth-conditioned descriptions of their intended domain, whether observable or unobservable, and are hence capable of being true or false.

3. The *epistemic* belief that mature and predictively successful

scientific theories are well confirmed, and are (at least approximately) true.

Although such ideas are widely held within the scientific community, they are not without their difficulties, and have been challenged in various ways. In the following section, I consider some of the alternatives, and the reasons that some have advanced in their favour.

Rivals to scientific realism

The three most significant alternatives to scientific realism may be identified as idealism, positivism and instrumentalism. Each of these continues to have its supporters. Although these are relatively few within the scientific community, they are considerably more numerous outside it, particularly within the postmodern community. In what follows, we shall consider these positions briefly.[20]

Idealism holds that the 'reality' that we experience or encounter is *not* independent of the human mind, but is the outcome of the organizational and correlational activity of an order-imposing human mind. Most (but not all) forms of idealism hold that there is no access to reality apart from whatever the mind provides. Some go further, insisting that the mind can only reveal its own contents. This kind of philosophy is in tension with the natural sciences, which hold that presupposing an engagement with the structures of the real world – rather than just the ideas of the human mind – is the only reasonable explanation of the experimental evidence.

Positivism regards scientific theories as essentially nothing more than summaries of experimental data or observations. The viewpoint is best explored from the writings of the Austrian physicist

Ernst Mach (1838–1916), who held that the natural sciences concern that which is immediately given by the senses. Science concerns nothing more and other than the investigation of the 'dependence of phenomena on one another'. The world consists only of our sensations; knowledge is merely a conceptual organization of the data of sensory experience or observation.

This led Mach to take a strongly negative view of the atomic hypothesis, in which he argued that atoms were merely theoretical constructs which cannot be perceived. On being told by his colleagues that there was excellent evidence for the atomic hypothesis, Mach responded with a demand to be *shown* one. Mach was certainly prepared to concede that 'talk about atoms' could be used; it was, he argued, a useful form of shorthand, which allowed a large number of experimental observations to be categorized. It was observations that were 'real'; beyond those, everything else was either fantasy or useful ways of organizing the observational material without any commitment to the ideas or entities that might seem to be proposed.

Instrumentalism is perhaps the most serious rival to scientific realism. On this view, scientific theories are to be seen as useful 'instruments' which enable us to order and anticipate the observable world. On this approach, a scientific theory is best understood as a rule, principle or calculating device for deriving predictions from sets of observational data. It makes no assumptions about any putative 'reality' behind these observations, but merely aims to predict from what can be observed. There is a serious difficulty with this position, which concerns its historical erosion. Many 'instrumentalist' approaches eventually came to be reclassified as 'realist'. Good examples are provided by the Copernican model of the solar system, which was initially seen as little more than a convenient way of calculating planetary motion, and Einstein's introduction of what later came to be

called the 'photon' to explain the puzzling observations associated with the photoelectric effect. In both cases, what started as
instrumentalist approaches ended up being recategorized as
'realist'.

While the vulnerability of the rivals of realism is one important
reason for preferring the latter approach, it is important to realize
that there are excellent additional reasons for accepting a realist
approach. I shall outline the main points in the following section.

The all-important notion of 'laws of nature' is widely regarded
as one of the most telling pieces of evidence for a realist approach
to the world. Not only are these 'laws' seen as important in relation to the debate over realism; they are also of direct relevance to
any discussion of the scientific significance of the Christian doctrine of creation. Historically, it is relatively easy to demonstrate
that the notion of the 'laws of nature' is firmly grounded in a
Christian doctrine of creation. They are to be regarded not as arbitrary regulations imposed upon the world from without on an
occasional basis, but as a permanent expression and embodiment
within the world of the mind of God as creator. The idea that
nature is governed by 'laws' does not appear to be a significant
feature of Greek, Roman or Asian conceptions of science; it is
firmly entrenched within the Judaeo-Christian tradition,
reflecting the specifics of a Christian doctrine of creation.

A second factor of importance is the scientific process of
'abduction to the best explanation', sometimes still referred to
using Gilbert Harman's somewhat misleading phrase 'inference to
the best explanation' (one can infer *that A* is the best explanation,
but not *infer* to *A* as the best explanation).[21] That there is a 'best'
explanation is seen to rest on the assumption that there exists a
reality which, once grasped, is capable of offering at least a partial
explanation of a variety of experimental and observational evidence. The ability of a hypothesis to explain something better

than its rivals must be seen as a mark of its truth, especially when those rivals include options such as 'treating the world *as if* it is made up of molecules, while believing that in reality it is not'. 'As if' theories have, as we have seen, a remarkably vulnerability to historical erosion, in that instrumentalist ways of viewing things often subsequently give way to realist approaches.

Nevertheless, there still remain some classic objections to scientific realism, which need to be considered. One of the most important challenges to realism concerns the shifting patterns of scientific theories in the early modern period – a phenomenon often referred to as 'radical theory change in science'. A theory which was widely held to be necessitated by the experimental or observational evidence in 1700 is abandoned by 1900, and replaced with a quite different theory. Is this not a clear indication that the central tenet of realism is vulnerable, in that theoretical entities which were so confidently proposed by one generation were abandoned by another?

The force of this point must be conceded; it is not, however, fatal to realism. In an important defence of realism, the historian and philosopher of science Ernan McMullin argues that the case for realism may still be maintained in the face of theory change. McMullin initially points out that 'realism had to do with the existence implications of successful theories'. Yet this raises the question of theories, regarded as valid in their day, yet now considered to be discredited. For McMullin, this point may be conceded, yet must be set against the considerable body of theories which have proved resilient.[22]

> The value of this sort of reminder, however, is that it warns the realist that the ontological claim he makes is at best tentative, for surprising reversals have happened in the history of science. But the nonreversible (a long list is easy to construct here also) still require some form of (philosophic) explanation.

A second difficulty is often known as the 'underdetermination thesis'. This thesis is based on the fact that the empirical evidence is often not sufficient to identify precisely which of several competing theories is correct. There may, it is argued, be two or more quite distinct metaphysical understandings of reality which have identical or indistinguishable empirical consequences. This being the case, it is not possible to adjudicate between their claims on the basis of the working assumptions and methods of the natural sciences. It is therefore not necessary or appropriate to adopt a realist approach, given this factor.

Yet for a scientific realist, there is no particular difficulty here. In those situations in which we are confronted with two empirically equivalent yet clearly different theories which are equally 'elegant', 'simple' and so forth, there is no compelling reason for choosing between them. The forms of quantum theories associated with the Copenhagen School on the one hand, and David Bohm on the other, are quite distinct – yet they are equally consistent with the observed evidence. The correct epistemic attitude here is that of deferring judgement until additional data can be acquired. A judgement cannot yet be made; yet we believe that the uncovering of new data will eventually lead to one theory being preferred over another. The 'underdetermination of theory by data' does not in any way compel us to abandon a realist outlook. As I show later, it is an important theme in understanding the *theological* relationship between orthodoxy and heresy.

Yet perhaps the most serious difficulty for anti-realism is that the underdetermination thesis can easily be turned against it. If anti-realism is to be 'proved', a case must be made from the available evidence, including historical case studies. As many scholars have pointed out, this inevitably means that such theories are *themselves* underdetermined by the evidence, and hence can never hope to have the explanatory power and appeal which are essential to their gaining acceptance. If the underdetermination theory is *itself* underdetermined by evidence, what reasons may be given to prefer this above other accounts of the situation? Underdetermination is thus a two-edged sword, in that the underdetermination thesis turns out to be just as vulnerable to the problem of self-referentiality as any other theory. Realism and anti-realism are equally affected by the issue.

At this point, we return to the question of the mathematical representation of reality. An appeal to the world of mathematics has already been made in relation to the implications of the doctrine of creation. I now return to consider the importance of what is usually referred to as 'mathematical realism', noting in particular how mathematical theorizing often surges ahead of experimental observation, predicting the existence of theoretical entities or relationships which are only confirmed much later. An excellent example of this is provided by Paul Dirac's 1928 prediction of the existence of the positron on the basis of his 'free particle equation', or James Clerk Maxwell's demonstration of the mathematical interrelatedness of electric and magnetic fields. Once more, a realist approach appears to offer the best explanation of such developments.

Yet the rise of postmodernity has posed a non-realist (or anti-realist) challenge to the working assumptions of the natural sciences. I therefore move to consider some aspects of these criticisms of realism.

Retreating from reality: postmodern anti-realism

A number of postmodern writers regard the natural sciences essentially as a human construction which may be deconstructed, in common with all other human endeavours. While natural scientists regard their research programmes as attempting to uncover the deep structure of the world through rigorous empirical investigation, postmodernity sees the sciences as culturally or socially constructed entities, which can be deconstructed to expose and ultimately eliminate the power structures which they embody. I illustrate this general attitude by considering a famous essay by the French postmodern writer Jacques Derrida, entitled 'Plato's Pharmacy'.

It is important to appreciate that the natural sciences do not fit easily into either a 'modern' or a 'postmodern' worldview. The former mistakenly holds that it is possible to have purely 'objective' judgements in all things, and especially in the natural sciences. The latter regards everything as being socially constructed – in other words, being a free creation of the individual, rather than a response to the way things actually are in the world. Both these positions are untenable; neither are necessitated by scientific realism, or a scientific theology. In view of the importance of this point, it may be explored a little further.

The natural sciences recognize a spectrum of possibilities between 'objectivity' and 'social construction', reflecting their different subject matters and approaches. While physics may be taken as an example of a natural science which makes little use of social construction, psychology makes much more extensive use of this device. An example of such a social construct is 'intelligence', which is constructed as a way of making sense of our observation of the world, rather than being directly observed itself within the world. Yet proponents of the 'strong programme' of social constructivism argue that the external world plays no role in the development of scientific theories. This is quite untenable.

The 'strong programme' is intensely vulnerable, both in terms of its own self-referentiality (how does it account for itself? Is it also a social construction, rather than a response to the way things are?) and the account it offers of the natural sciences. The suggestion that an attempt to encounter or engage with the external world plays no role in natural scientific methods is patently untrue. As Bruno Latour pointed out, the approach is implausible, to say the least: it requires us to believe that 'society had to produce everything arbitrarily, including the cosmic order, biology, chemistry and the laws of physics'.

The term 'social construct' is used throughout this project to refer to the fact that, when attempting to offer an account of the real world, one is often obliged to use models or constructs as provisional devices to allow a greater degree of understanding of how a system functions, or how a complex entity is to be mentally pictured. The model or construct is ultimately to be judged in terms of how effectively it accounts for the observational data, and the predictions it allows concerning hitherto unknown or uncorrelated phenomena.

Yet contrary to the postmodern trend, 'social construction' is *not* to be understood as an arbitrary determination or the pure invention of ideas on the basis of the free choice of the individual thinker or a community of discourse. The development of these constructs represents a principled exercise in attempting to understand the world as best as possible, and to develop for this purpose whatever tools or conceptualities are best suited to the tasks of the individual natural science in question, and the level of reality it engages. Within the natural sciences, such constructs are empirically based, and represent legitimate and warranted means of gaining a tighter grasp on the reality being studied.

Three observations must be made immediately to counter possible misunderstandings at this point. As we saw earlier, 'nature' designates a wide range of entities, all of which come within the scope of the 'natural sciences'. Physics and psychology alike must be regarded as natural sciences, whose working methods and assumptions are to be critically appropriated by a scientific theology. Some sciences make greater use of social constructs than others; yet these constructs are to be understood as arising out of the experimental evidence under consideration, and are to be regarded as interpretative and predictive tools for the better understanding of the reality under investigation. They are not arbitrary, free constructions of the human imagination, but are evoked by, and derive their validity from, the nature of the reality under investigation. This leads to the three points we are concerned with.

1. The extent of 'objectivism' or 'social constructivism' is dependent upon the tasks and subject-matter of the natural science in question.
2. The legitimate use of social constructions simply does *not* entail anti-realism, even in its weak instrumentalist version. Thus to recognize that 'intelligence' is a social construct does not mean that there is no such thing as 'intelligence'; it means that it is to be understood as a specific means of understanding a body of observational data which has a claim to reality by virtue of its explanatory and predictive fecundity, whose status is anticipated as being finally confirmed through the accumulation of additional data and interpretative devices.
3. Social constructs are subject to constant reappraisal and revision in the light of advancing knowledge and experimental observation.

Objectivity and social constructivism are thus not *contradictory* (as both the Enlightenment and postmodernity appear to believe, although in different ways and for different reasons). The intermingling of these notions is inevitable, given the complexity of the world which the natural sciences seek to encounter and explain. Above all, a realist approach to the world is not called into question through the recognition of socially constructed aspects of the explanations offered by the natural sciences. As John Searle points out in his highly important work *The Construction of Social Reality* (1995), a distinction may be made between 'brute facts' and 'social facts' – but they are still both *real*.[23] Furthermore, the use of social constructs is completely consistent with – even demanded by – a realist approach to the world.

For Searle, 'social facts' are not inventions, or free constructions of the human mind. They are to be regarded as realities consisting of objective facts. Thus the factual statement 'John Searle is a citizen of the United States of America' rests upon the fact that there is indeed a nation called the United States of America. This is not a 'natural' or 'empirical' entity such as a river or mountain, but one depending for its very existence upon human conventions and laws. Though based upon the 'brute fact' of the landmass of America, the concept of the 'United States of America' represents a political and social overlay on this physical entity. Though a social construction, it is none the less 'real' – as any citizen of the United States would testify.

Searle argues that those who reject realism in favour, for example, of pure social constructivism ultimately depend upon realist assumptions further down the line – for example, by holding that social beings exist, and that they are able to construct entities. Those who argue that things are constructed out of (or in response to) specific contexts are obliged to suppose that these contexts exist in order to explain the process of construction. And so on. Searle's argument, followed through to its logical conclusion, is that alternatives to realism – whether in the natural or social sciences – are ultimately obliged to presuppose the truth of realism in order to carry weight.

The debate over postmodern interpretations of the natural sciences took a new, unexpected and rather amusing turn in 1996, through what has widely become known as the 'Sokal hoax'. Irritated by the pseudo-scientific nonsense littering the pages of fashionable postmodern writers such as Lucy Irigaray, Sokal published a spoof article in *Social Text*, one of the leading journals of postmodern theory. The article was entitled 'Transgressing the Boundaries: Toward a Transformative Hermeneutics of Quantum Gravity'.

Throughout the article, Sokal imitated the dense style of postmodern writers, incorporating a series of completely nonsensical statements concerning the natural sciences. An example: 'The π of Euclid and the G of Newton, formerly thought to be constant and universal, are now perceived in their ineluctable historicity.' The statement, along with many others in the same vein, is empirically false and theoretically ludicrous – yet it was regarded as acceptable by this state-of-the-art journal.

So what was the result of this article? Sokal's hoax severely undermined credibility in social constructive accounts of the scientific enterprise by raising serious questions as to whether postmodern writers actually understood the scientific notions they brandished about in their discussions, and thence eroded credibility of their judgements concerning them. It naturally led many to look for alternatives to the manifest public failures of both the modernist and postmodernist accounts of the social construction of reality, and led many to seek an alternative – above all, the critical realism explored in the next chapter.

10. Critical Realism: Engaging with a Stratified Reality

I have found the form of 'critical realism' associated with Roy Bhaskar to be a particularly congenial dialogue partner in formulating a scientific theology. I first encountered this approach to realism in 1998. I had been aware of the importance of Alasdair MacIntyre's tradition-mediated approach to rationality since 1989, and – especially as a historian, with a keen sense of the historical

vulnerability of the modernist project – found it a highly persuasive means of dealing with the impasse arising from the failure of
the Enlightenment. It also had a powerful resonance for Christian
theology, on account of its implications for the role of the
Christian community or the institution of the Church in theological and ethical reflection – an agenda advanced with particular skill
by Stanley Hauerwas.

This did not, however, resolve the many issues arising from
another aspect of the scientific theology project – namely, the
question of the involvement of the knower in the process of
knowing. I had long been dissatisfied with certain realist accounts
of pure 'objectivity' which seemed to fail to take account of either
the observer's involvement in the process of knowing, or the
observer's location within history and hence at least partial conditioning by the contingencies and particularities of that location.
I was perfectly prepared to develop my own approach to this,
based on reflection on the natural sciences. However, it seemed
much more appropriate to interact with an existing model, which
could be adapted for the purposes of a scientific theology.

This is an important observation, as a perfectly reasonable
objection to the theological use of Bhaskar's ideas might be stated
like this: Does not the use of philosophical notions such as these
run the risk of making theology dependent upon such a philosophy? Is not what is being proposed tantamount to the enslave-
ment of theology to a philosophy – a development that Karl Barth
and others so vigorously opposed? I respond with three points.

1. Bhaskar's critical realism is not being adopted as an *a priori*
    foundation for theology, which would be to determine its
    foundation and norms in advance.
2. Bhaskar's critical realism is being used in an *ancillary*, not a
    foundational role.

3. Bhaskar's critical realism is grounded *a posteriori*, in that its central ideas rest on a sustained engagement with the social and natural structures of the world, rather than a dogmatic *a priori* determination of what those structures should be, and consequently how they should be investigated.

My discovery of Bhaskar's critical realism dates from late in 1998, when I came across his *Possibility of Naturalism*, then in its third edition. It immediately became clear to me that this approach made considerable sense, not least on account of its obvious resonance with the actual working assumptions of the natural sciences, and I then went on to explore this further.[24]

In this chapter, I explore the importance of Bhaskar's approach, and distinguish it from other forms of 'critical realism' currently in circulation, especially within 'science and religion' circles. Bhaskar sets out the 'basic principle of a realist philosophy of science' as the belief 'that perception gives us access to things and experimental activity access to structures that exist independently of us'. Yet what is interesting is not where Bhaskar begins, but where he ends.

A helpful way of beginning to clarify the concept of 'critical realism' is to compare it with two alternative approaches, as follows:

Naive realism: Reality impacts directly upon the human mind, without any reflection on the part of the human knower. The resulting knowledge is directly determined by an objective reality within the world.

Critical realism: Reality is apprehended by the human mind, which attempts to express and accommodate that reality as best it can with the tools at its disposal – such as mathematical formulae or mental models.

Postmodern anti-realism: The human mind freely constructs its ideas without any reference to an alleged external world.

This contrast immediately identifies the distinctive features of the approach. Against postmodernism, critical realism affirms that there is a reality, which may be known, and which we are under a moral and intellectual obligation to investigate and represent as best as we can. Against certain types of modernism, critical realism affirms that the human knower is involved in the process of knowing, thus raising immediately the possibility of the use of 'constructions' – such as analogies, models, and more specifically social constructs – as suitably adapted means for representing what is encountered.

The importance of the active involvement of the knower was stressed by the noted psychologist William James. In his 1878 essay 'Remarks on Spencer's Definition of Mind as Correspondence', James drew attention to the fact that the knowing agent received knowledge actively, not passively:[25]

> The knower is an actor, and co-efficient of the truth on the one side, whilst on the other he registers the truth which he helps to create. Mental interests, hypotheses, postulates, so far as they are bases for human action – action which to a great extent transforms the world – help to *make* the truth which they declare.

James's important point does not pose a challenge to the notion that there exists a world, independent of the observer. The point he is making is that the knower is involved in the process of knowing, and that this involvement must somehow be expressed within a realist perspective on the world.

The basic point is set out well by the leading British New Testament scholar N. T. Wright, who describes critical realism as:[26]

> a way of describing the process of 'knowing' that acknowledges the *reality of the thing known, as something other than the knower* (hence 'realism'), while also fully acknowledging that the only access we have to this reality lies along the spiralling path of *appropriate dialogue or*

conversation between the knower and the thing known (hence 'critical').
This path leads to critical reflection on the products of our enquiry
into 'reality', so that our assertions about 'reality' acknowledge their
own provisionality. Knowledge, in other words, although in principle
concerning realities independent of the knower, is never itself independent of the knower.

There are a variety of 'critical realisms' now in circulation. These
include the ideas associated with the 'American critical realism' of
the 1920s and 1930s, which is particularly associated with Arthur
Lovejoy (1873–1962) and Roy Wood Sellars (1880–1967). These
have now generally faded from view, having little impact on the
contemporary discussion of this issue. In more recent years,
however, the term has come to play an increasingly important role
in the 'science and religion' community, with writers such as Ian
Barbour, Arthur Peacocke and John Polkinghorne contributing to
the discussion.

In view of his clarity of presentation of the issue, we may briefly
note some of the characteristics of critical realism as set out by
Polkinghorne in his 1996 Terry Lectures at Yale University:[27]

> I believe that the advance of science is not just concerned with our
> ability to manipulate the physical world, but to gain knowledge of its
> actual nature. In a word, I am a realist. Of course, such knowledge is
> to a degree partial and corrigible. Our attainment is verisimilitude,
> not absolute truth. Our method is the creative interpretation of ex-
> perience, not rigorous deduction from it. Thus I am a critical realist.

Polkinghorne goes on to set out six distinctive characteristics of
the theological critical realism he wishes to commend. Several of
these are illuminating, not least in clarifying the points at which
this form of realism is 'critical':

1. The recognition that 'theory and practice are inexplicably
   intertwined in scientific thought', as a result of which

scientific facts are to be understood as having already been interpreted. 'There is an inescapable self-sustaining circularity in the mutual relationship of theory and experiment.'

2. The recognition that 'there is no universal epistemology, but rather entities are knowable only through ways that conform to their idiosyncratic nature'.

In certain ways, Bhaskar echoes such ideas. For Bhaskar, the world of reality possesses an ordering which is independent of the human recognition of its existence. Human agents thus find themselves existing, acting and reflecting within a world that is already structured, and find that they are 'always acting in a world of structural constraints and possibility that they did not produce'. We are born into pre-existing structures, some of which can be transformed by our activity and others not. The physical, biological and social worlds are always pre-structured; the question is how that structuring is to be investigated, and subsequently how it is to be represented.

However, Bhaskar's approach has some distinctive features, which set it apart from other forms of critical realism.

First, Bhaskar sets out what he terms the '*epistemic fallacy*'. By this, he means the seductive belief that ontology – the way things actually are – is determined by what can be known. If we cannot perceive something, on this view, it cannot be there. For Bhaskar, ontology determines epistemology – in other words, the specific nature of some aspect of reality determines the *manner* in which it is to be known, and the *extent* to which it can be known. Bhaskar illustrates this difficult point by pointing out that a stone may be picked up and thrown *because* it is solid; it is not solid because it can be picked up and thrown. While Bhaskar concedes that the fact that stones may be handled in this way 'may be a contingently necessary condition for our *knowledge* of their solidity', his basic point is that the ontology of the object determines how we know and use it. The nature of something determines how we handle it – and how we know it.

In his *Realist Theory of Science* (1975) Bhaskar argued that the concept of 'being' was an absolutely necessary and irreducible category for any understanding of the natural sciences. An ontology is therefore essential in any responsible account of the natural sciences. It was in this work that Bhaskar first introduced the notion of the 'epistemic fallacy', which reduced issues of ontology to issues of epistemology.[28]

> Empirical realism is underpinned by a metaphysical dogma, which I call the epistemic fallacy, that statements about being can always be transposed into statements about knowledge of being.

For Bhaskar, ontology is determined by neither methodology nor epistemology. The 'epistemic fallacy' rests on the false assumption that the structures of the world rest or depend upon human observation. Bhaskar is quite clear that the world is not limited to what can be observed. To put this another way: existence is not dependent on observation, or being observable. Bhaskar insists that certain aspects of reality – for example, what he calls 'generative mechanisms' – may exist yet not be observed or observable.

Much the same point might be made about such things as electrons, quarks and other such entities. They may not be capable of being observed – but we nevertheless believe that they are there. Furthermore, with the development of new technology, what was once not capable of being observed can become observable. The philosopher of science William Newton-Smith made this point as follows.[29]

> Consider the following typical development in the history of science. At one stage genes were posited in order to explain observed phenomena. At that time no one had in any sense observed or detected the

existences of genes. However, with the development of sophisticated microscopes scientists came to describe themselves as seeing genes.

The importance of this point to both scientific and theological reflection will be obvious. John Polkinghorne makes the point with characteristic lucidity, when he stresses that there are many things which we cannot observe, yet which we nevertheless believe, with good reason, to be there.[30]

> We habitually speak of entities which are not directly observable. No one has ever seen a gene (though there are X-ray photographs which, suitably interpreted, led Crick and Watson to the helical structure of DNA) or an electron (though there are tracks in bubble chambers which, suitably interpreted, indicate the existence of a particle of negative electric charge of about 4.8×10^{-10} esu and mass about 10^{-27} gm). No one has ever seen God (though there is the astonishing Christian claim that 'the only Son, who is in the bosom of the Father, he has made him known' (John 1.18)).

The second major theme developed by Bhaskar is that of the *stratification of reality*. Critical realism insists that the world must be regarded as differentiated and stratified. Each individual science deals with a different stratum of this reality, which in turn obliges it to develop and use methods of investigation adapted and appropriate to this stratum. Stratum *B* might be grounded in, and emerge from, Stratum *A*. Yet despite this relation of origin, the same methods of investigation cannot be used in dealing with these two different strata. These methods must be established *a posteriori*, through an engagement with each of these strata of reality.

Bhaskar offers a critical realist account of the relation of the natural and social sciences which affirms their methodological commonalities, while respecting their distinctions, particularly when these arise on account of their objects of investigation.[31]

Naturalism holds that it is possible to give an account of science under which the proper and more or less specific methods of both the natural and social sciences can fall. But it does not deny that there are significant differences in these methods, grounded in real differences in their subject-matters and in the relationships in which these sciences stand to them. . . . It is the nature of the object that determines the form of its possible science.

We see here a clear recognition of each science being determined by the nature of its object, and being obligated to respond to it *kata physin*, in a manner which is appropriate to its distinctive nature.

Bhaskar is stridently opposed to any form of reductionism – the rather crude and wooden approach which seems to collapse everything into one allegedly fundamental level. There is no shortage of scientists prepared to take such reductionist positions, despite their obvious difficulties. The Harvard biologist Edward O. Wilson, one of the founders of sociobiology, argues that social behaviour is to be explained by the principles of biology, biology by the principles of chemistry, and chemistry by the principles of physics. Similarly, Nobel Laureate Francis Crick has argued that the goal of the sciences is to reduce all knowledge to the laws of chemistry and physics. It is essential to note that Bhaskar argues that, because level A is rooted in and emerges from level B, it does not follow that level A is therefore 'nothing but' level B. Emergent strata possess features that are 'irreducible' – that is, which cannot be conceived solely in terms of lower levels.

For Bhaskar, biology cannot be 'reduced' to chemistry or physics, precisely because the biological stratum possesses characteristics which go beyond those of the stratum in which it is rooted. If it were possible to explain the origins of biological life in chemical or physical terms, that would not amount to the reduction of biology to either of these disciplines.[32]

Would biologists lose their object of inquiry? Would living things cease to be real? Our apprehension of them unmasked as an illusion? No, for in as much as living things were capable of acting back on the materials out of which they were formed, biology were not otiose. For a knowledge of biological structures and principles would still be necessary to account for any determinate state of the physical world. Whatever is capable of producing a physical effect is real, and a proper object of scientific study.

Bhaskar insists that each stratum – whether physical, biological or cultural – is to be seen as 'real', and capable of investigation using means appropriate to its distinctive identity. An overall vision of 'reality' does not entail that every level of that reality must be investigated in the same manner.

Bhaskar's idea of the stratification of reality is difficult to grasp. It may therefore be helpful to consider an illustration to make it clearer. The world of medicine offers a helpful analogy – not used by Bhaskar, I must add – which illustrates the failure of a single-level approach to the concerns of the natural sciences. What is meant by the notion of 'illness'? It turns out that 'illness' is a highly complex notion, which cannot be 'reduced' to the malfunctioning of some bodily organ or system. While 'illness' naturally includes pathological elements (such as damage to the liver, or the presence of a tumour), it also extends to socially constructed elements (such as radical changes in the individual's social role consequent to this, perhaps leading to unemployment or social isolation).

In 1980, the World Health Organization set out an 'International Classification of Impairments, Disabilities and Handicaps' (ICIDH).[33] On the basis of the revised ICIDH-2 model, four 'levels of illness' may be discerned. These can be set out in the following way:

Level of Illness	Alternative Terms	Comments
Pathology	Disease; diagnosis	Abnormalities in the structure or function of an organ or organ system
Impairment	Symptoms; signs	Abnormalities or changes in the structure or function of the whole body
Activity	Function; observed behaviour	Abnormalities, changes or restrictions in the interaction between a person and his or her environment or physical context
Participation	Social positions and roles	Changes, limitations or abnormalities in the position of the person in their social context

Exploring this in a little more detail will help explain the basic point at issue. At the *pathological* level, someone might develop a brain tumour. This leads to *impairment* in the form of certain observable changes in the functioning of the human body, including potential memory loss or other loss of cognitive functions. At the level of *activities*, this leads to the individual experiencing difficulties with certain – but not all – routine tasks, which have implications for his or her lifestyle. At the level of *participation*, this could lead to loss of social role and unemployment if the person's job required good memory and cognitive skills.

Illness can therefore be studied and addressed at several

different levels. It would be absurd to suggest that one level is 'real', and the others not. Unemployment may be argued to be a social construction; it is, nevertheless, decidedly real for those unfortunate enough to experience it. Each of the levels demands a different mode of investigation (and a different mode of treatment). A stratified reality thus leads to a plurality of methods of investigation. *Each stratum demands its own methodology.* A reductionist approach which demands that everything is stated and investigated only in terms of the most basic stratum cannot hope to do justice to the real life situations which critical realism aims to explore and illuminate.

The same point is true of religions, such as Christianity, which also represent stratified realities, each demanding to be investigated on its own terms, and refusing to be sidelined in the interests of a reductionist agenda. Later, I point out that at least eight strata may be discerned within Christianity, each representing a distinct level of the embedding of divine revelation within the world. These may be set out very briefly as follows, in anticipation of a more detailed subsequent discussion:

Texts, supremely Scripture;
Patterns of worship;
Ideas, such as those set out in creeds;
Communities;
Institutional structures;
Images;
Words;
Religious experience.

Others could easily be added to this list – such as narratives of faith. The point is that each stratum possesses its own distinct identity and significance, and must be given due weight in any attempt to engage with the greater reality of which it is part. Thus

George Lindbeck's sociolinguistic approach to doctrine gives something approaching due weight to the fourth stratum, but makes the regrettable and unsustainable assumption that this is the *only* stratum that needs to be addressed. Equally, the experiential approach of F. D. E. Schleiermacher unquestionably takes the eighth stratum with great seriousness – yet again neglects the remaining strata. A stratified approach to reality allows the multi-levelled embeddedness of revelation in reality to be fully and thoroughly explored, and its impact on the maintenance of the Christian tradition to be identified.

Two leading features of a scientific theology are lent support by Bhaskar's analysis, namely:

1. A scientific theology may legitimately be regarded as a response to an existing reality, whose existence is independent of the actuality or possibility of human observation.
2. Each intellectual discipline must adopt a methodology which is appropriate to, and determined by, the ontology of its specific object. Its methodology is thus determined *a posteriori* rather than *a priori*.

The stratified understanding of reality affirmed by critical realism thus allows us to argue that the natural sciences investigate the stratified structures of contingent existence *at every level open to human enquiry*, while a theological science addresses itself to God their creator *who is revealed through them*. The doctrine of the incarnation – the affirmation that the God who created space, time and history entered into this created zone in the person of Jesus Christ – affirms both historical and theological realities.

Once more, this can be related to the doctrine of the creation: the divine logos through which the world was created was incarnate in Jesus Christ. Creation and incarnation thus belong to the same theological trajectory.

However, I express some concern over the failure of some existing theologies to do justice to the stratification of reality. A case in point is Karl Barth's concept of the 'threefold form of the Word of God', which creates a significant theological link between a divine event (revelation), a historically mediated text (Scripture), and a social activity (preaching). Yet Barth treats each of these 'forms' as if they were purely ideational concepts, located at a single level of reality, despite the fact that they clearly represent different strata. To use Bhaskar's terminology, Barth locates them at differing horizontal positions within the same stratum, whereas a critical realist analysis would locate them on different vertical strata. The continuity which Barth discerns within a single stratum can just as convincingly be identified as existing across three vertical strata.

Nature, history and experience have all been argued to be foundational theological resources by theologians. Yet none of these need be regarded as the *only* such resource. The key points to appreciate here are these:

1. Critical realism denies that reality may be reduced to any specific level of reality – such as religious experience, culture or the social concept of religion – thus challenging reductionist approaches to theology in particular, and Christianity in general.

2. Critical realism encourages a connectivist approach to theology, by insisting that its correlation with the various strata of reality be explored, both as a means of intellectual enrichment and as a matter of intellectual responsibility. Thus to explore the relationship between theology and one such stratum – let us say, 'experience' – does not preclude recognizing the importance of other such relationships, involving other strata such as 'history'.

11. The Encounter with Reality: The Contours of a Scientific Theology

A scientific theology characterized by its critical realist approach to an enounter with reality has four fundamental characteristics. It

1. takes the form of a coherent response to an existing reality;
2. is an *a posteriori* discipline;
3. takes account of the unique character of its object;
4. offers an explanation of reality.

Yet it is important to note that these considerations arise from the generally scientific character of theology; there is also one specific feature which is a response to its distinctively Christian approach – namely, its focus on the person of Jesus Christ as being of critical importance to theological reflection. This fifth aspect of a scientific theology is thus discussed in a final section.

Scientific theology as a response to reality

The first major characteristic of a scientific theology is that it responds coherently to reality. A scientific theology should be seen as a response to reality – a deliberate and principled attempt to give a faithful and adequate account of the way things are, subject to the limits placed upon human knowledge on account of our status as sinful creatures and our location in history. To put this another way, it is *responsible*, in two senses of that term:

1. It represents a *response to reality*. We do not create our theological concepts through our free and unrestrained mental activity, but recognize and respond to a situation which already exists, independent of and prior to our reflections.

2. It is *accountable* for its insights and themes – that is to say, there are criteria against which it may be judged; there is a community who may judge how faithful that theology is as a positive yet critical affirmation of its insights and beliefs; and ultimately, in the Christian way of viewing things, a God who will hold the theologian accountable for the manner in which God's character and nature are rendered.

The notion of theology as a scientific discipline which gives an account of its apprehension of reality is thoroughly traditional. In more recent times, the substantial theological project of Karl Barth has given this new significance. For Barth, theology is an exercise in *Nachdenken*, a following through of the objectivity of reality. (The German term *Nachdenken*, which means something like 'reflection', is here interpreted by Barth as *Nach-Denken*, 'after-thinking'). Such an objectivity exists prior to any operation of the human mind. Our reflections disclose and illuminate the structures of this reality, but do not call that reality or its structures into being. We are not speaking of a human mind imposing order in any way it pleases, but of a principled attempt to recognize and represent the way things are.

This may be contrasted with the anti-realism which has gained considerable influence, especially within more liberal theological circles and others influenced by postmodernity. The origins of modern theological anti-realism – that is, an anti-realism conditioned by the ideas of modernity, not the most recent form of anti-realism – can be traced back to Ludwig Feuerbach. It is, however, the postmodern forms of anti-realism that are now of greatest importance. To explore their vulnerability, I consider the development of this approach in the writings of Don Cupitt.

In his more recent writings, Cupitt argues for a form of anti-realism which allows us to create our concepts of God as we please. There is no 'objectively real' God which we are under some kind of obligation to respect. The world, he argues, has been completely cut adrift from the moorings of realism. Instead of responding to reality, we create whatever we choose to regard as real. Reality is thus something which we construct, not something to which we respond. 'We constructed all the world-views, we made all the theories . . . They depend on us, not we on them.'[34] Over the years, Cupitt has gradually shifted from his early commitment to a form of critical realism (which recognizes that what we say about God never fully represents the reality of God) to a robust anti-realism, which insists that there is no objective reality 'out there': all our language about 'reality' – including God – is really about ourselves.

There are some obvious problems here. Cupitt's rather strident anti-realist rhetoric never quite seems to manage to engage with the critical questions thrown up by the explanatory and predictive successes of the natural sciences, or the growing discontent with anti-realist philosophies. Instead, we find a studied evasion of such questions, shored up by a manipulative rhetoric which describes realism as 'simplistic' and 'outmoded'. Yet Cupitt merely asserts this, as the consensus of our day; he does not justify his assertion.

The problems with Cupitt's approach are probably best seen in the sections of *The Sea of Faith* which survey the radical changes that have come about in our understanding of the world as the result of Newtonian mechanics and Darwin's theory of evolution. These new insights have, he insists, transformed our religious situation, making it impossible to go back to earlier forms of belief. Yet Cupitt assumes that the reason we must abandon these earlier beliefs is that these scientific insights are *correct*. He assumes that Darwin's theory of evolution is more or less true, and that it offers a reliable account of the real world. As a result of this, Christianity has to rethink its ideas about human origins, and the place of humanity within nature. The blindingly obvious fact is that a form of scientific realism has been smuggled in here; indeed, without it, Cupitt would have to speak merely of arbitrary shifts in intellectual fashion, rather than permanent changes in our understanding of the world. To discredit theological realism, Cupitt is obliged to assume its historical or scientific counterparts. So it seems that all of our ideas are not free creations of the autonomous human mind after all. Cupitt's anti-realism simply is not capable of dealing with the natural sciences.

Cupitt's rather puzzling account of the interaction of experience and knowledge simply fails to correspond with the known facts of history. More robust forms of theological realism are associated with Karl Barth and Thomas F. Torrance. Barth's realism is firmly grounded in his Christology, rather than an engagement with its alternatives in the worlds of philosophy or theology. Although I will endorse much of what he has to say concerning the importance of grounding a Christian conception of reality in Christ, I do not endorse his disengagement with the public arena. A scientific theology is a *public* theology, which expects to engage with its alternatives in the ideological marketplace. As I made clear earlier when critiquing the approach of John Milbank, I am resolutely opposed to the intellectual and cultural isolationism which seeks to disconnect Christian discourse and debate from that of the world around us.

Torrance's approach is much more satisfying. Although thoroughly grounded in Barth's distinctive approach to reality, Torrance is prepared to engage in a dialogue with culture at large over the issues he wishes to defend, including the all-important question of theological realism. This is seen above all in his insistence on the importance of the dialogue between theology and the natural sciences. Although this was publicly demonstrated in his landmark work *Theological Science* (1969), it was already evident earlier in his career – for example, in a series of lectures on the sciences and theology delivered in 1938–9 at Auburn Theological Seminary, in the state of New York. Barth, it must be said with regret, never regarded this interaction as being of particular importance. For Torrance, the dialogue with the sciences offers a means of defending and exploring a realist approach to theology.

The merits of this approach are probably best seen in his Richards Lectures, delivered at the University of Virginia at Charlottesville during 1978.[35] Torrance here argued that he wished to explore 'the ground and grammar of a realist theology'. Whereas writers such as George Lindbeck had argued for an essentially coherentist approach to theology, Torrance supplemented this with an insistence that theology is *grounded* in reality. For Lindbeck, theology was about the *grammar* of faith; for Torrance, theology is about the *ground and grammar* – that is to say, the external foundation and internal coherence of Christian theology.

One more, we find some of the fundamental themes of a scientific theology being set out. We must 'allow objective being to reveal itself to us' out of 'its own inner *logos* or intelligibility'. Torrance argues for an approach to theology which recognizes the incarnation as its 'ground and grammar' and is thus essentially realist in its orientation, and Christological in its focus – an important element of Barth's theology, which Torrance develops in a helpful direction. Adopting the great Greek patristic writer Athanasius of Alexandria as his dialogue partner, Torrance argues that theology takes its proper form 'in movements of thought in which we seek to know God strictly in accordance with his nature, and in terms of his own internal relations as they become disclosed to us through the incarnation'. We see here a theology which is as realist as it is Christocentric – yet which Torrance affirms to be thoroughly *scientific* in its approach.

We now move on to consider the second distinctive feature of a scientific theology, which stresses that it arises as a response to an existing reality rather than an attempt to create reality on the basis of prior beliefs.

Scientific theology as an a posteriori *discipline*

Some approaches to theology which developed during the Enlightenment held that the existence and attributes of God could be deduced from first principles, which were in turn derived by the human mind without the need for engagement with an external reality. These *a priori* ways of conceiving the theological task were regarded as liberating, in that they offered a universal way of reasoning, independent of the contingencies of history and culture. What pure reason disclosed, it was argued, was true for all people at all times. While foundationalism was in fashion, this was just fine. But it isn't in fashion any more.

Two fundamental objections were duly raised against this. First, it was simply untrue that there was only one, universal, form of reasoning – one rationality which was valid and operational for all peoples, at all times, and in all places. At best, this was just wishful thinking on the part of the apologists of the Enlightenment; at worst, it was imperialist aggressiveness, which demanded that all peoples accept the Enlightenment's specific view of the nature and place of reason. As we have seen, recognition of this failure of the Enlightenment project was perhaps the most significant factor in leading Alasdair MacIntyre to propose his concept of 'tradition-mediated rationality'. As MacIntyre commented, 'the legacy of the Enlightenment has been the provision of an ideal of rational justification which it has proved impossible to attain'.[36]

The second objection is that, as a matter of historical fact, many beliefs which were asserted to be *a priori* truths turned out to be nothing of the sort. In fact, many turned out to be *a pos-*

teriori truths which had become so widely accepted that they were treated as self-evidently true. An excellent example of this trend is provided by Immanuel Kant's assumption that Newton's problematic notion of 'absolute space' was to be regarded as 'pure *a priori* experience' – when it is, in fact, a somewhat tentative hypothesis, grounded in *a posteriori* reasoning.

However, a still more fundamental objection may be raised – namely, that the natural sciences owe their successes to *a posteriori* reasoning. In fact, if anything, they have been considerably inhibited in their development by those who insisted that they already knew the deep structuring of the world on the basis of *a priori* concepts. The natural sciences refused to allow themselves to be held back by preconceived ideas about what can and what cannot be known, in advance of an engagement with the natural world. The history of science shows that this does little beyond temporarily restraining advances in scientific understanding, and generally causing natural scientists to take a less than positive view of the place and propriety of philosophy in their scientific enterprises. A good example of the way in which *a priori* dogmas got in the way of scientific advance is provided by the rigid Aristotelianism of the late sixteenth and early seventeenth centuries, which seriously held up advances in the fields of mechanics and astronomy.

In the case of theology, the issue is also the distorting impact of preconceived ideas about God and the world. One of Karl Barth's most fundamental concerns was to liberate theology from the stranglehold of philosophy. On close reading, it becomes clear that Barth's chief anxiety was that *a priori* philosophical assumptions would be allowed to determine the possibility of revelation. A responsible theology, for Barth, takes the form of *a posteriori* reflection on a revelation that has already taken place. As Barth states this point in his 1924–5 Göttingen lectures:[37]

The problem of the possibility of revelation can only be seriously raised and treated where its *reality* is known. The possibility of revelation can, as a matter of principle, only be comprehended *a posteriori*. All reflection on how God *can* reveal himself is really only a thinking-after of the fact that God *has* revealed himself.

A similar position is taken by Torrance in his 1969 landmark work *Theological Science*:[38]

A genuine theology is distrustful of all speculative thinking or of all *a priori* thought. Theological thinking is essentially positive, thinking that keeps its feet on the ground of actuality; *a posteriori*, thinking that follows and is obedient to the given and communicated Word and Act of God as the material for its reflection; and *empirical*, thinking out of real experience of God determined by God. It is because it is through this given fact that theological knowledge has reality, and on its basis alone that it can be established as knowledge.

An excellent example of the importance of this point is provided by the debate about the incarnation. Many of a more philosophical outlook held that it is illogical or inconceivable that God should become incarnate in Christ. When stripped down to its bare essentials, this simply amounts to the assertion that an *a priori* concept of God is inconsistent with the incarnation. But what is the value of such an argument, when such *a priori* notions of God – or just about anything else – are far from being the universal and necessary truths that the Enlightenment believed them to be? Once more, we find that many have simply come to believe that certain ideas of God are self-evidently correct, and mistakenly assumed that they are therefore possessed of a universal and necessary character. In fact, they are often the product of western cultural conditioning.

The alternative approach is to have recourse to divine revelation, in effect arguing like this: if God has indeed become incarnate in

Christ, as the Christian revelation holds to be the case, then we must adjust our thinking about God so that it comes into line with this. We are simply not in a position to say that the incarnation 'cannot' take place; rather, we must argue that, since the incarnation has taken place, our thinking about God must be consistent with this.

The basic point, then, is that we cannot do theology in advance of, and independent of, an engagement with the reality which we are under obligation to explore and represent. Martin Luther's celebrated 'theology of the cross' is an excellent example of a theology which insists that prior ideas about God must be critiqued, perhaps even discarded, in the light of the specifics of the Christian revelation, above all its emphasis on the centrality of the cross of Christ.

Scientific theology as a response to its distinctive object

One of the basic themes of scientific theology is that theology, like any science, represents an *a posteriori* response to a distinct existing reality, which it attempts to describe, represent and communicate. The distinctiveness of the object of a science must be reflected in the methodology of that science. The Enlightenment insisted that all sciences were committed to using the same working methods and assumptions; a scientific theology insists that the distinctive identity of the object of a science determines its response to that object.

To suggest that theology is a distinct discipline with its own integrity might at first sight appear to call into question any unitary conception of knowledge, or any conception of 'the real', as opposed to an aggregate of discrete realities. This is an issue of considerable importance; indeed, it could be argued that any attempt to construct a unitary conception of reality or of human knowledge must be able to offer a satisfactory response to this concern. We may therefore open our discussion of this point by considering its grounding and application in the natural sciences.

A wide variety of methodologies are deployed across the spectrum of these disciplines. Physics, evolutionary biology and psychology each have their own vocabularies, methods and procedures, and engage with nature at their own distinctive levels. This point has long been understood, and is not controversial. Each science develops a vocabulary and a working method which is appropriate or adapted to its object. The more complex that object, the more levels of explanation are required. A classic example is the human body, which can be investigated at a series of levels – anatomical, physiological and psychological – each of which illuminates one aspect of the greater whole, but none of which is adequate by itself to give a full account. The issue of levels of explanation or multi-layered description is well established in the natural sciences.

It will be clear from the analysis thus far that there is therefore no generalized scientific methodology which can be applied without variance and uncritically to all sciences. While certain general principles may be argued to lie behind the specific approaches found in any given natural science, the point is that the nature of the field to be investigated shapes the approach to be adopted. In that each science deals with a different object, it is under an obligation to respond to that object according to its distinctive nature. The methods which are appropriate to the study of one object cannot be abstracted and applied uncritically and universally. Each science develops procedures which it deems or discovers to be appropriate to the nature of its own particular object in which it 'has solved its own inductive problem of how to arrive at a general conclusion from a limited set of particular observations'.[39]

This can be illustrated from some developments in quantum mechanics. Werner Heisenberg's famous 'uncertainty principle' represents the theoretical outcome of the application of the principle that we must encounter reality on its own terms, and accept the limitations which this entails. The distinctive nature of electrons, Heisenberg insists, is such that they cannot be 'perceived'. Unlike the particles of classical physics, they are not 'observable'. The question of how this affects the way in which they were to be studied thus became a matter of critical importance. The normal procedures of measurement and observation – which were virtually unproblematic in classical physics – encountered fundamental difficulties at the quantum level. The nature of electrons were such that they placed fundamental limitations on the processes of observation and measurement. Entities are known only in ways that correspond to their idiosyncratic identities, which must be acknowledged and respected.

This insight allows us to revisit one of the more interesting theological debates of the twentieth century – the controversy between Karl Barth and Heinrich Scholz over whether Christian theology is 'scientific'. (The German term used is *wissenschaftlich*, which does not mean 'relating to the natural sciences', but has the more general sense of 'science', including the human and social sciences.) In 1931, Scholz published an article dealing with the question of whether Protestant theology could possibly be a science. The article was prompted by Karl Barth's insistence that Christian theology was indeed *wissenschaftlich* in that it responded to its object in an appropriate manner. It was not appropriate, he insisted, to develop a universal method, capable of being applied across disciplines; rather, it was necessary to identify the object of Christian theology, and respond in a manner which was consonant with its distinctive characteristics. Although the rudiments of this idea can be seen in earlier writings, the idea is set forth with particular clarity in the

1927 *Christian Dogmatics* and other works dating from this period. For Barth, it was essential to respect the unique subject matter of Christian theology, and respond accordingly.[40]

> The choice of the means of establishment of the objective truth, the type of epistemic connection, the critical norm, and possibility of proof in any discipline must be determined by the distinctiveness of the relevant object – not the inverse, in which the object is forced to conform to predetermined concepts of method and science.

In his 1931 article, Scholz challenged Barth's approach.[41] Scholz approached the question from the standpoint of a philosopher of religion who was not entirely hostile to Barth's theological position, yet had serious misgivings concerning Barth's hostility to engagement between theology and other disciplines, including philosophy. He set out three 'minimum conditions' for any theology to possess 'scientific' status:

1. That any scientific discipline must be capable of stating its beliefs as propositions whose truth is asserted.
2. That all such propositions must be related to a single aspect of reality.
3. That the truth claims made by theological statements should be capable of being tested and confirmed against the critical principles used in their formulation.

To this, Scholz then adds the most important condition of all – the requirement that a science must be able to state its propositions as axioms (or fundamental propositions) and as theorems which are deduced from these axioms.

It is surely possible to see that there are nuggets of truth in each thinker's approach. Scholz, for example, is surely right to insist that the principles which lead to theological statements being formulated require investigation and should be open to testing.

Theological statements do not appear magically from nowhere; their historical origins (rather de-emphasized by Scholz, by the way) and intellectual coherence must be open to critical examination.

Yet there is a major problem. Underlying Scholz's works appears to be a foundationalist view of knowledge, with priority being given to deduction from fundamental propositions. While the demise of foundationalism does not require us to reject the idea of a foundation for Christian theology, it frees us from any obligation to insist that theology mimics other disciplines, such as analytical philosophy. Scholz's supreme demand – that theology should be able to formulate axioms, apparently by analogy with mathematics and logic – rests upon an understanding of method which seems firmly rooted in the Enlightenment. While Scholz is no uncritical rationalist, his article is deeply influenced by the Enlightenment assumption that at least some degree of universality of method is possible.

Barth is surely right to challenge this. It is impossible to lay down *a priori* what conditions must apply to theology as the science (*Wissenschaft*) of God, or to assume that norms and working assumptions drawn from other disciplines can be transposed to theology without doing violence to its integrity. In this, he is followed by Torrance, who argues for a 'kataphysical' approach to theology (from the Greek *kata physin*, 'according to its own nature'), which takes into account the distinctive nature of its object, while nevertheless embodying a methodology which is capable of application across disciplines.

Scientific theology offers an explanation of reality

The notion of explanation plays a significant role in Christian theology. Both the natural sciences and a scientific theology attempt to offer explanations of reality, by disclosing the way things truly are, so that the correlations established by observation may be accounted for, and additional observations and correlations proposed, so that they may be subjected to the appropriate validatory processes. The Oxford philosopher of religion Basil Mitchell summarizes a widely held consensus within the Christian tradition as follows:[42]

> It would be somewhat perverse to deny that both within a system of religious belief and in the individual's approach to such a system there appear what look like explanations or demands for explanation. The perplexed individual who asks 'What is this all for, what does it mean?' is ostensibly looking for some explanation of the 'changes and chances of this transitory life'. And if he becomes persuaded that all these things have a purpose in the providence of God, than it would seem that he has found an explanation.

Yet this position has been challenged, and thus requires closer examination. D. Z. Phillips argued vigorously against those who proposed any significant explanatory dimension to religion.[43] His approach here is shaped to no small extent by the writings of Wittgenstein, especially his caustic remarks on Sir James Frazer's *Golden Bough*. This is especially evident in his discussion of the problem of evil, in which he appears to suggest that the potential explanatory difficulties which suffering poses to the existence of God are not of particular importance.[44] Again, in dealing with the cosmological argument for the existence of God, Phillips marginalizes the explanatory aspects of God, arguing that it is quite wrong to suggest that God is a hypothetical postulate on the part of believers.

A similar point is made by the philosopher of religion Alvin Plantinga, who stresses that the origins of Christian belief do not lie in the human longing for explanation; rather, they lie in the self-revelation of God, and the human attempt to respond to that revelation.[45]

> Believers in God do not ordinarily postulate that there is such a person, just as believers in other persons or material objects do not ordinarily postulate that there are such things. Postulation is a process that goes with scientific theories; one postulates entities of a certain sort (e.g. quarks or gluons) as part of an explanatory theory. Christians, however, do not ordinarily propose the existence of God as an *explanation* of anything at all.

Plantinga does not, it must be stressed, deny that Christian doctrine possesses an explanatory dimension; he insists, however, that this is neither the cause nor the primary focus of the Christian vision of God.

In turning to criticize Phillips or Plantinga at this point, it is essential to concede that they have made important points. For the community of faith, God is most emphatically *not* conceived simply as an explanatory hypothesis. Within the context of a scientific theology, the Christian network of doctrines is conceived as a response to revelation, in the belief that such doctrines will possess explanatory potential. Yet the primary reason for developing them is to respond to divine self-disclosure – to gain an understanding of God, in the belief that this will indirectly yield explanations of the world.

The explanatory aspects of theology have been reaffirmed in a number of recent works specifically engaging with the relationship of Christianity and the natural sciences. Though not its primary task, theology cannot avoid offering explanations of reality by virtue of its nature and scope. In his careful study *Explanation from Physics to Theology*, Philip Clayton brings out the significance of 'the meaning dimension' in religion.[46] While there are variations between writers on what 'explanation' means in a religious context, most are firmly convinced that religious worldviews both encourage and expect explanations of reality. Michael Banner argues that the objections against explanation advanced by Phillips can be countered and refuted, on account both of internal difficulties within his approach and of the need for a more nuanced account of the nature of faith than that which he offers.[47]

The considerations set out by Banner and Clayton are widely regarded as at least neutralizing the objections to a 'religion as explanation' model in general, and more specifically to the explanatory aspects of a scientific theology. For the specific purposes of the present work, it is not my intention to argue that a scientific theology is primarily concerned with offering explanations of the way things are. My concern is simply to note that the vision of reality set out by a scientific theology cannot help but offer at least some explanation of the nature of things, irrespective of the degree of comprehensiveness of that explanation or the emphasis which would be placed upon 'explanation' alongside other aspects of religious existence, such as 'salvation'. As Richard Swinburne points out in his carefully argued defence of the existence of God, the explanatory power of theism in relation to such matters as the existence and ordering of the universe must never be understated.[48] The world displays phenomena which 'cry out for explanation'; part of the coherence of theism is its (alleged) ability to offer an explanation for what is observed.

We turn to a detailed examination of the manner in which a scientific theology offers an explanation of reality in Chapter 4. At this stage, however, it is my intention only to affirm that this is indeed a distinctive feature of a scientific theology.

Why a scientific theology is Christocentric

The internal logic of the Christian faith is such that the person of Jesus Christ plays a critical role in its reflections and deliberations. In stressing that a scientific theology explores both the 'ground and grammar of theology' (to borrow a phrase from Thomas F. Torrance), it is important to identify the implications of this procedure – one of which is the way in which the person of Christ functions as both the foundation and criterion of Christian theology. The basic theme I endorse can be found throughout the writings of Torrance, who develops the view that Christology is central to Christian theology, in terms of both its method and its substance, at a number of points, including his landmark 1969 work *Theological Science*. This work affirms the centrality of the 'logic of Christ' – note the implicit reference to the *coherence* of faith – in the theological enterprise:[49]

> We do not seek to impose a pattern upon theological knowledge, but rather to discern the pattern inhering in its material content, or to let it reveal itself to us as we direct our questions toward it to find out its central frame of reference. When we do that we are directed to Jesus Christ, to the Incarnation, to the hypostatic union, the unique togetherness of God and man in Christ which is normative for every other relationship between man and God. . . . It is from that centre that we take our bearings as we consider the doctrine of the Trinity, of the Father and of the Holy Spirit as well as of the Son, and therefore of creation as well as of redemption.

I have shown that the critical realist approach is both intellectually habitable and theologically responsible. It is a distinctive feature of a scientific theology. However, it will be obvious to the reader that the emphasis which I place on the interaction of knower and known within critical realism leads to a corresponding importance being attached to the manner in which reality is portrayed and represented. We must therefore move on to consider how scientific theories and Christian doctrines are developed in response to reality. In other words, we need to move on from *reality* to *theory*.

4

Theory

Ascientific theology holds that theories, whether scientific or theological, are not free creations of the human mind, but are rather constructed in response to an encounter with an existing reality. Theory is to be seen as 'responsible', in the double sense that it represents a considered and faithful *response* to reality, and that it is *accountable* to the community of faith for the manner in which its corporate vision of reality is depicted.

Even to speak of 'theory' in a theological context is to raise a number of hackles, which must be taken with the utmost seriousness. Chief among these is a deep-rooted suspicion of the reductionist ambitions of theory. How can the mystery of God be expressed in words? How can the radiant glory of the Lord be captured in a doctrine? While I concede immediately that theory must, by its very nature, be reductionist, I must also insist that it need not detract from the glorious vision of God which sustains the community of faith. Only when theory is divorced from the particulars upon which it is ultimately grounded can such an unsatisfactory situation arise. Yet this, I concede, is often the case, in that theology often offers us theories about Jesus Christ rather than an encouragement to foster a sense of 'lingering delight' (Ludolf of Saxony) over the particulars of the Gospel narratives.

In what follows, I consider the legitimacy of theory in the natural sciences and theology. This involves dealing with the concerns raised by those who regard any attempt to develop theories within theology as premature and inappropriate. After arguing for the propriety of theory in the Christian life, I move on to deal with the complex question of how reality may be represented in any intellectual engagement with reality, before turning to deal specifically with the explanatory aspects of theory. Finally, a defence is offered of the place of metaphysics in any theological or scientific attempt to represent reality, in which I criticize those who reject metaphysics on *a priori* grounds.

We begin to reflect on the nature of theory by considering the pressures that create it in the first place.

12. The Legitimacy of Theory within a Scientific Theology

The driving force behind theory is an 'eros of the mind' (Augustine of Hippo) – an intellectual curiosity, fuelled and powered by a deep sense that a greater account of the coherence of reality lies beneath the surface of what may be observed. The relentless human yearning to see the 'big picture' which provides a framework for the myriad of particular observations leads inexorably to the formulation and testing of theories. Both the natural sciences and Christian theology offer such theories as a means of explaining what may be observed in the world. We are like spectators contemplating the theatre of the world – to use one of the great Renaissance metaphors of nature. What account can we offer of what we observe? Yet alongside this intellectual longing to penetrate to the heart of reality, another pressure must be noted –

the sociological pressure for communities to differentiate themselves from other such groupings, particularly when they are, in many respects, similar. It is important to appreciate that the Christian church is located in human history and culture, and is not immune from factors which might be categorized as 'social' rather than 'intellectual'.

Yet there is no doubt that the most important factor leading to the development of theory within Christian theology is a longing to give a full and proper account of the vision of God. As Irenaeus of Lyons, writing in the second century, declares, 'the glory of God is a living human being, while the life of humanity is the vision of God' (*Gloria enim Dei vivens homo; vita autem hominis visio Dei*).[1]

We have already stressed the importance of observation, noting that this means *seeing* something *as* something – an insight especially associated with Norbert R. Hanson, but widely accepted within the scientific community. Theory can be regarded as the 'communal observing of reality', or the 'communal *beholding* of reality'. In speaking in this way, I am drawing attention to the important lines of thought developed by writers such as Martin Heidegger and Jürgen Habermas, who argued that the Greek term *theoria* (from which we derive our English term 'theory') designated a 'community beholding reality', and attempting to express in words what it observed. They appealed to the Greek idea of the *theoros* – the official 'observer' sent to certain sacred rites by cities, in order that they might report back on what they saw.

This idea is expressed particularly well by Wlad Godzich, formerly Professor of English and Comparative Literature at the University of Geneva, who argues that theory represents the public beholding of the world and society, through which private perceptions were transcended and reconfigured into socially normative beliefs 'invested with undeniable authority by the polity'.[2]

The act of looking at, of surveying, designated by *theorein*, does not designate a private act carried out by a cogitating philosopher but a very public one with important social consequences. The Greeks designated certain individuals . . . to act as legates on certain formal occasions in other city states or in matters of considerable political importance. These individuals bore the title of *theoros*, and collectively constituted a *theoria*.

On this understanding of the idea, 'theory' designates the reflective activity of a community.

So is theory inevitable, like 'death and taxes' (Benjamin Franklin)? There are certainly some within the theological community who hold that the case for Christianity would be significantly advanced if its apparent obsession with doctrine were to be abandoned. Judaism, many point out, is much more concerned with issues of practical living than with doctrines. So might not Christianity have made a false move in developing such a preoccupation? Is not an 'undogmatic Christianity' the faith of the future?

Such concerns have a genuine point to make. However, I argue that it is ultimately quite irresponsible for Christianity to fail to give an intellectual account of itself in this way. Theory arises precisely because human beings are rational creatures, and feel impelled, both morally and intellectually, to give an account of things. It is part of our nature to wish to respond to reality in this way. To illustrate this, I turn to consider Francis Bacon's 1620 work *Novum Organum*, in which he compares three groups of insects:

1. Ants, which 'heap up and use what they accumulate'. Bacon is here criticizing those who believe that the business of the natural sciences is merely to accumulate observations about the external world.

2. Spiders, which 'spin webs out of their own resources'. Bacon's target here are those who reason *a priori*, constructing philosophical systems out of their own minds, without any engagement with the external world.

3. Bees, which both accumulate material about the external world, and mentally digest it. Noting that a bee 'gathers material from the flowers of the garden and the field, but then works and digests it by its own faculties', Bacon argues that the task of a natural philosophy is to analyse observations, and synthesize theories as a result.

We see here the fundamental patterns which underlie the natural sciences – the quest for universal patterns underlying specific and particular phenomena. The natural sciences and Christian theology are both rooted in human experience and culture; yet they also aspire to transcend the particularities of time and place to yield truths that claim a more universal significance. Particularities give rise to theories, which in turn give rise to worldviews, as follows:

$$observation \rightarrow theory \rightarrow worldview$$

I illustrate this transition from the biological and physical sciences. The basic issue is best understood by considering the approach of the eighteenth-century Swedish biologist Carl von Linné (1707–78), more generally known by the Latinized form of his name, 'Linnaeus'. Much of Linnaeus's career was given over to cataloguing existing forms of plant and animal life, attempting to discover various patterns of order within the natural world. Having established that a certain form of ordering seemed to exist, the question then arose concerning how this was to be interpreted. What did it point to? What theory of the development of the natural world might account for this observed ordering? In the end, it was Darwin's account of how such ordering arose which would eventually win the day, largely on account of its elegance and the relatively few assumptions it required, and its resonance with prevailing social assumptions. The Linnaean taxonomy can thus be seen as providing a significant conceptual foundation for Darwin's subsequent reflections. Linnaeus provided the observations which led to Darwin's theories.

In the case of physics, a series of puzzling observations concerning the diffraction of electrons and other phenomena gave rise to quantum theory. Once more, the basic pattern can be discerned: the *particularities* of observation give rise to the *universalities* of theory. Certain universal patterns are shown to lie behind specific observations. A deeper universal pattern is uncovered as underlying a series of specific individual observations.

A similar pattern of thought lies behind the development of Christian doctrine, which I argue represents a specifically Christian form of theory. This can be seen from the emergence of Christology during the patristic period. The essential point is that patristic writers – such as Athanasius of Alexandria – found themselves confronted with a series of particularities concerning Jesus Christ, in the form of the gospel accounts of what he did, his impact upon people, what was said about him, and what happened to him. So what theoretical account of the identity of Jesus Christ best explained these observations?

Athanasius argued that the totality of the biblical witness to and Christian experience of Jesus Christ required him to be conceptualized as both divine and human. Only this theoretical framework, he argued, was capable of doing justice to the gospel narratives. Simplistic, reductionist modes of representing the identity and significance of Jesus Christ were judged inadequate with reference to the phenomena which they were required or intended to represent. In particular, the model of Jesus of Nazareth as a purely human figure (the Ebionite heresy) or as a purely divine figure (the

Docetic heresy) were regarded as quite inadequate. Both the representation of Jesus in the New Testament and the manner in which the Christian church incorporated Jesus into its life of prayer and worship required a more complex and nuanced understanding of his identity and significance than either of these simpler models were able to offer. A theory of the identity of Jesus Christ capable of embracing all of his activities was required, rather than one which could explain only some.

Christian theology uses the term 'doctrine', in preference to 'theory'. It is necessary to draw a distinction between 'doctrines' (meaning 'theories' that the Christian church has come to regard as authentic representations of the consensus of faith) and 'opinions' (meaning 'theories' that have been developed by individual theologians or groups, but are not regarded as binding by the Christian community). The term 'dogma' is used in classic Christian theology to mean something like 'communally authoritative and authorized theories, which are held to be essential to the identity and mission of the Christian community'. Although this term has now come to have rather unsavoury associations for many, it nevertheless makes an important distinction. For this reason, the term 'dogma' has found its way into Roman Catholic, Lutheran and Reformed dogmatics to refer to 'an accepted teaching of the Church'.

Given the slightly problematic historical associations of the term 'dogma', I prefer to use the term 'doctrine' to mean 'a theory which is an accepted teaching of the Church', as opposed to 'a theory which has the support of some academics and religious groups, but has failed to win the support of the Church as a whole'. The importance of this distinction is obvious from the history of the Church in the late Middle Ages, when immense confusion arose over what counted as the official teaching of the Church, and what was the private opinion of academics or pressure groups.

Drawing on earlier reflections on the role of the *theoros* in ancient Greece, as developed in recent writings, I argue that doctrine may thus be provisionally defined as communally authoritative teachings regarded as essential to the identity of the Christian community, in which the community *tells* itself and outsiders what it has *seen*, and what it has become in response to this vision.

It will therefore be clear that the concept of 'doctrine' has both intellectual and social dimensions. A doctrine is a theory; it is also something which distinguishes the Church from other groupings. This double aspect of doctrine can be seen from the earliest of times. In the course of his controversy against Gnosticism in the second century, Irenaeus of Lyons developed credal statements and formularies designed to differentiate Christianity from its intellectual rivals, and offer both a social and an intellectual demarcation of the two movements. This has important implications in relation to the social function of doctrine, which we shall turn to presently.

We now turn to consider some important anxieties which are regularly expressed over the place of theory in Christian theology, and elsewhere.

Reductionist foreclosures: some hesitations over theory

The great concern that is regularly expressed about any theoretical account of reality is that it seems austere and impoverished in relation to the phenomena it is meant to represent. A classic example is provided by the rainbow, one of the most beautiful and awe-inspiring phenomena in the natural world. Many writers, including John Keats, have compared the majestic splendour of the original phenomenon rather unfavourably with the mathematical formulae which describe the optical process of refraction which generates it in the first place. Similar anxieties have been expressed about God. How can the awesome reality of God ever be expressed in words? Do not theological doctrines seem rather severe and meagre in comparison to the great vision of God, as set out in the Christian liturgy and embodied in the architecture of Gothic cathedrals? C. S. Lewis recalls precisely such concern being expressed after a talk he once gave to the Royal Air Force:[3]

> I remember once when I had been giving a talk to the RAF, an old, hard-bitten officer got up and said, 'I've no use for all that stuff. But mind you, I'm a religious man too. I know there's a God. I've felt him: And that's just why I don't believe all your neat little dogmas and formulas about Him. To anyone who's met the real thing they all seem so petty and pedantic and unreal!'

The same concern can also be illustrated from the field of literary theory. A good example is provided by the 'story of the swan-geese', a rather touching Russian folk tale which relates how a young girl attempts to recover her brother from the clutches of the evil witch Baba Yaga before her parents notice he is missing. Her ultimately successful efforts to find him and bring him safely home are assisted in various ways by an oven, an apple tree, a river of milk and a little mouse. Some years ago, Vladimir Propp developed a theoretical model for Russian folk tales. Propp argued that these folktales all make use of the same basic structural building blocks, set out in the same order. The story may thus be reduced to an abstract theoretical representation, identifying which of the 31 elements are used. His theoretical representation of the 'story of the swan-geese' looks like this:[4]

$$\gamma^1\beta^1\delta^1A^1C\uparrow \left\{ \begin{array}{l} [DE^1 \text{ neg. F neg.}] \\ d^7E^7F^9 \end{array} \right\} G^4K^1\downarrow[Pr^1D^1E^1F^9 = Rs^4]^3$$

So a story has been reduced to an equation. Its drama, characters, pace and excitement have evaporated; in its place, we find something that looks unspeakably dull. It is easy to understand

why many have expressed concerns about the reductionist trajectory of theory. As the case of the 'swan-geese' story makes clear,
theory reduces narratives to formulae. This is also an issue in the area
of Christology, where one of the most persistent criticisms
directed against the Chalcedonian definition is that it likewise
reduces the richly textured biblical narrative concerning Christ to
a neat little formula. So what purpose does theory serve, which
might in some way excuse this rather troubling matter?

In responding to such concerns about theory, it is clearly
important not to deny the obvious fact that theory is reductionist. To criticize theory for being 'reductionist' is like criticizing
water because it is wet; that is just the way things are. The problem
lies in how we use theory, not in the nature of theory itself. The
entire purpose of scientific theories may be said to be the uncovering of universal principles which lie behind specific patterns of
behaviour, which may be empirically observed – as, for example,
Darwin's theory of natural selection offers an explanation of the
observable features of the natural world of plants and animals by
reducing those complex observations to a common pattern,
capable of theoretical formulation. The quest to find basic explanations for observed patterns of behaviour is inevitably formulated in terms of reducing phenomena to theories.

A scientific theology recognizes and welcomes the intellectual
demands that reality places upon us, realizing that the formulation
of a theoretical account of things is an essential aspect of any true
engagement with reality. This does not mean that theory displaces
observation; it is simply to acknowledge the need for an additional
layer of reflection, which adds to what is already known. John
Keats's famous protest against 'philosophical' (we might say 'theoretical') accounts of such natural wonders as the rainbow is not
intended to invalidate its beauty, or the sense of aesthetic delight
that it occasions. It is an additional layer of reflection, which adds

rational integrity to aesthetic emotions. Theory aims to offer a representation of reality, which allows us to engage that reality at a new and deeper level, while in no way obliging us to abandon its impact on our imaginations and emotions.

The real difficulty with theory concerns its potential abuse – namely, that the theory comes to displace and overshadow the individual phenomena which it represents. This can happen in two ways:

> Through insisting on a theory-driven engagement with reality, which relentlessly sees reality through the lens of a predetermined theory. This results in an impoverished encounter with the world, in that there is a marked tendency to simply see natural phenomena as another example of some general theoretical principle, without appreciating it in its own right. This was the concern that John Keats expressed about 'unweaving' the rainbow – that a hasty assignment of the phenomenon to a theoretical category robbed it of its beauty and wonder.
>
> Through failing to appreciate that theory is actually dependent upon an engagement with reality. A universal theory is grounded on a series of particulars, with reference to which it is justified. The particulars that once were cited in support of a theory may subsequently be seen to support an alternative theoretical reading. For this reason, the 'redemption of particulars' is an important corrective to placing an excessive reliance on theory.

We shall explore each of these points in greater detail.

Theory and defamiliarization

It is widely conceded that there is something of a problem with purely theoretical approaches to such natural wonders as rainbows, or theological mysteries such as the death of Christ on the cross. An emphasis on theory encourages the automatic, unthinking assignment of such phenomena to ready-made categories. It causes the observer to pigeon-hole complex phenomena in terms of simplistic categories, bypassing the immensely important and productive process of deep reflection which any meaningful encounter with reality is meant to engender. So how can this impoverishing process of premature theoretical assignation and reduction be forestalled? How can theoretical analysis proceed without robbing reality of its wonder?

In trying to answer this question, I turn to the field of literary theory. The Russian formalist Victor Shklovsky (1893–1984) develops a notion which is of profound importance to this problem of theoretical representation in a scientific theology – the idea of 'defamiliarization'. The basic idea is widely attributed to the German Romantic poet Novalis (Friedrich von Hardenberg, 1772–1801), who declared that the essence of romanticism was 'to make the familiar strange, and the strange familiar'. This theme is developed in a significant direction by Shklovsky. Any artistic object, according to Shklovsky, runs the risk of becoming routine, habitual or overfamiliar, and thus loses its power as an artistic object. 'As perception becomes habitual, it becomes automatic.'[5] This inevitable process of 'automatization' or 'habitualization' leads to a loss of potency of the form. It is essential to recover the vitality of such modes of representation; this takes place through the process of 'defamiliarization' or 'making strange' (a process Shklovsky describes using the Russian word *ostranenie*).

Shklovsky's concern is that things may become so familiar that they lack the potential to stimulate or provoke their intended reaction from their audience. Overfamiliarity leads to the erosion of their aesthetic potential, and consequently an impoverishment of the experience of the reader. Shklovsky's insistence on the need to 'increase the difficulty and length of perception' has important parallels with Christian spirituality, which deplores the brevity and superficiality of the Christian engagement with biblical texts and images, and thus aims to foster an extended and more profound engagement with their form and contents.

From a theoretical point of view, Shklovsky's concerns help reduce the risks associated with theorizing – evident, for example, through Norbert R. Hanson's famous assertion that we always *see* things *as* something – for example, the Christian *sees* nature *as* God's creation. Yet this process of perception can become automatic and reflex. We learn to recognize objects 'by their main characteristics' and automatically place them in predetermined categories instead of seeing them 'in their entirety'.[6] We need to make the familiar strange, so that we can encounter it as if for the first time, and appreciate it all over again.

An approach to theology which places an emphasis on theory runs the risk of failing to engage properly with reality precisely because it hastens towards a theory-driven reading of things. Reality is automatically and hastily assimilated to theoretically predetermined theological categories. According to Shklovsky, the essential function of 'defamiliarization' is to counteract the process of habituation encouraged by routine everyday modes of perception – processes which prevent us from fully perceiving the world around us, in that we become anaesthetized to its distinctive features. We are called upon to defamiliarize that with which we are overly familiar.

It is possible to see the world and its events through a rigid theoretical framework, which not merely disinclines us to engage with the particular, but represents a foreclosure of the interpretative process. While theory is a legitimate aspect of the theological enterprise, it cannot be regarded as its ultimate goal. As Dante pointed out, the supreme end of life is to see 'the love that moves the sun and the other stars' – something that transcends our feeble human attempts to describe it, even though those attempts point us directly towards this greater reality.

Theory and the redemption of particulars

The second concern is how theoretical accounts of reality – whether in the natural sciences or theology – seem to lose their grounding in particularities, and assume an independent life of their own, almost as though the question of how they came into being could be disregarded. Both in the natural sciences and in Christian theology, theory emerges from particulars, and is accountable to them. In an article entitled 'On Behalf of Theory', Frank Lentricchia – currently Katherine Everett Gilbert Professor of Literature and Theater Studies at Duke University – points to the way in which a theoretical reading of things can lose sight of its origins in experience and observation.[7]

> Theory is primarily a *process* of discovery of the lesson that I am calling historical; any single, formulable theory is a reduced version of the process, a frozen proposition which will tend to cover up the process it grew out of by projecting itself as an uncontingent system of ideas.

Lentricchia's concern was that theory had come to see itself as possessing the character of an *a priori* truth, and had chosen to ignore its *a posteriori* origins in an engagement with particulars – whether literary texts or empirical observations.

An excellent example of the continuing importance of particularities is provided by Joseph Prout's atomic hypothesis, first put forward in 1815. According to Prout, all elements were composed of hydrogen. On the basis of this hypothesis, it would be expected that the atomic weights of the elements would be integral multiples of that of hydrogen. The precise measurements of the

Swedish chemist Jöns Berzelius called this into question, in that a number of elements clearly possessed non-integral atomic weights – such as chlorine (35.45). This was widely seen as a decisive contradiction of Prout's hypothesis. However, the discovery of isotopes in 1910 reversed this judgement. It was established that a number of elements existed with different atomic weights, while having the same atomic numbers. Each of these isotopes possessed an atomic weight which was an integral multiple of that of hydrogen. As Larry Laudan comments: 'The very phenomena which had earlier constituted anomalies for Prout's hypothesis became positive instances for it.'[8]

Countless other examples could be provided from the history of science to demonstrate how the assembly of meticulously recorded observations – whether of planetary movements, ocean temperatures, or the frequencies of solar or stellar spectral lines – proved to be decisive for the confirmation or disconfirmation of theories. The particulars always take epistemological precedence over the universal, precisely because the validity of the allegedly 'universal' is to be regarded as provisional, rather than final.

Both these concerns relate to potential abuses or misunderstandings of theory. When rightly understood, theory liberates, rather than imprisons, in that it allows us to 'see' or 'behold' a particular in a new manner – for example, to see a rainbow as a specific instance of a general optical principle, or the orbiting of the satellites of the planet Jupiter as a specific instance of the general theory of gravitation. Theologically, it allows us to gain new and potentially dramatic readings of the particularities of the Gospels – for example, reading the birth of Christ in a theoretical manner, so that it speaks of the humility and condescension of God in the incarnation. Some such interpenetration of particularities and theory can, of course, be argued to be implicit within the New Testament itself, both in the Gospels and in the Pauline letters.

The issue of closure in theory

I now move on to address another concern often raised about theoretical approaches to both the natural sciences and Christian theology – that these 'theories' represent premature closure of debates that ought to be declared permanently open. A particularly important representative of this position is the philosopher Hilary Lawson.[9] 'Closure', for Lawson, represents the crystallization of the world into differentiated entities:

> It is through closure that openness is divided into things. Without closure, we would be lost in a sea of openness: a sea without character and without form. For in openness, there is no colour, no sound, no distinguishing mark, no difference, no thing. . . . Closure enables us to realize objects of every type and variety. Closure is responsible for our being able to describe the atoms of hydrogen and the molecules of water that make up the sea . . . Closure can be understood as the imposition of fixity on openness. The closing of that which is open.

Lawson argues that the world is open; it is the human observer who secures (or imposes) closure. For Lawson, the human observer is active in this process. Far from representing a passive response to observation, closure represents an active imposition of meaning or pattern upon the world.

In effect, Lawson argues that we are confronted with two possibilities – the modernist and postmodernist construals of reality. According to the former, there exists one universal means of securing closure, which would be accepted by all people at all times. According to the latter – which Lawson favours – we are constantly searching for theoretical closure, yet have to learn to live with the fact that this cannot be secured. 'The failure of closure has the consequence that there can be no final resting place.'[10]

Yet a scientific theology takes a markedly different approach, insisting, as we have seen, that *ontology determines epistemology* – in other words, that the degree of theoretical closure that may be secured for any aspect of reality is determined by its intrinsic nature. We are thus obliged to think in terms of a range of possibilities of closure, depending on which stratum of reality is being encountered and represented in this manner. The category of 'mystery' plays a particularly important role in any discussion about theological closure. The key point here is that the category of 'mystery' affirms both the *coherence* of a multi-levelled reality, and its *complexity*, which is such that its meaning cannot be totally determined by any one writer or era. As a result, what one generation inherits from another is not so much definitive answers as a shared commitment to the process of wrestling.

There are three fundamental theses concerning theoretical closure within a scientific theology, taking into account the fundamental notion of a multi-layered reality, with each stratum demanding a mode of representation appropriate to its own distinctive nature:

1. Closure is an activity which takes place, to the extent that it can, within a communal context.
2. Closure is always partial, not total, in matters of Christian doctrine.
3. The extent of closure is determined by the subject matter. The nature of the object determines the extent of closure possible, according to its own distinctive nature.

For example, the Council of Chalcedon may be said to have secured 'closure' of the Christological debate at one level, while directing it into fresh channels on the other. As Karl Rahner has argued, Chalcedon thus represents a beginning rather than an end, in that it lays down a 'line of demarcation' on essentials, while leaving open the question how lesser issues are to be addressed and understood.

In the liberal Protestant intellectual environment in which I began to study theology at Oxford in the 1970s, it was regarded as axiomatic that it is more blessed to pursue truth than to achieve it. We are questing for something that cannot be achieved; only fools and knaves believed that it was possible to *know* the truth. Like all overstatements, this incorporates genuine insights – most notably, that the belief that one has firmly secured the truth (and may thus cease questing and enquiring) is intellectually stifling, inhibiting its further exploration. Yet as Rahner points out in relation to Chalcedon, far from shutting down discussion, the partial closure of a debate opens out a new vista of exploration.

The problem of a 'non-dogmatic' Christianity

From what has been said thus far, it will be clear that I believe that Christianity cannot avoid theoretical reflection and formulation, however tentative. Yet this is by no means universally accepted, and would be vigorously contested by some. There continues to be resistance to the notion of a 'dogmatic' Christianity, reflecting unease about the very nature of 'dogma', as well as the idea of shutting down what ought to be an ongoing discussion (echoing some of the concerns expressed by Hilary Lawson).

There are a number of particularly important factors which create this sense of unease and distrust about doctrinally shaped approaches to Christianity. Among these may be noted the lingering concerns about the relation between dogma and conflict, as in the European Wars of Religion and the fading impact of the 'History of Dogma' movement, which argued that theoretical developments within Christianity were something of an historical aberration, resulting from a malignant Greek influence on the development of Christianity as it expanded from Palestine into new geographical territories.

I respond with three points in arguing for the inevitability of doctrine:

1. The demand for an 'undogmatic' Christianity often seems to amount to little more than imposing a global embargo on critical reflection in matters of faith. It represents a retreat from precisely the kind of intellectual engagement which makes Christian theology such a genuinely exciting and challenging discipline. Instead of encouraging Christians to think about their faith, it represents a demand that they suspend use of their intellectual faculties in any matters to do with God, Christ or human destiny. Precisely because human beings think, they will wish to develop theories concerning the nature of God and Jesus Christ – whatever form those theories may take.

2. Some use the term 'undogmatic Christianity' in a highly invidious manner, meaning something like 'an understanding of Jesus Christ which is opposed to the official teachings of the Christian faith'. Yet the ideas which are held to displace these are generally as dogmatic as their predecessors. It is a new set of dogmas that is being proposed, not the elimination of dogma as such. Theoretical statements, whether implicit or explicit, lie behind all reflection on the nature of God or Christ. To pretend that they do not is to close one's eyes to the pervasive influence of theories in religion, which must be honestly addressed and acknowledged at every point.

3. To demand an 'undogmatic' Christianity often involves confusion over the *tone* and *substance* of Christian doctrine.

'Dogmatic' can rightly be understood as meaning 'enclosed within a framework of theoretical or doctrinal beliefs', and in this sense, I must insist, reflects some integral themes of the Christian faith. Yet the term can also bear the meaning of 'uncritical', 'unreflective' or 'authoritarian' – referring, in other words, to the tone of voice in which Christian theological affirmations are made, rather than to their substance. I have no interest in supporting shrill, strident, imperious and overbearing assertions of Christian doctrine, which demand silent unthinking compliance on the part of their audiences, and lead to conflict and tension. Yet I remain convinced that such statements are necessary and legitimate, while insisting that they can and should be stated more graciously and humbly.

A number of people have defended the continuing necessity of theoretical statements in Christian thought and life, four of whom are the British writers Charles Gore (1853–1932), James Orr (1844–1913), Peter Taylor Forsyth (1848–1921) and John Seldon Whale (1896–1997). Each of these offers a highly competent defence of the necessity of dogmatic statements. As an example of some of the points made, we may consider briefly some of the points made by Forsyth in his landmark work *The Person and Place of Jesus Christ* (1909).

Earlier, we noted both the intellectual and social pressures for doctrinal definition. Developing such a line of thought, Forsyth contends that the identity of the Church requires definition if it is to continue in existence as a distinct entity within the historical process. Dogma, according to Forsyth, is essential to the life of the Church, in that it both arises from and *expresses* that life.[11]

A Church must always have a dogma, implicit or explicit. A cohesive Church must have a coherent creed. But it must be a dogma the

Church holds, not one that holds the Church. The life is in the body, not in the system. . . . The idea of a dogma, as the organized declaration or confession by any Church of its collective doctrine, is only the intellectual counterpart of the idea of the organized Church itself.

There thus exist two pressures which make dogma inevitable: the human desire to make sense of things and extend the horizons of understanding; and the social need for the Church to offer a definition of its identity and boundaries – a matter to which we shall return presently.

An 'undogmatic' Christianity is only a possibility if individual Christians cease to exercise their intellectual faculties and if the Church ceases to regard itself as having anything distinctive to say to the world around it. As Forsyth points out, the faith of the Church must be capable of statement – and that process of formulation of a statement inevitably leads to the development of dogma.[12]

Revelation did not come in a statement, but in a person; yet stated it must be. Faith must go on to specify. It must be capable of statement, else it could not be spread; for it is not an ineffable, incommunicable mysticism. It has its truth, yet it is not a mere truth but a power; its truth, its statement, is part of it.

The proper debate thus concerns which dogmas should be adopted, rather than whether dogma as such is a good or necessary thing.

The social function of doctrine

An examination of the question of the social function of doctrine must begin with the recognition that

1. The social role of a doctrine has no bearing on its truth.
2. Recognition of the social role of a doctrine does not in any way entail a non- or anti-realist approach to doctrine.

3. The social function of a given doctrine is determined by historical circumstances, and may change from one period or culture to another.

I begin by considering the social function of doctrine in relation to the demarcation of Christianity from its parent Judaism, where Paul's doctrine of justification by faith plays a particularly important role in clarifying the relation of these two religious groups. This ecclesial function of the doctrine represents a 'social construction' – but on a critical realist approach to matters, I emphasize that this cannot be regarded as implying that the doctrine is an invention or is untrue. It is simply an observation that this doctrine came to play a critical role in the demarcation of communities.

Doctrine also plays an important role in distinguishing the Christian community from the world around it, thus aiding its preservation as a distinct entity in the face of assimilationist pressures from its cultural environment. Doctrine came to be of increasing importance in distinguishing the Church from secular culture at large, and increasing a sense of identity and cohesion within its ranks. Yet with the rise of Christendom in western Europe, the social function of doctrine began to become of lesser importance. If the culture as a whole was Christian, there was little point in a church emphasizing doctrinal distinctives.

With the Reformation, a new situation emerged. The religious homogeneity of western Europe was swept aside, as new religious groupings – Lutheran, Reformed and Anabaptist – came into being, each anxious to distinguish itself from Catholicism on the one hand, and from its Protestant rivals on the other. Doctrine assumed a new importance, as the pressure for self-definition became intense. In England, a rather different situation arose. The older 'Christendom' model was retained, with the king's authority substituted for that of the Pope. As a result, doctrinal debates played a far smaller role in the English Reformation than in its continental counterpart.

Recognizing that certain doctrines function as social demarcators between Christian churches, and that this function is historically situated, opens the way to an understanding of how ecumenical rapprochement is possible. It is not that the truth of certain doctrines is being denied or marginalized; rather, their *social function* – which is superimposed upon the theological truth of those doctrines – is recognized as being specific to a past age, and hence not permanently valid. Their intellectual truth remains; their social function changes.

Recognizing (a) that certain doctrines function as social demarcators between ecclesial traditions, and (b) that this function is historically situated, opens the way to an understanding of how ecumenical agreement is possible. It is not the truth of certain doctrines that is being denied or marginalized; a social function of those doctrines, specific to a past age, is declared to be no longer valid. This can be seen in the social role played by the doctrine of justification in the sixteenth century. Ecumenical agreement on the doctrine of justification involves the recognition that doctrinal matters which were, as a matter of historical contingency, essential to the self-definition of either Lutheranism or Roman Catholicism at the time of the Reformation need no longer be regarded as having this function. The self-identity of Lutheranism is no longer perceived to be shaped by this doctrine. No longer need this doctrine serve as a marker of division between Lutheranism and Roman Catholicism.

As I stressed earlier, the recognition of the social function of doctrines in no way weakens their truth-claims. Certain specific contingent historical circumstances lead to a given doctrine becoming of normative importance for the self-definition of a community in that situation. With the passing of those circumstances, its social

function is eroded, possibly to the point at which it plays no
significant role. Central to modern ecumenical discussions is the
fact that doctrines which functioned as social demarcators in the
Reformation period – or other periods of critical importance to
the identity of the ecclesial community in question – have lost that
function, partly by a process of historical erosion and partly on
account of a more recent willingness to set that function aside in
the interests of the unity of Christendom.

13. The Representation of Reality in a Scientific Theology

Having reflected on the importance of theory, we must now turn
to consider how reality may be represented. A stratified reality
may be represented in three major ways: through words, propositions and images.

Representation through *words* raises the issue of how terminology is developed to cope with advances in the natural sciences, or
the particular demands of Christian theology. New advances
demand new words. Thus terms such as electron, mitochondria
and entropy were developed in response to new scientific
advances, which had to be described and designated. A particularly good theological example of this development is the technical Greek term *homoousios* ('of the same substance'), which was
coined to define a very specific understanding of the relationship
of Christ to God the Father.

An engagement with reality often demands new concepts,
which need to be expressed verbally. The theological use of words
demands particularly careful attention. Often words are 'borrowed' from their original secular context to serve new theological
purposes, with significant shifts in their meaning as a result.
Thomas F. Torrance points out how Athanasius of Alexandria
insisted that Christian theology had to develop a distinctive

vocabulary in response to the realities it engaged with, building on existing concepts as it tried to express the new ideas of the gospel:[13]

> So far as scientific theology is concerned, this means that we are forced to adapt our common language to the nature and reality of God who is disclosed to us in Jesus Christ, and even where necessary to coin new terms, to express what we thus apprehend. Hence Athanasius insisted that when our ordinary terms are applied to God, they must be *stretched* beyond their natural sense and reference, and must be employed in such a way that they indicate more than the actual terms can naturally specify.

Whether theology coins its own vocabulary, or borrows terms from other contexts, it is essential to ensure that they are used and understood as they relate to the object of the Christian faith, rather that recapitulating the presuppositions of their original context.

Representation can also take place through *propositions*, despite much contemporary anxiety about the ability of such statements to depict a complex reality. Thus Newton's laws of motion can be stated in purely propositional form. Although George Lindbeck expressed severe misgivings concerning what he styled 'cognitive-propositional' approaches to doctrine, these are now widely regarded as inflated reactions, based on a misreading of their leading representatives. It is clear that propositional revelational statements can be found in Scripture, such as 'God is love' (1 John 4:8, 16). Far from being a proposition derived from *a priori* theological axioms – to note a distinguishing theological pretension of the Enlightenment – it represents an *a posteriori* account of the significance of the death of Christ, seen from the unique perspective of the Christian tradition.

Representation can also take place through *images*. At the theological level, this raises the important question of the relation between the image and the reality it depicts. Why are such images capable of reflecting God's nature? Is this capacity intrinsic to them? Or is it conferred or acquired, perhaps through some external process of authorization or internal process of illumination? A Christian doctrine of creation certainly points to a form of created correspondence between images within the material world and what lies beyond it. Yet the situation is rather more complex than this, as Karl Barth's formidable criticism of the notion of any 'analogy of being' (*analogia entis*) makes clear. We shall presently move on to a detailed analysis of the place of analogies in a scientific theology, and explore the concepts of 'analogy of being' and 'analogy of faith' in a little more detail.

Before moving on to consider such analogies, however, it is appropriate to reflect a little on the concept of 'mystery'. We have already explored how the concept allows us to argue that a failure to grasp fully the rationality of a complex reality does not oblige us to draw the conclusion that it is incoherent. The fundamental point that a scientific theology makes at this point is that there are limits to our understanding and capacity to represent the divine, fixed both by our limitations as fallen, finite human beings and by the nature and extent of divine self-revelation. It has long been recognized that systematic theology encounters serious difficulties of language and imagery in attempting to convey even a hint of the wonder of the vision of God.

When Augustine wrote his famous words 'if you can grasp it, it is not God' (*si comprehendis non est Deus*),[14] he was making the fundamental point that the coherence of divine reality cannot be adequately grasped by human reason, or represented by human language. To affirm that this reality may, in some sense of the word, be *explained* is not to suggest that it may be reduced to the level of our comprehension. Rather, it means that we are enabled to catch such a glimpse of its structures as is sufficient to allow us to grasp its fundamental characteristics. To affirm that it may be *represented* is not to suggest that it may be fully and exhaustively disclosed in human words and images, but rather that such words and images are pointers to a greater whole which simply cannot be conveyed in all its totality. The essence of a mystery is the fact that it simply cannot be reduced to something smaller, or even to its individual parts – and part of our task as theologians is to acknowledge the reality of this situation, and respond and work within the limits it imposes upon us.

I explore this further by considering how C. S. Lewis and Dante Alighieri attempt to represent the divine mystery in their writings, before reaffirming the limitations placed upon human language and conceptualities when confronted with the Christian vision of God. Words fail when faced with such a vision – a thought famously expressed by T. S. Eliot in *Burnt Norton*:[15]

> Words strain
> Crack and sometimes break, under the burden
> Under the tension, slip, slide, perish,
> Decay with imprecision, will not stay in place.
> Will not stay still.

Analogical reasoning in a scientific theology

I now turn to consider how reality may be represented analogically, one of the most debated and important themes in classic Christian theology, which assumes a position of considerable significance within a scientific theology. The importance of the question is largely, though by no means totally, linked with the extensive use of 'analogies' or 'models' within the natural sciences as a means of both representing and prompting further investigation of reality.

Giambattista Vico once commented that it was a distinctive 'property of the human mind, that whenever men can form no idea of distant and unknown things, they judge them by what is familiar and at hand'.[16] This general principle has played a major role in both science and religion. It is widely agreed that analogies play a major role in many forms of argumentation and inference, whether in philosophy, theology or the natural sciences. The manner in which analogies are generated, validated and applied provides one of the most interesting parallels between Christianity and the natural sciences, and illuminates their commonalities and divergences.

One of the central difficulties encountered in dealing with analogies is that no general theory of analogical argument is widely accepted. This is not to say that no such theory has been set out; the point is that none has managed to secure general acceptance. One of the most intriguing questions is whether older justifications of argumentation by analogy can be retrieved. For example, there is a clear understanding in classical philosophy that the concept of analogy is somehow grounded in mathematical proportions, so that there is some form of proportionality between entities which are held to be analogically related. The Renaissance witnessed the growing influence of a Neoplatonic ontology which affirmed a linkage between an image and its original. One of the more interesting aspects of classical Christian theology concerns its grounding of the use of analogies concerning God in a series of theological beliefs, to which we shall turn presently.

The logical structure of arguments from analogy can be set out in the following manner:

1. *a*, *b*, *c* and *d* all have properties *P* and *Q* in common.
2. *a*, *b* and *c* all have property *R* in common.

Therefore it is likely that

3. *d* probably also has property *R*.

This principle can be seen at work in the development of models of the atom during the early twentieth century. For example, in December 1910 Ernest Rutherford developed a simple model of the atom, based on the solar system. The atom consists of a central body (the nucleus), in which practically the entire mass of the atom is concentrated. Electrons orbit this nucleus, in much the same way as the planets orbit the sun. Whereas the orbits of the planets were determined by the gravitational attraction of the sun, Rutherford argued that the orbits of the electrons were determined by the electrostatic attraction between the negatively charged electrons and the positively charged nucleus.

Interestingly, Rutherford developed this 'solar system' analogy further by arguing that the way in which alpha-particles were scattered by atoms could be explained if the alpha-particles were assumed to behave like certain types of comets, whose orbits around the sun took the form of hyperbolae. The behaviour of these alpha-particles, as recently observed by Hans Wilhelm Geiger, was thus analogous to that of other members of the solar system (non-periodic comets). The model was visually simple and easy to understand, and offered a theoretical framework which explained at least some of the known behaviour of atoms at this time.

It is clear that the natural sciences have gone some considerable way towards establishing and regulating the use of analogies in the depiction and explanation of the world, and have led to comparisons between the ways in which analogies and models function in the sciences and religion. It is not entirely clear, however, how far these comparisons have taken us. As Janet Martin Soskice has suggested, the level of discussion on the part of theologians has tended to be little more than something along the lines of 'religion need not be ashamed of its reliance on models if science proceeds in the same way'.[17] The clear (if unstated) assumption here is that the explanatory successes of the

natural sciences lend credence to its use of models, and hence
justify theology doing the same thing.

Yet this is clearly inadequate as the basis for detailed theological engagement with reality. From the perspective of a scientific
theology, the grounding of analogies is of central importance. The
fundamental point that needs to be made here is that a Christian
doctrine of creation entails an analogical mode of argumentation.
The created correspondences between humanity, the world and
their divine creator entails the use of analogies in both scientific
and theological explanation. In each case, four fundamental issues
arise:

1. The capacity of an analogy to model or represent another
    system.
2. The authority of the analogy, which establishes and vali-
    dates its use as a model.
3. The extent to which an analogy may be deployed before its
    similarity to the system to be modelled breaks down.
4. The complementary interaction of analogies in represent-
    ing a system.

In what follows, I consider each of these points in more detail.

1. The 'analogy of being' (analogia entis)

One of the most interesting consequences of a Christian doctrine
of creation is that a 'created correspondence' may be posited
between God and the created order. This correspondence arises
specifically from the fact that God, in freely creating the world,
was not constrained in the manner of its fashioning, but was able
to create things in such a way that they mirror, in however attenuated a manner, the divine nature. Thomas F. Torrance explored
this point in some detail in his essay 'Divine and Contingent
Order', in which he stresses that this correspondence can be

expressed in terms of the notion of 'contingent order', which is the 'direct product of the Christian understanding of the constitutive relation between God and the universe, which he freely created out of nothing, yet not without reason, conferring upon what he has made and continues to sustain a created rationality of its own dependent on his uncreated transcendent reality'.[18] This idea underlies the concept of the 'analogy of being', which came to be a subject of intense debate in twentieth-century theology, not least due to the influence of Karl Barth.

Thomas Aquinas is of critical importance in the development of the medieval notion of analogy, largely on account of his explorations of the ontological foundations of the concept. For Aquinas, there exists a fundamental 'likeness (*similitudo*) to God' within the created order as a consequence of God being the cause, in some sense of the word, of all created things. In that no created thing can be said to come into existence spontaneously, the existence of all things can be considered to be a consequence of a relationship of causal dependence between the creation and its creator. For Aquinas, the capacity of analogies to model God therefore rests upon a *created correspondence* between the creation and creator, arising directly from the doctrine of creation.

This idea was developed and intensified by Erich Przywara (1889–1972), perhaps best known in the English-language world through Karl Barth's extended critique of his views. Przywara's concept of the 'analogy of being' is based upon a Christian doctrine of creation which affirmed the absolute distinction between creator and creation. This leads him to conclude that there is a created capacity on the part of an analogy to model God. Barth regarded this as an assertion of the revelational autonomy of the creation over its creator, which is not entirely fair to Przywara. To follow this through, we may move on immediately to consider Barth's concerns in a little more detail.

2. The 'analogy of faith' (analogia fidei)

We have explored how a Christian doctrine of creation allows us to propose a 'created correspondence' between the world and God. Yet the *potential* of an image to represent the vision of God must be complemented by its *authorization* to function in such a capacity. In the natural sciences, the concept of 'authorization' of an analogy or model to represent a given complex reality is cast in terms of its explanatory and predictive successes, and assessed empirically, often in terms of the 'degree of fit' between the model and what is being modelled.

There are two major issues at the centre of this debate, each of which relates directly to the theological use of analogy.

1. Does the ultimate theological justification for the use of a given analogy as a model of God, or of the divine activity, reside in the *intrinsic capacity* of the analogy to represent God, or *divine authorization* of the analogy to function in this manner?

2. Does not the affirmation of the intrinsic capacity of some aspect of the creation to model God represent a compromise of the divine freedom in revelation, in that revelation can occur without the divine will that it *should* occur?

Both these issues emerge in Karl Barth's critique of Erich Przywara's doctrine of the 'analogy of being', and in his proposed counter-understanding of the theological basis of analogy in the doctrine of the 'analogy of faith', to which we now turn.

While Thomas Aquinas and Erich Przywara ground the analogical basis of theological language and divine revelation in the doctrine of creation, Barth insists that the proper grounding of any such analogy must lie in the event of revelation itself. For Barth, any analogy between human language and the reality of God is grounded in the divine decision that this shall be the case.

The analogy in question is called into being by the free revelational act of God; it is not something that is uncovered by human reflection on the created order. Analogies rest upon a covenant, not upon nature.

Barth is clearly worried that the distinctive language of the Christian faith might lose its foundation in God's revelation, and instead become rooted in natural events or objects. Such a danger exists, and it is entirely proper to forestall any such development through the formulation of appropriate theological strategies, particularly when these involve gaining an enhanced appreciation of some fundamental themes of the doctrine of revelation. Yet it is reasonable to ask whether this is actually the case.

A scientific theology intentionally *sees* nature *as* creation, including the critical insight (which distinguishes Christianity from Judaism and Islam at this point) that the agency of creation is Christ. A responsible approach to the 'analogy of being' – which I believe can be found in the writings of Thomas Aquinas and Jonathan Edwards – cannot be conceived as an assertion of the ability of unaided human reason to find and fully know God, but is rather to be seen as reflecting a desire to follow through the implications of the revealed notion of the divine creation of the world in and through Christ. The capacity of the created order to model God is thus a revealed, not a natural, insight. I argue that the same Scripture which affirms that only certain analogies are authorized to model God and things of God also affirms that, through the act of creation, the created order possesses a created capacity to witness to its creator. No tension need exist between the two analogies, which are both presupposed by a responsible Christian doctrine of revelation. Rightly understood, they are as two sides of the same revelatory coin. Both have a constructive and important role to play in a scientific theology.

3. The limits of analogies

Having considered some aspects of analogies in theological analysis, I now turn to consider the limits of analogies, focusing particularly on the use of such models in the natural sciences and more especially on the 'kinetic theory of gases', which aims to explain the behaviour of gases based on a 'billiard-ball' model. Scientific analogies are often developed on the basis of a perceived congruence between a reality and its proposed analogue. Thus light was widely held to be related to sound, so that modes of sonic propagation were assumed to be cognate to those of light. In a similar way, Darwin perceived points of similarity between the outcomes of the methods of cattle breeders and the patterns he discerned within the natural world, and thus assumed that an analogy existed between 'artificial' and 'natural' modes of selection.

Yet analogies possess a remarkable ability to mislead. For many years, it was assumed that light was analogous to sound, in requiring a medium for its propagation. It was only in the early twentieth century that this assumption was challenged, and eventually realized to be incorrect. Similar difficulties arise in theology, as can be seen in the patristic discussion of the redemption of the world through Christ, especially the idea that Christ's death can be said to represent a 'ransom' for humanity. Four elements to the analogy were identified: human bondage to Satan; a price paid to achieve liberation; the achievement of liberation; and Satan as the one to whom the ransom was paid. The first three such elements were common elements of the patristic doctrine of redemption; the fourth was widely regarded as unorthodox. Unorthodox it may have been; it was, nevertheless, hugely attractive. Rufinus of Aquileia was one of many writers who held that Christ's death was a ransom paid to Satan – an idea which went on to play a decisive role in Middle English literature, often developed in terms of the imagery of Christ jousting with Satan, or outwitting Satan to gain control of humanity.

This is widely regarded as theologically illegitimate, pressing an analogy beyond its clearly intended limits. There are two principles that must always be borne in mind when using analogies, in either science or Christian theology.

1. It cannot be assumed that analogies are *identical* with the systems with which they are associated. Gas molecules are not minute inelastic spheres; the point is that they behave, in some respects only, *as if* they are. An analogy offers a visualizible representation of a system, which assists explanation and interpretation, and stimulates exploration. Yet analogy is not the same as identity.

2. The degree of ontological transference from analogy to the reality being depicted must be established *a posteriori*. It cannot be assumed *a priori* that every aspect, or any given individual aspect, of the analogy is necessarily to be transferred to its subject.

The correct use of analogies in Christian theology proceeds by bearing these two general principles in mind, and supplementing them with two additional considerations.

1. Any given theological analogy or image is to be interpreted with a matrix of doctrinal affirmations, which establish the context within which an analogy is to be interpreted, and provide an important check against the improper overinterpretation of any single given analogy. It does not stand on its own.

2. The Christian representation of reality does not take the form of a single, isolated analogy, but a network of interlocking images, whose interpretation is determined to a substantial extent by their mutual relationship.

In view of the importance of this second point to a scientific theology, I now move on to explore it in greater detail.

4. *The interlocking of analogies*

The more complex the reality, the more analogies or models are required to describe it. A single analogy is often quite inadequate. This is especially evident from the early phase of the Copenhagen school of quantum mechanics, which postulated the 'principle of complementarity' as a means of modelling quantum phenomena. The Danish physicist Niels Bohr (1885–1962) argued, on the basis of the experimental evidence at his disposal, that two quite distinct models are required to account for the behaviour of quantum entities – a wave model and a particle model. The fact that these two models are mutually inconsistent was not seen as a fundamental obstacle to this process of representation. The phenomena appeared to require to be visualized in this manner, thus forcing Bohr and his colleagues to proceed in this way. The episode is an excellent case study of adapting means of investigation and representation to the aspect of reality under consideration.

But what of its theological implications? Once more, the general point is that a complex entity requires many levels of representation, and a correspondingly large number of models or analogies. Arthur Peacocke makes a similar point in relation to both science and theology.[19]

> The scientific and theological enterprises share alike the tools of groping humanity – our stock of words, ideas and images that have been handed down, tools that we refashion in our own way for our own times in the light of experiment and experience to relate to the natural world and that are available, with God's guidance, to steer our own paths from birth to death.

Peacocke, it may be noted, holds that we are at liberty to modify the traditional Christian imagery, including that inherited from

Scripture; I do not agree with him at this point, believing that the critical issue is how these traditional images are to be understood and deployed.

This chapter has considered some issues that arise in any attempt at the representation of reality, noting the difficulties and challenges that face any intellectual discipline as it attempts to depict or describe what it encounters in the world, and offer frameworks allowing an enhanced appreciation of the relationships and interconnections that are observed. While doubtless made more complex through the recognition of the stratification of reality, the representation of the world may be concluded to be a theoretically valid and constructive enterprise. Theology may face some particular challenges of its own, but there can be no doubt that most of those challenges are the common property of any attempt to represent and describe the world, especially the natural sciences.

Yet the enquiring human mind has never been content merely to *describe* things; it longs to *explain* them. In the following chapter, I therefore move on to consider the explanatory aspects of a scientific theology.

14. The Place of Explanation in a Scientific Theology

To speak of 'explanation' is to affirm that the world possesses a rationality and coherence which may be grasped and understood, thus affirming the intelligibility of reality by its beholders. We have already seen how some such assumption underlies the entire scientific enterprise, and how it is given a rigorous theological foundation through a doctrine of creation. Again, some preliminary thought has also been given to the importance of affirming the explanatory aspects of a scientific theology in the face of criticisms directed against such a possibility by writers such as D. Z. Phillips and others.

There are three areas in which a scientific theology is capable of offering an explanation, where such an explanation is clearly demanded. Reverting once more to Alasdair MacIntyre's important emphasis upon traditions as a means of constituting and transmitting ideas and values, I argue that

1. A tradition must be able to offer an account of its own specific form and contents, and explicate their interconnection. While Schleiermacher, Barth and the Yale School understand this task and its implications in somewhat different manners, it could be argued that this aspect of the theological enterprise is common to most approaches.

2. A tradition must be able to offer an account of why alternative traditions exist. Following the collapse of the artificial modernist notion of a 'universal rationality', any given tradition is under an obligation to explain both its own existence and that of its rivals. The particularity of a tradition does not call into question its universal applicability; it does, however, demand that it demonstrate this wider validity.

3. A tradition must be capable of seeing the world through theoretical spectacles in such a manner that it is able to offer explanations which may reasonably be regarded as appropriate and convincing to those within that tradition.

Explanation thus possesses both intrasystemic and extrasystemic dimensions – issues which we shall explore throughout this chapter. I turn first to consider how the Christian tradition is able to give an account of its own shape, form and contents. This brings us to the concept of revelation, widely agreed to be of critical importance to Christian theology. How is this concept understood by a scientific theology?

The concept of 'revelation' in a scientific theology

Traditionally, the term 'revelation' designates the critically important notion that the central ideas of the Christian faith owe their
origins directly or indirectly to God, rather than to unaided
human reason. Human opinions about God can only be a true
knowledge of God if they somehow correspond to the divine
reality. This can be secured by insisting that such knowledge of
God has, in the first place, its *origins* in God, and in the second
place, is *authorized* by God. The Pauline contrast of the 'wisdom
of God' with human wisdom (1 Corinthians 2:1–4) is one of the
most important examples of the pervasive biblical insistence upon
the priority of God in the acquisition of true knowledge of divine
things.

So how is this revelation encountered? Barth's vigorous defence
of the autonomy of divine revelation is stated in uncompromis-
ing terms in his *Romans* commentary and other early works. For
Barth, the reality of God cannot be statically and objectively
described. Revelation itself must be conceived as 'a revealing and
not a state of being revealed'.[20] The revealing God remains
unknown and unknowable; all that may be seen of the reality of
this unknown God in the history of the world are the effects of
revelation, rather than a static revelation itself. Revelation is like
a bird in flight; it is the free act of a God who cannot be pinned
down nor controlled by human interpreters.

Revelation is first and foremost a divine *act*. But it is a divine
act which impacts upon humanity. Barth, presumably with the
shell-pocked battlefields of the recent Great War in mind, refers
to the impact of revelation as 'shellholes and craters'. The revelational imprint on history is like the explosion of an artillery shell,
leaving a crater which may be investigated long after the immense
power of the detonation has passed. Yet it is the detonation, rather

than the resulting crater, which is to be considered as 'revelation' in the proper sense of the word. It refers to a divine action, not a permanent state – but an action which leaves an imprint on history, at various levels.

The basic idea I want to develop maintains Barth's emphasis upon God's freedom in revelation, and especially that revelation is an *act* of God rather than a permanent state of 'revealedness'. A revelational act gives rise to revelational interpretations of these acts, which we find recorded in Scripture – an idea which the New Testament itself sets out when speaking of the meaning and significance of the death and resurrection of Jesus Christ, to note but one example. An act gives rise to a deposit – the 'deposit of faith'. These are insights which any orthodox Christian would regard as acceptable. The act of revelation has made an impact – or left an imprint – on history. It is embedded at various levels of historical reality. One of the tasks of a scientific theology is to clarify precisely what those strata are, and how they relate to the revelational events that brought Christianity into being.

While cosmologists are concerned to trace the universe back to its first few seconds, and evolutionary biologists to trace the complex ancestry of humanity, a scientific theology sets itself the agenda of determining what called the Christian tradition into being, and how this can and should continue to sculpture its intellectual contours. The only adequate explanation, as will become clear, is that of a series of original revelational events, which give rise to a 'deposit of faith' *which is itself revelational*. The essential point here is that we do not *presently* have access to the totality of whatever 'revelation' might be. We know it primarily by its effects, by the impact it has had upon history – such as Scripture, various ecclesiastical institutions, and the liturgy – which point to something decisive having happened, and mediate its perceived significance to us. Yet we are not in a position to predetermine what can or cannot have happened in history; we are confronted with a complex multi-levelled amalgam of historical, literary, institutional and experiential clues, embedded at various strata of reality, to what once happened, which is traditionally designated as 'revelation'.

I therefore turn to consider the multi-levelled imprint of revelation upon reality. These different levels of reality are all affirmed to be integral aspects of the same fundamental notion, whose interconnectedness may be explored and confirmed by historical and theological analysis. I identify eight such levels, although others could easily be added. The critical point is that the original revelational events are embedded in a stratified way in historical reality. The eight levels I note are the following.

1. *Texts*, which are understood both to mediate the events which constitute revelation, and to set the context for the events of revelation, providing a means by which certain events are to be interpreted. The canonical scriptures of the Christian tradition both bear witness to the foundational events of the Christian faith and offer narrated interpretations of their significance. Narrative and proclamation are thus interspersed and interconnected within this textual medium. As an evangelical, I place supreme theological weight upon Scripture, while recognizing that revelation has also impacted elsewhere. Other Christian traditions might place an emphasis elsewhere (for example, a Catholic might wish to emphasize the fifth level I note).

2. *Patterns of worship*, already evident in the New Testament, which are to be regarded both as social realities (in that they involve a quite definite set of actions) and ideas (in that the words associated with these actions have certain quite specific meanings). The importance of doxology to theology

has often been noted; what has not been sufficiently appreciated is that Christian patterns of worship are to be thought of as constituting a distinct stratum of reality, capable of illuminating the original revelational events of faith.

3. *Ideas*, which occasionally build on existing notions, and at other times go beyond or negate existing ideas. Such ideas are clearly evident within the textual level, and play an increasingly important role through the growing emphasis placed upon formal 'creeds' as both a means of defining membership of Christian communities and a way of articulating and communicating their ideas.

4. *Communities*, brought together through a shared faith in the revelational events, which found their sense of identity and purpose to be consolidated through the public and private reading of such texts, and the liturgical commemoration of both the foundational events of faith and their perceived significance. Of particular importance is the manner in which Christian communities came to be differentiated from Jewish communities, which involves perceptions on both sides of this growing divide concerning the distinctive identities of the two communities.

5. *Institutional structures*, such as the episcopacy, as means of securing the faithful transmission and embodiment of the ideas and values of the Christian communities. While critical of aspects of existing ecclesiastical institutions, the Protestant reformers of the sixteenth century were fully aware of the importance of institutions in this process of transmission, and established variants on existing structures which they believed were more consonant with Scripture.

6. *Images*, above all the cross as the distinctive icon of the Christian faith – a complex process of development of

transformation involving the re-reception of traditional images and the forging of new images.

7. The distinctive *vocabulary* of the Christian tradition, which may take the form of new words minted to meet theological needs – such as the Greek term *homoousios* as a technical term representing the relationship of Christ to God the Father – or the investment of existing terms with new meanings.

8. *Religious experience*, which may be taken to include – without being restricted to – the specifically religious experience identified by Schleiermacher as the 'feeling of absolute dependence'.

Each of these eight interconnected strata – to which others could easily be added – may be regarded as something encountered within the ambit of contemporary experience, whose existence requires explanation, with each level requiring investigation and exploration using techniques appropriate to its stratification. Institutional aspects of the 'deposit of faith' may be investigated, within limits, by sociological methods, without being restricted by the assumption that only a social explanation of its origins may be offered. Doctrines may be explored at a more intellectual level, without assuming that the 'deposit of faith' is simply a set of ideas. It is clearly much more than this, extending to include institutions and practices.

So how is this complex multi-layered reality to be explained? Given what we observe, how can we account for it? If the various levels of an illness are all to be accounted for by a pathological development, according to the ICIDH model of illness (see p. 149), what revelational development accounts for the various levels of revelation within the Christian tradition? The issue here is 'abduction', in the sense developed by the American philosopher Charles Sanders Peirce (1839–1914), by which he meant the way in which it is appropriate to argue from observations to their presumed explanation. We therefore need to reason backwards from what is accessible and may be observed in the present to what may be argued to lie behind it – in other words, to set in place a process of *abduction to the past*. In what follows, we shall explore how this process of abduction is developed in both the natural sciences and Christian theology.

The natural sciences are frequently forced to find an explanation for a number of present-day observations. In some cases, observations relating to the past must also be brought into consideration – for example, fossil or other geological records. The question asked is this: given these present observations, what is their best explanation? What happened to bring this state of affairs about?

An excellent case study is provided by the physical sciences in trying to answer the following question: why did dinosaurs die out? What factors, in other words, caused their extinction? In the late 1970s Luis and Walter Alvarez, along with a team of scientists from the University of California, were making a study of the rocks marking the Cretaceous–Tertiary (K–T) boundary in Gubbio, Italy. They found a layer of clay at this boundary point which contained an unusually high concentration of the rare element iridium. The levels of iridium contained in the clay were roughly thirty times the normal levels. Now iridium is also known to be found in relatively high concentrations in asteroids and chondritic meteors. To explain their otherwise puzzling observations, Alvarez and his team proposed that an asteroid hit the earth at the end of the Cretaceous period, 65 million years ago, throwing up a dust layer that encircled the earth and led to the extinction of the dinosaurs.

Two particularly strong contenders for the site of such a collision have been identified, both under the ocean; indeed, it is possible that both relate to the same cataclysmic event, representing separate impact craters from an asteroid collision with the earth. One is the 180-kilometre-wide impact crater Chicxulub, located at the tip of the Yucatán Peninsula in the Gulf of Mexico, which dates back to 65 million years ago. The second is the Shiva crater – thus named by the palaeontologist Sankar Chatterjee – located under the Arabian Sea off the coast of India near Bombay. This crater also dates from the K–T boundary, 65 million years ago.

A process of abduction to the past is also evident in the biological sciences, especially the theory of evolution. For example, consider the four observations which weighed heavily on Charles Darwin's mind, as he sought to identify the best explanation of their origins.

1. *Adaptation.* An explanation was required of the manner in which organisms' forms are adapted to their needs. A ready explanation of one type was available from the doctrine of special creation, which posited that the creator caused each organism's form to be related to its environmental needs.
2. *Extinction.* Darwin's discovery of Thomas Malthus's theories on population growth had a significant impact on his thinking on this issue. It was not initially clear how the extinction of seemingly well-adapted and successful species could be explained without recourse to 'catastrophe' theories.
3. *Distribution.* The uneven geographical distribution of life forms throughout the world was the source of some puzzlement. Darwin's personal research trips on the *Beagle* convinced him of the importance of developing a theory which could explain the peculiarities of island populations, such as those found on the Galapagos.
4. *Vestigial structures.* The apparent biological redundancy of

certain animal structures – such as the nipples of male mammals – was difficult to accommodate on the basis of the concept of special creation, in that they appeared to serve no apparent purpose. Darwin hoped to offer a superior explanation of non-functional or rudimentary anatomical features.

All these observations were accessible and verifiable to the present-day observer. Darwin's task was to develop an explanation which would account for them more satisfactorily than the alternatives which were then available. It is clear that the driving force behind Darwin's reflections was the belief that the phenomena could be more convincingly accounted for by a single theory of natural selection than anything else. Darwin himself was quite clear that his explanation of the biological evidence was not the only one which could be adduced. He did, however, believe that it possessed greater explanatory power than its rivals, such as the doctrine of special creation. 'Light', he wrote, 'has been shown on several facts, which on the theory of special creation are utterly obscure.'

A similar process can also be employed by Christian theology. There is already a well-established pattern within the Christian theological tradition of arguing from a present effect to a revelational cause. This can be illustrated from F. D. E. Schleiermacher's analysis of present religious experience to its putative historical cause. For Schleiermacher, the present experience of the individual Christian believer requires explanation. Why does she or he have such an experience? How is it to be accounted for? How do individuals come to develop this feeling of absolute dependence upon God?

Schleiermacher holds that the origins of this feeling are to be located in the impact of Jesus of Nazareth upon the collective consciousness of the Christian community. Schleiermacher then argues that a specific Christology can be *inferred* from the present impact of Jesus of Nazareth upon believers within the Church. It is possible to argue back from the observed effect in the present experience of believers to its sufficient cause in the person of Jesus of Nazareth. Schleiermacher thus begins this abductive analysis with a single specific stratum of reality, as currently experienced within the life of the Church, and proceeds to trace it back to its cause. Schleiermacher's strategy has weaknesses and limitations, primarily on account of Schleiermacher's single-level approach to Christian experience, which fails to take into account the multi-levelled character of the Christian faith. Given the multi-levelled nature of the present-day Christian experience, a correspondingly stratified notion of revelation is required to account for it.

The process of abduction exemplified, although in a limited and not entirely satisfactory form, by Schleiermacher may be applied to the eight strata identified earlier as corporately constituting the dogmatic concept of revelation. In every case, the argument may be made that the fundamental impetus to the development of this stratum is the words and deeds of God in history, culminating in the death and resurrection of Jesus Christ. It is this which has impacted upon history, and resulted in what is now accessible to our investigation.

The discussion of the way in which revelation has impacted on history naturally leads to an examination of the theme of 'revelation in history'. Wolfhart Pannenberg and Alan Richardson offer significantly different approaches to the question. For Pannenberg (born 1928), history is a publicly accessible resource, whose revelatory dimensions can be grasped and understood by everyone. The 'revelation of God is open to anyone who has eyes to see, and does not need any supplementary inspired interpretation'.[21] As James Barr pointed out, Pannenberg's entire approach seemed to rest on the notion of 'plain history' being 'revelatory'.[22] This is a characteristically modernist approach, which I criticized earlier for failing to appreciate the difficulties created by the collapse of the Enlightenment project.

Alan Richardson (1905–75), formerly Professor of Christian Theology in the University of Nottingham, sets out a very different and altogether more satisfying approach. Richardson avoids locking himself into such a modernist trap, partly through his careful engagement with the philosophy of history, especially some of the themes developed in Edward Hallett Carr's George Macaulay Trevelyan Lectures delivered in the University of Cambridge, over the period January–March 1961, which mounted a sustained attack on the objectivist idea of historical 'facts'. In 1962, Richardson set out an approach to revelation which grounded it in universal history, while simultaneously affirming its particularity within the Christian tradition.[23]

Richardson explicitly recognizes that, while history requires interpretation, that same history itself does not provide an interpretative framework through which the process of interpretation may take place. The revelatory events do indeed take place in 'real' history; their significance, however, is only rightly perceived from the standpoint of faith – that is to say, they are only revelatory if they are recognized as divine revelation, in that they do not interpret themselves as such. It is therefore entirely correct for Richardson to conclude that 'Christian dogmatics is, in essence, the Christian interpretation of history.'[24]

Richardson proposes an understanding of revelation in history which continues to be fruitful for Christian theology, as it reflects on its identity and tasks. The past cannot be replicated in the present, nor can it be encountered and known *directly*. This process of transmission can be summed up under three broad categories:

1. A summary account of the historical events which are held to constitute revelation.

2. A summary of the perceived significance of those events for faith.
3. A community which is brought into being by those revelational events and their perceived significance, which regards its identity as being constituted and safeguarded by them, and which proclaims them in word and action. In effect (3) is generated by (1) and (2); and (3) subsequently 'hands down' or 'hands over' (1) and (2) within the historical process.

We may proceed immediately to a consideration of how such revelation, here understood in its developed sense of the 'deposit of faith' (*depositum fidei*), is transmitted through the historico-social reality of the Christian tradition. I therefore now turn to consider the concept of tradition, noting especially its stratification.

The transmission of revelation

The New Testament plays a decisive role in Christian theology. In addition to setting out the narrative concerning Jesus, it provides reflection on his identity and significance, in order that these may be passed on to subsequent generations. 'Tradition' is a thoroughly biblical notion. Paul reminded his readers that he was handing on to them core teachings of the Christian faith which he had received from others (1 Corinthians 15:1–4). The term can refer both to the action of passing teachings on to others – something which Paul insists must be done within the Church – and to the body of teachings which are passed on in this manner. Tradition can thus be understood as a process as well as a body of teaching. The Pastoral Epistles in particular stress the importance of 'guarding the good deposit which was entrusted to you' (1 Timothy 6:20; 2 Timothy 1:14).

The notion of tradition extends to both the process by which

the Christian proclamation is transmitted, and to the actual
content of what is transmitted. The Latin term *traditio* thus designates a process of 'handing over' and 'handing on', which can
be thought of as the faithful and responsible transference from
one generation to another of the central realities of the Christian
faith. It will immediately be clear that tradition – considered both
as process of transmission and as transmitted reality – is a socially
embedded concept. This becomes clearer by considering the two
aspects of tradition individually.

1. Considered as *process of transmission*, the notion of tradition
    embraces far more than the mere oral transfer of ideas from
    one individual to another. The process of inter-generational
    transmission of the faith has been institutionalized. This
    process is already evident in the Pastoral Epistles, where the
    importance of offices and institutions in preserving the integ-
    rity of the 'deposit of faith' is heavily emphasized. This would
    become increasingly important during the patristic period,
    when bishops and ecumenical councils played a decisive role
    in determining and subsequently preserving orthodoxy. It is
    impossible to overlook the sociological substructure which
    increasingly upholds and transmits the realities of faith.
2. Considered as *transmitted reality*, tradition includes institu-
    tions, practices, systems of symbols, values and beliefs. It is
    unacceptable to limit the notion of tradition merely to
    ideas; what is passed on from one generation to another are
    ways of thinking, existing, seeing, living, belonging and
    behaving. It is a deeply socially embedded concept, which
    embraces matters of doctrine while at the same time
    transcending them.

Rudolf Bultmann's much-criticized notion of the *kerygma* could
be reconceptualized to serve the purposes of a scientific theology.

For Bultmann, continuity with the identity-giving past can be maintained through its impact upon the present – namely, through the *kerygma*, which can be seen as a 'distillation' of the significance of Jesus for the community of faith, passed down through proclamation to subsequent generations. Bultmann fails to appreciate that the *kerygma* is more than mere ideas. It takes the form of social realities, embedded at differing levels, and thus making it amenable to a critical realist analysis, as defended throughout this project.

A scientific theology and the explanation of reality

We now come to the major focus of this chapter: the way in which a scientific theology can be said to *explain* reality. In an earlier engagement with Alasdair MacIntyre's concept of 'tradition-mediated rationality', I made the point that a tradition-mediated rationality may thus be *universal* in the scope of its application, while being *particular* in the extent to which it is accepted. If its universal scope is to be taken seriously, MacIntyre points out that it must be able to demonstrate this in two respects:

First, such a tradition must be able to account for its own existence.

Second, this tradition must also be able to account for the existence of rival traditions.

We have already seen how a scientific theology is able to offer an account of the existence, shape and form of the Christian community, drawing on a critical realist account of the stratified impact of the original revelational events. It is perhaps easiest for a tradition to account for its own existence, and undue weight must therefore not be placed on this point. However, a scientific theology, especially through its deployment of natural theology as an explanatory tool, is able to deal with MacIntyre's second point.

First, I point out that a scientific theology is able to offer an *explanation of other traditions.* The kind of natural theology set out by a scientific theology offers a way of making sense of the common human quest for truth, beauty and goodness. A Christian natural theology is tradition-specific, yet possesses a universal applicability, thus offering an explanation of other traditions, while at the same time reinforcing the plausibility of its own tradition.

Second, a scientific theology is able to offer a coherent *explanation of the world.* As I argued earlier, a Christian doctrine of creation offers an explanatory window into both the ordering of the natural world and the capacity of the human mind to discern and represent this ordering. These points may be supplemented by the arguments of works such as Richard Swinburne's classic *The Existence of God,* one of the most important twentieth-century affirmations of the explanatory capacity of theism. An important aspect of his argument concerns the potential of the Christian understanding of God to make sense of the ordering of the world.[25] Rather than suggesting that God offers an explanation of what the natural sciences are currently unable to explain, more recent theistic writers have stressed the importance of belief in God in explaining the 'big picture' – that is to say, the overall patterns of ordering which are discerned within the universe. Swinburne thus insists that the explanatory aspects of theism are not limited to the fine details of reality, but extend far beyond these to embrace the great questions of life – those things that are either 'too big' or 'too odd' for science to explain.

However, this raises the question of how a scientific theology copes with aspects of nature which it does not seem capable of explaining, or which appear to be inconsistent with a Christian worldview. A scientific theology here adopts a similar approach to dealing with the place of anomalies within scientific theories, which allows it to cope with such explanatory challenges. The writer whose ideas have been of seminal importance in this respect is the French philosopher and physicist Pierre Duhem (1861–1916).

Duhem's analysis is concentrated on the question of how a theory can be shown to be false. If observational data and a given theory are seen to be in conflict, can one draw the conclusion that any particular theoretical statement is responsible for this tension, and must therefore be rejected? Duhem points out that this is far from being a simple question. The root of the problem may lie in an auxiliary assumption used in the theoretical analysis, or the manner of observation which leads to the suggestion that such a conflict does in fact exist. Duhem's most fundamental assertion could be stated in terms of 'the thesis of inseparability'. According to Duhem, the physicist simply is not in a position to submit an isolated hypothesis to experimental test. 'An experiment in physics can never condemn an isolated hypothesis but only a whole theoretical group.'[26]

So what does Duhem mean by this? The easiest way to understand his point is to consider a case study. Newton's theory of planetary motion can be thought of as a composition of his three laws of motion and the gravitational principle. Suppose that observation is made which seems inconsistent with this theory – for example, a series of observations, made in the early nineteenth century, that the observed orbit of the recently discovered planet Uranus is not consistent with its predicted theoretical values. This therefore calls into question the group of hypotheses consisting of both the central and auxiliary hypotheses of the Newtonian theory. But how was this anomaly to be explained?

Which of these hypotheses is wrong? Or was the entire theory wrong? Did Newton's entire understanding of the solar system have to be abandoned, or was a modification required to only one hypothesis, which allows the theory as a whole to be saved? And if so, which one? Duhem's point is that experimental observation is simply incapable of identifying the level of the problem.

As things turned out, in this specific case, it was an auxiliary assumption which proved to be incorrect – namely, the assumption that the solar system did not extend beyond the planet Uranus. It was suggested that these anomalies could be explained by proposing that there was a planet beyond Uranus, which exercised a gravitational pull on it and thus produced the distortions to its orbit that had been observed. The planet in question (Neptune) was duly discovered independently (but on the basis of the same calculations) by Adams and Leverrier in 1846.

The implications of Duhem's approach are thus considerable. Suppose that something is observed which appears anomalous – for example, a departure of a planetary orbit from predicted values. Is this merely an anomaly, which will be resolved through theoretical or observational advances? If this is so, we will just have to live with this anomaly until it is eventually reconciled with the theory through theoretical advance. Or does it demand that the theory be abandoned? Or just modified – and if so, at which point?

Duhem's analysis raises a significant theological question: does an anomaly necessitate the abandonment or modification of the central teachings of the Christian faith, or merely one of its many subsidiary aspects? And if the latter, what conceivable means exist for the identification of the deficient subsidiary hypothesis? We can consider this further in relation to what many regard as the greatest anomaly of faith – the existence of suffering in the world.

In particular, is the existence of suffering in the world to be regarded as an anomaly, which will one day be resolved, as a difficulty with an ancillary assumption of some theological systems, or as a fatal incoherency within the Christian worldview as a whole? The problem can be set out in terms of two hypotheses, H_1 and H_2, as follows:

H_1 God is omnipotent and omniscient.
H_2 God is completely good.

Now add the following observation statement, O:

O The world contains instances of suffering and evil.

Does the observation statement O require that the group of hypotheses (H_1 and H_2) be abandoned? Or that just one of them should be revised? And if so, which one? Or that there is a problem with a yet unidentified auxiliary hypothesis? Or that this is merely an apparent difficulty, which will be resolved with theoretical advance? Duhem's argument leads inexorably to the troubling conclusion that we simply cannot tell.

Each of the two fundamental hypotheses needs careful examination, as they are not quite as straightforward as they seem. For example, both could be argued, at least to some extent, to rest on Cartesian rather than Christian foundations. The Cartesian emphasis upon the perfection of God is subverted by the existence of evil, which may clearly be viewed as a defect. The issue of suffering thus constitutes the grounds for disconfirmation of the Cartesian God, whereas in the Middle Ages – which was generally innocent of such assumptions – the same problem was seen as a riddle or puzzle, but most emphatically not the grounds for abandoning faith. As Alasdair MacIntyre remarked, 'the God in whom the nineteenth and twentieth centuries came to disbelieve had been invented only in the seventeenth century'.[27]

It might also be pointed out that O does not really cause difficulties for Christianity unless a third hypothesis is brought into the equation, as follows:

H_3 A good omnipotent God would eliminate suffering and evil.

This ancillary assumption is also vulnerable, as many theologians would argue that God is under no such obligation. Perhaps this is the ancillary hypothesis that Duhem's critique suggests should be eliminated?

On the basis of the application of Duhem's theory of anomalies to the question of suffering, I conclude that Christian theology takes a similar stand to Duhem, holding that its explanatory potency allows the many puzzles and anomalies of life – such as suffering – to be seen as noetic rather than ontic, resulting from limitations on our perception of the situation, rather than from the situation itself. Those puzzles or anomalies, it is argued, will ultimately only be resolved at the end of time, when all is finally revealed.

I conclude this discussion of Duhem's relevance to Christian theology by considering his concept of 'good sense' (*le bon sens*). In setting out this idea, Duhem was drawing on the idea that a scientific community develops an intuitive sense of its subject, allowing it to reach conclusions when the experimental evidence is actually insufficient to allow, for example, two rival theories to be distinguished. Duhem's concept expresses the idea that such theoretical choices are not irrational or arbitrary, but represent the best judgement of the scientific community in the light of its past experience and accumulated experience of engaging with nature. In a similar way, the theological community develops a related way of coping with such theoretical anomalies as the existence of suffering in the world.

Finally, I turn to consider some aspects of theological explanation which have been intensely debated – the validity of the concepts of 'heresy' and 'orthodoxy', and the development of doctrine.

Heresy, orthodoxy, and the development of doctrine

Both the natural sciences and Christian theology develop theories in response to observation; in both cases, these theories develop over time. There is no doubt that scientific theories have undergone development, including the displacement of those which were once widely accepted and regarded as the best available explanation of the known evidence. In the case of Christian theology, 'the development of doctrine' deals with the history and theory of the emergence of more complex forms of doctrinal statements. There are clearly important parallels between science and theology in relation to the formulation and development of theory. In this concluding section of the present chapter, I set out two new models for understanding some aspects of theoretical development within Christian theology, and briefly explore their potential. The first relates to the phenomenon of the development of doctrine, the second to the concepts of 'heresy' and 'orthodoxy'.

1. The development of doctrine

Many approaches to the development of Christian doctrine have argued that the process can be compared to the growth of a seed. John Henry Newman (1801–90) developed what is perhaps the best-known approach of this kind, which in effect argues that the Church can be seen as a 'gardener', nurturing the development of a Spirit-led process of growth and development. Yet the development of doctrine is far from linear, as this organic model might suggest. At times, there is regression to older approaches; at times, what seems to be stagnation; at others, radical and innovative development. I point out that the process of scientific theory development can be regarded as analogous to doctrinal development, and that these same features are common to each process. The patterns that Thomas Kuhn observed in the development of

scientific theories clarify how a scientific realism does not necessarily lead to a linear development of theories. The authenticity of
theoretical advance is not determined by the linearity of the
process, but by the empirical adequacy and intra-theoretical excellence of the outcome of that process.

My alternative model is based on an image found in the writings of Otto von Neurath. Neurath's argument is that philosophical reflection does not take place from nothing and out of
nowhere; it is about engaging with existing ideas. He uses the
image of a ship at sea to illuminate our situation:[28]

> We are like sailors who on the open sea must reconstruct their ship
> but are never able to start afresh from the bottom. Where a beam is
> taken away a new one must at once be put there, and for this the rest
> of the ship is used as support. In this way, by using the old beams and
> driftwood, the ship can be shaped entirely anew, but only by gradual
> reconstruction.

Neurath's metaphor, applied to the Church as it seeks to sort out
its beliefs, offers a means of making sense of the empirical development of doctrine, rather than forcing the material into a preconceived dogmatic pattern.

My approach has three leading features:

1. It is descriptive, rather than prescriptive – that is, it is based
   on the actual historical study of Christian theology without
   reference to preconceived notions of what form that development ought to have taken.
2. It acknowledges that the development of scientific theories
   has not been straightforward, but has involved major shifts
   in understanding along the way. Applied to the development of Christian doctrine, this insight avoids the simplistic and very problematic notion of the continuous
   development of doctrine – as found in the model of a seed

sprouting – which is difficult to reconcile with the actual historical evidence.

3. It avoids foundationalist assumptions which have so often found their way into alternative accounts of the process of the genesis, development and reception of doctrine.

Neurath's image of a ship at sea helps us in this matter by allowing us to discern at least three major patterns of doctrinal development. Using Neurath's imagery, these patterns may be described as follows:

1. *The unpacking of resources.* The process of inhabiting the Christian tradition entails becoming acquainted with its basic features, and establishing certain connections. The image of 'unpacking' conveys the notion of identifying what is already present within the Christian tradition, and establishing connections between the various resources that are found to be present. In some ways, this aspect of the metaphor of a boat corresponds to certain aspects of the 'organic' model of doctrinal development, in that it proposes a simple unfolding of what is already present, through the establishment of interrelationships.

2. *The reconstruction of the boat.* The ship exists in the sea; if the sea penetrates the ship, it will sink. The defence of the ship against internal and external threats is of paramount importance to its continuing existence. Holes need to be plugged, broken masts to be repaired. As Neurath points out, this task is to be undertaken at sea, using materials already present within the boat. Retrogression in doctrinal development is thus easily understood as a process of reassembling resources, with a view to improving the overall structure and coherence of the ship. The sixteenth-century Reformation can be seen as a clear example of this process

of reconstruction. The mainline reformers were not attempting to construct a new church, but to renew an existing church. Nor did they see themselves as introducing any new ideas or methods to the Christian theological tradition. The fundamental intention of reformers such as Luther was to reconstruct the Church on the basis of its fundamental theological resources, in response to developments and accretions during the later Middle Ages which he regarded as prejudicial to the future existence and integrity of the Church. Luther's agenda was renovation, not innovation.

3. *The incorporation of driftwood into the structure of the boat.* Neurath points out that his hypothetical sailors were able to reconstruct the boat using material to hand within the boat, or driftwood around them. The history of the Christian tradition demonstrates a marked propensity to avail itself of intellectual and cultural resources it encountered around it, floating in the water of history. These may be incorporated into the fabric of the boat. Once worn out, they may be replaced by new driftwood, scooped up from another historical location. Such driftwood is not part of the original fabric of the boat, and its incorporation must be seen as temporary, not permanent. Medieval theology incorporated the Ptolemaic model of the solar system into its deliberations; today, a Copernican model has displaced it. Both are driftwood. Various ancillary hypotheses and working methods – including those of the natural sciences – may be adopted and incorporated, until such time as their utility has been exhausted, and new material needs to be incorporated.

This new approach demands a book-length treatment, and this is currently under way.

2. Heresy and orthodoxy

Purely theoretical and historical accounts of the relation of orthodoxy and heresy are widely agreed to have failed. The noted Berlin theologian F. D. E. Schleiermacher offered a purely theoretical account of what he called the 'four natural heresies of Christianity' – meaning Docetism, Ebionitism, Pelagianism and Manichaeism. (The precise details of these need not concern us here.) Yet the very theoretical account he offered led to the historical aspects of heresies such as Docetism being suppressed to facilitate accommodation to his dogmatic model. A purely theoretical account of heresy fails to take into account such historical questions as the social dimensions of the heresy, or cultural factors which played an important role in its development and appeal.

Yet purely historical accounts are also intensely problematic. The German Lutheran theologian Philip Melanchthon argued that orthodoxy could be identified with the earliest teachings of the Church. The earliest form of a teaching was the most authentic. Yet this criterion proved impossible to sustain. More recently, Walter Bauer argued that the earliest and most authentic form of belief was likely to be heretical, not orthodox, and set out a rather ambitious – and ultimately unsustainable – thesis concerning the relation of orthodoxy and heresy.[29] Bauer argued that a variety of views which were tolerated in the early Church gradually began to be regarded with suspicion by the later Church. Teachings which were accepted in the earliest decades of the Church's existence were later condemned, particularly from the end of the second century onwards, as an orthodox consensus began to emerge. Bauer's hostility to the idea of doctrinal norms can be seen particularly clearly in his conviction that these were a late development within Christianity. Opinions that had once been tolerated were now discarded as inadequate.

Bauer's theory is now widely regarded as discredited, generally on historical grounds. Instead, there has been a renewed appreciation of the merits of a more traditional view, which holds that second-century Christianity ought to be viewed essentially as an orthodox core surrounded by a penumbra within which the borderline between 'orthodoxy' and 'heresy' was still somewhat blurred, and open to further clarification through controversy and debate.[30] It has also been pointed out that the historical observation that heresy existed prior to orthodoxy in some given location cannot legitimately be used to justify the rather more ambitious theory that heresy is to be seen as existing on historically equal terms with orthodoxy.

So if purely theoretical and purely historical approaches fail to deal adequately with the categories of 'orthodoxy' and 'heresy', how can a scientific theology improve on things? The parallels between the patterns and issues of scientific and theological theory development illuminate this matter considerably, possibly offering a model for revalidating these important concepts. The compelling similarities between the manners in which the scientific community generates and evaluates theories and the Christian community receives doctrines point to two fundamental theoretical issues which make the notion of 'heresy' an inevitability:

1. The *underdetermination of theory by evidence*, which means that any given event is open to a number of interpretations, with the evidence often not being sufficient to secure closure of the issue.

2. The *dynamics of the reception of theory*, which account for the manner in which certain theories may enjoy a temporary degree of popularity or acceptance, before being discarded in favour of another as the process of evaluation and reception continues.

Taken together, these two factors determine that there are likely to be divergent interpretations of the person of Jesus Christ, in that interpretations of his identity and significance are at least to some extent underdetermined by the evidence; and that the process of evaluating these alternatives within the community through a process of 'reception' takes some time.

How then might this approach apply to the development of Christology? There is no doubt that one of the most formidable tasks facing the early Church was the clarification of the complex biblical witness to the identity of Christ. The process of Christological clarification cannot be conceived simply as a linear trajectory from the New Testament to Chalcedon, involving organic metaphors such as a seed growing to maturity. The pattern of development which emerges can, however, be understood satisfactorily if two complex interactive processes are recognized to have been in operation during the first five centuries of Christian reflection on the matter.

1. A process of *interpretation* of a complex biblical witness to the identity and significance of Jesus Christ, which was open to more than one interpretation. The underdetermination of theory by evidence led to the realization that the biblical witness did not decisively discriminate between the various models of the person of Christ. A series of approaches was proposed and evaluated, some involving 'ready-to-hand Jewish models',[31] others involving models borrowed from Hellenistic culture. To use Gilbert Harman's phrase, the Christian community was attempting to 'infer to the best explanation' of Jesus Christ on the basis of a body of evidence which seemed to be capable of multiple interpretations. But which was the best?

2. A process of *reception*, in which the community of faith

explored and assessed the proposed models, testing them against the testimony of Scripture, and the tradition and worship of the Church. This process of testing cannot be regarded as universal throughout the Church, in that it was clearly catalysed by local factors, such as certain key individuals and debates, and crystallized by certain events, not least ecumenical councils. This process can be regarded as being shaped to some extent by a theological or ecclesiological equivalent of Pierre Duhem's concept of 'good sense', and was often framed in terms of a doctrine of divine providence or the guidance of the Holy Spirit.

To the external observer, these two processes – especially when interlocked – appear decidedly non-linear, involving what seems to be backtracking, digression and stagnation. To attempt to 'freeze' this process at any one time, particularly in its earlier stages, would be to disclose a complex pattern of variations, rather than a uniform picture, representing a debate which was proceeding at different paces in different ways at different locations. Yet the overall process is immediately recognizable to anyone concerned with the reception of ideas – namely, a communal attempt to explore, evaluate and appropriate theoretical models on the basis of the available evidence, which is catalysed by both individuals and institutions.

Once more, this model demands a book-length study, which is currently being pursued.

15. The Place of Metaphysics in a Scientific Theology

A final question is whether metaphysics has any place in a scientific theology. Recent discussions of the theological role of metaphysics have been somewhat hesitant to offer firm definitions of the concept, reflecting a widespread lack of agreement on what the term denotes. Perhaps the most helpful understanding of the term is the study of 'ultimate reality', including such questions as why the world exists, and what place humanity has within it. On this broad definition of the term, metaphysics denotes the knowledge of entities or matters which transcend the realm of empirically grounded sciences, including the idea of 'God'.

One of the most significant philosophical movements to arise in the twentieth century had its origins in the Austrian capital city of Vienna. The 'Vienna Circle' is generally regarded as the group of philosophers, physicists, mathematicians, sociologists and economists who gathered around Moritz Schlick during the period 1924–36. The group fell apart after Schlick was shot dead by a student in 1936, and dispersed as a result of the rise of National Socialism in Austria prior to the Second World War. As a result, the ideas of the Vienna Circle were widely propagated, particularly in the United States.

One of its most distinctive emphases was its wholesale, thoroughgoing rejection of metaphysics. For the Vienna Circle, statements which did not directly connect up with or relate to the real world were of no value, and simply served to perpetuate fruitless conflicts of the past. The terms in statements or propositions had to be directly related to what we experience. Every proposition must therefore be capable of being stated in a manner which relates directly to the real world of experience.

The Vienna Circle developed this approach by making use of the forms of symbolic logic which had begun to appear in the late nineteenth century, and had been used very effectively by Bertrand Russell in the early twentieth century. The manner in which terms and sentences relate to each other can be clarified by an appropriate use of logic. As Schlick himself pointed out, the rigorous use of such logical principles could prevent absurd lapses in philosophical rigour. Schlick offered the following as elementary examples of such lapses which would be eliminated by this logical rigour:

> My friend died the day after tomorrow.
> The tower is both 100 and 150 metres high.

The overall programme which was thus proposed can be seen to fall into two parts, as follows.

> All meaningful statements can be reduced to, or are explicitly defined by, statements which contain only observational terms – usually referred to as 'protocol' statements;
> All such reductive statements must be capable of being stated in logical terms.

The most significant attempt to carry this programme through is to be seen in the works of Rudolph Carnap, particularly his 1928 work *The Logical Construction of the World*. In this work, Carnap set out to show how the world could be derived from experience by logical construction. It was, as he put it, an attempt at the 'reduction of "reality" to the "given"' by using the methods of logic on statements derived from experience. The only two sources of knowledge are thus sense perception and the analytical principles of logic. Statements are derived from and justified with reference to the former, and related to each other and their constituent terms by the latter. A. J. Ayer's *Language, Truth and Logic* (1936), widely seen as demolishing any metaphysical dimensions to the natural sciences – or, indeed, just about anything – drew part of its inspiration from this source.

Although theology, in its classical forms, had little difficulty with issues of metaphysics, this is no longer the case. There has been a growing revolt against allowing metaphysics into Christian theology. Gordon Kaufman asserted that 'there is an inescapable rivalry between metaphysics and theology',[32] and argued that the elimination of metaphysics was the only way of resolving this difficulty. More recently John Milbank's programme of 'radical orthodoxy' argues that metaphysics is tainted on account of its autonomous pretensions or anti-theistic presuppositions. The simplest way of ensuring that its claims to autonomy were eliminated from theology was to distance Christian theology from any involvement with this rival discipline.

However, these judgements are open to question. There has been a growing recognition of the many problems with Ayer's approach – not least, its failure to achieve compatibility with the actual working methods of the natural sciences. In its most rigorous form, Ayer's approach entails the *a priori* denial of the *a posteriori* possibility of metaphysics. Far from opening the way to a rigorous scientific assessment of the issues, in which the legitimacy of any form of metaphysical speculation will be judged on the basis of the nature and extent of its grounding in observation and experience, Ayer proposes to declare the entire metaphysical enterprise to be invalid in advance of any such engagement, on the basis of a methodologically confused reading of the traditions and tasks of the natural sciences. This has met with growing resistance, not least as confidence in the programme proposed by the Vienna Circle has sunk to near vanishing point.

The twentieth century witnessed a sustained attack on metaphysics. The origins of this trend are traditionally traced back to David Hume, particularly his caustic comments in his *Enquiry concerning Human Understanding*:[33]

> When we run over libraries, persuaded of these principles, what havoc must we make? If we take in our hand any volume; of divinity or school metaphysics, for instance; let us ask, Does it contain any abstract reasoning concerning quantity or number? No. *Does it contain any experimental reasoning concerning matter of fact and*

existence? No. Commit it then to the flames: for it can contain nothing but sophistry and illusion.

Hume thus proposes two criteria for meaningfulness: logical analysis, and empirical investigation.

In the twentieth century, the Vienna Circle developed related approaches to description which they believed avoided any metaphysical elements or commitments. The most important of these are so-called 'observation statements' or 'protocol statements'. The 'protocol statement' consists only of observable predicates and spatio-temporal coordinates; these are embedded in a three-fold manner which allows the observer and the general conditions of the process of observation to be established. This leads to the rather complex formulation of a protocol statement as follows:[34]

> A complete protocol statement might, for example, read: 'Otto's protocol at 3:17 o'clock [at 3:16 o'clock Otto said to himself: (at 3:15 o'clock there was a table in the room perceived by Otto)].'

This complexly embedded statement is intended to convey information concerning the circumstances of the observation, including the identity of the observer and the conditions of the observation. Any metaphysical dimension – for example, about the essence of a table – is eliminated as redundant.

The reception of 'protocol statements' since the Second World War has seen a growing recognition of their radical limitations, and a deepening awareness of the problems of the forms of empiricism which espoused them. Of particular concern to this critical debate is the issue of unobservable theoretical entities – such as subatomic particles – in the natural sciences. These cannot strictly be 'observed', yet cannot be regarded as 'non-existent' for that reason. This raises significant difficulties for logical positivism, and led some of its leading advocates to modify their position on the matter. Thus in a 1938 paper entitled 'Procedures of

Empirical Science', V. F. Lenzen argued that certain entities had to be *inferred* from experimental observation.[35] For example, the behaviour of oil droplets in an electric field leads one to infer the existence of electrons as negatively charged particles of a certain mass. They cannot be seen (and hence cannot be 'verified') – yet their existence is a reasonable inference from the observational evidence.

The concept of metaphysics has also come in for considerable criticism at the hands of postmodern writers, such as Jacques Derrida. To suggest that there exists an external reality which may be known or represented through a complex series of engagements and negotiations on the part of the human knowing agent is to raise the (at least, for postmodernity) spectre of claims of privilege on the part of the knower. This is seriously in tension with some core values of the movement, not least its concern to identify and neutralize power and privilege.

Those who are less troubled by this issue point out, not entirely unreasonably, that the issue is not *privilege* but *accountability*, in that the knower is under a legitimate obligation to give an account of what she believes and why. More significantly, any suggestion that we may simply dispense with metaphysics is much more problematic than might at first seem to be the case. Metaphysical assumptions are actually *implicit* within the ideologies of those who oppose the notion.

Metaphysical conclusions flow naturally and reasonably from scientific experimentation. In his 1993 Tanner Lectures at Cambridge University, Michael Redhead makes the point that physics cannot help but address metaphysical issues, whether its practitioners regard themselves as qualified to do so or not: 'Physics and metaphysics blend into a seamless whole, each enriching the other.'[36] The trajectory which links reflection on the observable world with metaphysics can be represented as follows:

Empirical observation → theory → metaphysics

Theory here functions as a bridge between experience and metaphysics. It is simply impossible to draw a theoretical line, and declare that nothing 'exists' beyond this point. An entirely legitimate debate is to be had about what those metaphysical conclusions might be.

Some recent Christian theologians have issued a more or less blanket prohibition on metaphysics within theology. John Milbank is a particularly strident voice on this issue. In his essay 'Only Theology Overcomes Metaphysics', Milbank argues that metaphysics is to be rejected on account of its pretensions to theological autonomy, in that it[37]

> claims to be able fully to define the conditions of finite knowability, or to arrive at possible being as something 'in itself'. . . . Modernity is metaphysical, for since it cannot refer the flux of time to the ungraspable infinite, it is forced to seek a graspable *immanent* security . . . By contrast, the Christian thought which flowed from Gregory of Nyssa and Augustine was able fully to concede the utter unknowability of creatures which continually alter and have no ground within themselves, for it derived them from the infinity of God which is unchanging and yet circumscribable, even in itself.

Milbank thus argues for the elimination of metaphysics from a radically orthodox theology, holding that metaphysics is in the first place theologically *unnecessary* (in that the Christian revelation of God is independent of the need of philosophical support), and in the second place *degrading* (in that metaphysics is intellectually contaminated by the presuppositions of a secular world).

This is a puzzling argument, which seems to rest on the assumption that metaphysics is an *a priori* discipline, which lays down in advance what can and cannot be said or thought – for example, about God. But the entire trajectory of a scientific theology points in a quite different direction. Within a scientific theology, metaphysics is understood to arise *a posteriori* – in other words, as a result of an engagement with reality. Far from being the *precondition* of any such investigation, metaphysics is its *outcome*.

A close reading of a representative range of Christian theologians suggests that the *theological* case for the elimination of metaphysics from theology simply has not been made. For example, Martin Luther's critique of metaphysics is actually directed against those who import preconceived metaphysical notions of God from outside the Christian tradition, and demand that theology adjusts its ideas accordingly; it is not strictly a criticism of the development of a metaphysics within Christian theology itself. Luther opposes those who smuggle an *a priori* metaphysical system into theology, not those who derive such a system *a posteriori* on the basis of an engagement with Scripture. Nor has the inner propensity of the Christian tradition to *generate* a metaphysic been fully appreciated, particularly by John Milbank, who commends writers such as Augustine of Hippo and Gregory of Nyssa for defending an 'anti-metaphysical tradition',[38] yet puzzlingly fails to concede that both engaged positively and constructively – some might even say 'uncritically' – with Neoplatonic metaphysics in developing that tradition.

On my reading of the Christian tradition, the inner dynamic of the Christian tradition is such that the emergence of some form of metaphysics within its theology is to be expected. Attempts to embargo metaphysical discussions are doomed to failure. Thus the remarkable re-emergence of metaphysics within both Lutheran and Reformed theology during the period 1590–1620 rested partly on the realization that debates between the two styles of theology could not be conducted without at least some degree of engagement with metaphysical questions.[39] Considerations

such as the above suggest that it is decidedly premature to declare
that theology can do – or has done – without metaphysics.

I follow this through by exploring the theological critiques of
metaphysics associated with liberal Protestant writers such as
Albrecht Benjamin Ritschl and Adolf von Harnack, and more tra-
ditionalist writers such as Martin Luther and Eberhard Jüngel.
The case of Christology is especially illuminating. Both Ritschl
and Harnack prefer functionalist approaches to Christology,
arguing that identifying what Jesus achieves need not lead on to
metaphysical reflection on his identity. For Harnack, such a development would represent a characteristically Hellenistic distortion
of an essentially Jewish gospel.

But is this so? As John Macquarrie points out in his careful
assessment of the Christological issues confronting contemporary
theology, a belief that the metaphysical beliefs and terminology
which undergird the patristic understanding of Christ are outmoded does *not* lead to the conclusion that all metaphysical
understandings of Christ are to be abandoned or declared illegitimate. The question concerns which metaphysics is legitimate for
the contemporary philosophical task. 'Metaphysics or ontology is
indispensable if one is going to give an account of Jesus Christ
that is intellectually well-founded.'[40] Functional statements entail
ontological commitments, which demand to be evaluated critically. It is part of the task of a scientific theology to assess which
set of ontological commitments is most appropriate, in the light
of the evidence available.

In the case of Luther and Jüngel, we find metaphysics denied a
controlling or *foundational* role in theology. Luther has no particular objection to metaphysics as such, as even a cursory reading
of his writings in the period 1515–21 demonstrates. His real
concern is to allow the scriptural narrative of Jesus of Nazareth, as
it is focused upon the crucified Christ, to generate its own frame-

work of conceptualities. Luther's assertion of the autonomy of the scriptural narrative does not involve the rejection of metaphysics; it merely denies to any preconceived metaphysics the right to impose its interpretative framework upon Scripture.

In the case of Jüngel, metaphysics is critiqued on account of its associations with the Cartesian worldview, which Jüngel holds to have had a severely detrimental impact on modern theology. Jüngel develops his insights in a vigorously polemical manner, demonstrating their destructive impact upon the whole Cartesian theological enterprise upon which the Enlightenment was ultimately grounded. His concern is that a specific strand of metaphysics – which he traces back to Descartes – makes certain imperialistic claims which, if conceded, leads to the erosion of an authentically Christian conception of God.[41] Thus Jüngel notes how J. G. Fichte, Ludwig Feuerbach and Friedrich Nietzsche derive their understanding of God (and hence, it may also be pointed out, their antithetically conceived atheisms) from the metaphysical tradition, not from the Christian tradition.[42] Yet Jüngel does not have fundamental misgivings about the development of a theological metaphysic within the parameters of a revelationally focused system; indeed, his own reflections on the doctrine of the Trinity constitute precisely such a metaphysical extension of theology.

The theological evasion of metaphysics is perhaps most evident in Christological debates. There has been no shortage of those – such as Ritschl and Harnack – who argue for the elimination of such metaphysical categories as static and outdated, insisting instead on a purely functional account of Christian beliefs. A functional approach to Christology is seen by some as legitimating a focus on what Jesus Christ can be said to have done or achieved, without entailing any awkward metaphysical questions. From a historical perspective, this distinction can be framed in terms of an essentially Jewish approach to the identity of Christ (which readily attributed certain specific functions to him) and a Greek approach (which sought to define his identity using categories of divinity being borrowed, rather uncritically, from Hellenistic philosophy).

Yet as Richard Bauckham has shown, on the basis of a detailed examination of critical passages, this simple model really will not do.[43]

> The dominance of the distinction between 'functional' and 'ontic' Christology has made it seem unproblematic to say that for early Christology Jesus exercises the 'functions' of Lordship without being regarded as 'ontologically' divine. In fact, such a distinction is highly problematic from the point of view of early Jewish monotheism, for in this understanding of the unique divine identity, the unique sovereignty of God was not a mere 'function' which God could delegate to someone else. It was one of the key identifying characteristics of the unique divine identity, which distinguishes the one God from all other reality.

For Bauckham, the New Testament 'identifies Jesus as intrinsic to who God is'.[44] The New Testament may not make significant use of the language of metaphysics; it nevertheless prepared the ground for those who realized that such categories would be needed to contain the new wine of the gospel proclamation. This naturally leads to the view that the New Testament contains the fundamental themes and pointers, in embryonic form, which would eventually lead to the Nicene theology of the fourth century. This theology thus brings to full and conscious articulation the somewhat more tentative metaphysical hints of the New Testament, developing – not distorting – them in doing so.

For such reasons, based on considerations deriving from both the natural sciences and Christian theology, I believe that metaphysics has a proper and legitimate role to play in a scientific theology. There is an ongoing legitimate place for metaphysics in Christian theology, where the nature and style of that metaphysic is determined *a posteriori*, in the light of the specific nature and characteristics of the gospel proclamation.

A scientific theology thus recognizes and welcomes a responsible metaphysics, grounded in and determined by an engagement with reality, rather than predetermined in advance, and shaped by the 'vision of God', which is the guiding star of a scientific theology. A scientific theology does not endorse a metaphysically inflationary account of reality, but insists that whatever account of reality we offer must represent a proper response to both our encounter with reality and the categories which that reality itself imposes upon us as we seek to represent and explain it. Metaphysics is not the precondition of any engagement with the world, but its inferred consequence.

Conclusion

In this introductory text, I have laid out some of the ideas that I explore in my 'scientific theology' trilogy, and explored some of them in a little detail. Space has prevented any extended discussion of these specific points. However, it is hoped that this introduction to the themes of a scientific theology will encourage readers to dig deeper into the three volumes, and explore their ideas in greater depth.

Where next?

So where do the three volumes of *A Scientific Theology* take us? What future agenda do they set?

I am clear that I shall have to await detailed scrutiny of my proposals at the hands of my peers before moving on to develop them further. However, both those processes are already under way. I can therefore sketch out what I think will be the likely future development of the scientific theology.

As I stressed earlier, a scientific theology is a system, rather than a loose collage of ideas. It offers a coherent vision of reality, and the manners in which this can be known and represented. It offers a 'big-picture' approach to the entire theological enterprise, which transcends the somewhat limited field of science-and-religion studies, and embraces the questions traditionally associated with systematic theology as a whole. This means that it is capable of being applied to detailed, small-scale theological questions, as well as to the great themes of classic dogmatics, from Aquinas through to Barth. I believe that, precisely because it is a coherent system, a scientific theology is capable of operating at both the microtheological and macrotheological levels.

As I have indicated, the next two projects are microtheological, aimed at applying the method to very well-defined concerns, which have proved intractable on the basis of previous approaches. These will aim to explore the intellectual fecundity and theological utility of the project by considering the two specific and highly focused issues in which the method adopted in these volumes has already been identified as having genuine potential – the development of doctrine, and orthodoxy and heresy.

1. A study on the development of doctrine, which will avoid the weaknesses of traditional approaches, both historical and theoretical, by exploring the parallels between the related processes of theoretical development in the natural sciences, and doctrinal development in Christian history. In particular, I shall be using Otto von Neurath's image of a 'ship at sea' as a model of the *ecclesia in via*, as it attempts to consolidate its grasp of its own doctrinal heritage. I have already begun to develop this model, and provided an interim report on its theological potential. However, it remains to be developed more fully, and set against the broadest background of Christian doctrinal reflection,

covering every period of Christian history, and as many aspects of that history as is practicable within the limits of a monograph.

2. A monograph aiming to revalidate the concepts of orthodoxy and heresy, once more avoiding the weaknesses of existing historical and theoretical models. This approach rests on the critically important notion of 'reception theory', which offers an account of the complex factors – both intellectual and cultural – which influence the manner in which theories are evaluated and appropriated. These can be seen in the manner in which both scientific theories, such as Copernicanism and Darwinism, and new Christian doctrinal developments were 'received' after their development. The concept of 'underdetermination' – including the issue of the 'empirical fit' of theory and evidence – will play a key role in this process.

Again, an interim report on the viability of this approach to date was presented in the final volume of the scientific theology trilogy. The model requires further development, and testing against a wide range of material drawn from Christian history. While it is far too early to draw definitive conclusions, the preliminary indications are that the method has real potential in this field, and offers important insights which will assist with the revalidation of the contested categories of 'heresy' and 'orthodoxy'.

Both will be scholarly works, characterized by an extensive and sustained engagement with primary and secondary sources. Yet my preliminary research on the macrotheological application of the approach has been equally encouraging. For this reason, I am happy to indicate that the ultimate goal of the scientific theology project is a set of (probably three) volumes with the overall working title *A Scientific Dogmatics*. As the title indicates, this will be a work of positive theology, based on the actualization of the approaches set out in the trilogy.

Yet this will not be a dogmatics, as traditionally conceived – that is, as an exploration of the interconnectedness of ideas. Faithful to the critical realism which underlies the project, these works will engage with the various strata at which theological ideas are embedded. These volumes will deal with themes traditionally seen as peripheral to the theological enterprise, yet which a critical realism demands be embraced as part of its legitimate task. A purely notional apprehension of Christian dogmatics will be set to one side, to allow a proper apprehension of its themes to be developed. It is impossible to undertake a critical realist dogmatics without addressing such issues as spirituality, apologetics, preaching, pastoral care, worship and prayer. Although evangelical in its foundation and orientation, the work will be of considerable interest to Christians of all traditions.

One of my concerns, for example, will be to develop a 'creation spirituality' which will affirm the role of the created order in devotion and contemplation, while avoiding the theological shortcomings of Matthew Fox's approach. Another will be to develop the significance of Alasdair MacIntyre's notion of tradition-constituted rationality for an ecclesiology, which will see the Church as a community of ideas and values, similar to the *polis* of ancient Greece.[1] Above all, these works will seek to convey the immensity of the Christian vision of God – what John Donne described as the 'exceeding weight of eternal glory'[2] – and its impact on the intellectual, spiritual and prayerful practice of the Christian faith.

That, however, lies in the future. It is at present the far horizon of the scientific theology project, with much work to be done during the interim. The enterprise of Christian theology is like civilization itself, characterized by Arnold Toynbee as 'a movement and not a condition, a voyage and not a harbour'. I do not for one moment imagine that the scientific theology project will settle anything. But it might make that voyage of faith more interesting, and make sense of some of the enigmas we encounter along the way.

Notes

Preface

1. Throughout this work, references to the three volumes will be abbreviated by citing the volume and page numbers. Thus '1:xviii' is to be understood as 'volume 1, page xviii', and '2:139–40' as 'volume 2, pages 139–40'.

Introduction

1. I later came back to explore the entire question of the plausibility and attraction of atheism: see Alister McGrath, *The Twilight of Atheism: The Rise and Fall of Disbelief in the Modern World.* New York: Doubleday, forthcoming 2004.
2. This led to three major publications: *Luther's Theology of the Cross: Martin Luther's Theological Breakthrough.* Oxford: Blackwell, 1985; *Iustitia Dei: A History of the Christian Doctrine of Justification,* 2 vols. Cambridge: Cambridge University Press, 1986, 2nd edn 1998, 3rd edn forthcoming

2005; *The Intellectual Origins of the European Reformation.* Oxford: Blackwell, 1987, 2nd edn 2003.

3. *The Genesis of Doctrine: A Study in the Foundations of Doctrinal Criticism.* Oxford: Blackwell, 1990.

4. *The Foundations of Dialogue in Science and Religion.* Oxford: Blackwell, 1998.

5. *Thomas F. Torrance: An Intellectual Biography.* Edinburgh: T&T Clark, 1999.

6. See below, pp. 120–5.

7. See Alister McGrath, 'Engaging the Great Tradition: Evangelical Theology and the Role of Tradition', in John G. Stackhouse (ed.), *Evangelical Futures: A Conversation on Theological Method.* Grand Rapids, MI: Baker, 2000, 139–58.

8. Mark Noll, *The Scandal of the Evangelical Mind.* Grand Rapids, MI: Eerdmans, 1994.

1. Prolegomena

1. The word 'ontology' refers to the structures of reality itself – the way things actually are.

2. C. P. Snow, *The Two Cultures and the Scientific Revolution.* Cambridge: Cambridge University Press, 1959, 3.

3. See below, pp. 139–53, and *Scientific Theology*, vol. 2.

4. Alister E. McGrath, *Thomas F. Torrance: An Intellectual Biography.* Edinburgh: T&T Clark, 1999.

5. The works which illustrate Torrance's approach best, in my view, are: *Theological Science.* London: Oxford University Press, 1969; *The Trinitarian Faith: The Evangelical Theology of the Ancient Catholic Church.* Edinburgh: T&T Clark, 1988; *The Christian Doctrine of God: One Being, Three Persons.* Edinburgh: T&T Clark, 1996.

6. Lawrence Sklar, *Theory and Truth: Philosophical Critique without Foundational Science*. Oxford: Oxford University Press, 2000, 79.

2. Nature

1. C. S. Lewis, *The Abolition of Man*. London: Collins, 1978, 43.
2. For these categories, I draw on Michael E. Soulé, 'The Social Siege of Nature', in Michael E. Soulé and Gary Lease (eds), *Reinventing Nature: Responses to Postmodern Deconstruction*. Washington, DC: Island Press, 1995, 137–70. This work includes excellent comments on the postmodern deconstruction of nature and its implications.
3. Sir Thomas Browne, *Religio Medici*, II.xiv–xviii.
4. The three most important such articles were published over a period of two years in the leading British journal of philosophy *Mind*: 'The Christian Doctrine of Creation and the Rise of Modern Science'. *Mind* 43 (1934), 446–68; 'Christian Theology and Modern Science of Nature (I)'. *Mind* 44 (1935), 439–66; and 'Christian Theology and Modern Science of Nature (II)'. *Mind* 45 (1936), 1–27.
5. Michael Foster, 'Greek and Christian Ideas of Nature'. *The Free University Quarterly* 6 (1959), 122–7, at 124.
6. John Polkinghorne, *Science and Creation: The Search for Understanding*. London: SPCK, 1988, 20–1.
7. Polkinghorne, *Science and Creation*, 22.
8. Augustine, *de Trinitate*, XVI.iv.6.
9. Athanasius, *de incarnatione Verbi*, 3.
10. Augustine, *Confessions*, I.i.1.
11. Plato, *Euthyphro*, 10a.
12. Paul Davies, *The Mind of God: Science and the Search for Ultimate Meaning*. London: Penguin, 1992, 77.

13. Oliver O'Donovan, *Resurrection and Moral Order*. Grand Rapids, MI: Eerdmans, 1986, 31–2.

14. O'Donovan, *Resurrection and Moral Order*, 36–7.

15. T. F. Torrance, 'Divine and Contingent Order', in A. R. Peacocke (ed.), *The Sciences and Theology in the Twentieth Century*. Notre Dame, IN: University of Notre Dame Press, 1981, 81–97, at 84–5.

16. Eric L. Mascall, *Christian Theology and Natural Science: Some Questions on their Relations*. London: Longmans, Green & Co., 1956, 94.

17. Thomas Aquinas, *Summa contra Gentiles*, II.ii.3–4.

18. John Calvin, *Institutes*, I.iii.1, 2.

19. *Confessio Gallicana*, 1559, article 3; in E. F. K. Müller (ed.), *Die Bekenntnisschriften der reformierten Kirche*. Leipzig: Böhme, 1903, 222.5–44.

20. *Confessio Belgica*, 1561, article 2; in E. F. K. Müller (ed.), *Die Bekenntnisschriften der reformierten Kirche*. Leipzig: Böhme, 1903, 233.11–21.

21. William P. Alston, *Perceiving God: The Epistemology of Religious Experience*. Ithaca, NY: Cornell University Press, 1991, 289.

22. James Barr, *Biblical Faith and Natural Theology*. Oxford: Clarendon Press, 1993, 138.

23. Theodore Beza, *Sermons sur l'histoire de la passion et sepultre de nostre Seignure Jesus Christ*. Geneva, 1592, 46.

24. T. F. Torrance, 'The Problem of Natural Theology in the Thought of Karl Barth'. *Religious Studies* 6 (1970), 121–35, at 125.

25. T. F. Torrance, *The Ground and Grammar of Theology*. Charlottesville, VA: University of Virginia Press, 1980, 89.

3. Reality

1. Richard Rorty, *Philosophy and the Mirror of Nature*. Princeton: Princeton University Press, 1979, 3
2. Rorty, *Consequences of Pragmatism*, 166.
3. Rorty, *Consequences of Pragmatism*, xlii.
4. Reuben Hersh, 'Introducing Imre Lakatos'. *Mathematical Intelligencer* 1 (1978), 148–51.
5. George Lindbeck, *The Nature of Doctrine: Religion and Theology in a Postliberal Age*. Philadelphia: Westminster Press, 1984, 19.
6. Lindbeck, *Nature of Doctrine*, 65.
7. David Tracy, 'Lindbeck's New Program for Theology: A Reflection'. *The Thomist* 49 (1985), 460–72.
8. Paul K. Feyerabend, *Science in a Free Society*. London: Verso, 1983, 82.
9. *After Virtue*. Notre Dame, IN: University of Notre Dame Press, 1981; *Whose Justice? Which Rationality?* Notre Dame, IN: University of Notre Dame Press, 1988; *Three Rival Versions of Moral Inquiry: Encyclopaedia, Genealogy, and Tradition*. Notre Dame, IN: University of Notre Dame Press, 1990.
10. MacIntyre, *Whose Justice? Which Rationality?*, 6.
11. MacIntyre, *Whose Justice? Which Rationality?*, 334.
12. MacIntyre, *Whose Justice? Which Rationality?*, 357.
13. Roger Penrose, *Shadows of the Mind: A Search for the Missing Science of Consciousness*. London: Vintage, 1995.
14. O'Donovan, *Resurrection and Moral Order*, 17.
15. Augustine of Hippo, *de doctrina Christiana*, II.xl.60–1.
16. John Polkinghorne, *One World: The Interaction of Science and Theology*. Princeton: Princeton University Press, 1986, 22.
17. Michael Redhead, *From Physics to Metaphysics*. Cambridge: Cambridge University Press, 1995, 9.

18. Richard Boyd, 'The Current Status of Scientific Realism', in Jarrett Leplin (ed.), *Scientific Realism*. Berkeley: University of California Press, 1984, 41–82.

19. Stathis Psillos, *Scientific Realism: How Science Tracks Truth*. London: Routledge, 1999.

20. Readers wishing to have a more extended defence of the realist position and criticism of its alternatives should consult the original volume *Reality*, rather than rely upon the brief summaries presented below.

21. Gilbert Harman, 'The Inference to the Best Explanation'. *Philosophical Review* 74 (1965), 88–95.

22. Ernan McMullin, 'A Case for Scientific Realism', in Jared Leplin (ed.), *Scientific Realism*. Berkeley, CA: University of California Press, 1984, 8–40.

23. John R. Searle, *The Construction of Social Reality*. New York: Free Press, 1995.

24. I used four of Bhaskar's works as primary sources for his ideas: *The Possibility of Naturalism: A Philosophical Critique of the Contemporary Human Sciences*, 3rd edn. London: Routledge, 1998; *A Realist Theory of Science*, 2nd edn. London: Verso, 1997; *Reclaiming Reality: A Critical Introduction to Contemporary Philosophy*. London: Verso, 1989; *Scientific Realism and Human Emancipation*. London: Verso, 1986.

25. William James, *Essays in Radical Empiricism*. Cambridge, MA: Harvard University Press, 1976, 21.

26. N. T. Wright, *The New Testament and the People of God*. London: SPCK, 1992, 35.

27. John Polkinghorne, *Belief in God in an Age of Science*. New Haven, CT: Yale University Press, 1998, 104.

28. Roy Bhaskar, *A Realist Theory of Science*, 2nd edn. London: Verso, 1997, 16.

29. W. H. Newton-Smith, *The Rationality of Science*. London: Routledge & Kegan Paul, 1981, 25.

30. John Polkinghorne, *Reason and Reality*. London: SPCK, 1991, 20.

31. Roy Bhaskar, *The Possibility of Naturalism: A Philosophical Critique of the Contemporary Human Sciences*, 3rd edn. London: Routledge, 1998, 3.

32. Roy Bhaskar, *A Realist Theory of Science*, 2nd edn. London: Verso, 1997, 113.

33. *International Classification of Impairments, Disabilities and Handicaps: A Manual of Classification Relating to the Consequences of Disease*. Geneva: World Health Organization, 1980. The classification was modified (ICIDH-2) in 1997, replacing the notion of 'disability' and 'handicap' with the categories of 'activity' and 'participation'.

34. Don Cupitt, *Only Human*. London: SCM Press, 1985, 9.

35. Published as Thomas F. Torrance, *The Ground and Grammar of Theology*. Charlottesville, VA: University of Virginia Press, 1980.

36. MacIntyre, *Whose Justice? Which Rationality?*, 6.

37. Karl Barth, *The Göttingen Dogmatics: Instruction in the Christian Religion*. Grand Rapids, MI: Eerdmans, 1991, 151.

38. Thomas F. Torrance, *Theological Science*. London: Oxford University Press, 1969, 33–4.

39. A. D. Ritchie, *Studies in the History and Methods of the Sciences*. Edinburgh: Edinburgh University Press, 1963, 7.

40. Karl Barth, *Die christliche Theologie im Entwurf*. Munich: Kaiser Verlag, 1927, 115.

41. Heinrich Scholz, 'Wie ist eine evangelische Theologie als Wissenschaft möglich?' *Zwischen den Zeiten* 9 (1931), 8–51.

42. Basil Mitchell, *The Justification of Religious Belief*. London: Macmillan, 1973, 100–101.

43. This is best seen from D. Z. Phillips, *Religion without Explanation*. Oxford: Blackwell, 1976.
44. D. Z. Phillips, *Wittgenstein and Religion*. London: Macmillan, 1993, 152–70.
45. Alvin Plantinga, *Warranted Christian Belief*. Oxford: Oxford University Press, 2000, 370.
46. Philip Clayton, *Explanation from Physics to Theology: An Essay in Rationality and Religion*. New Haven, CT: Yale University Press, 1989, 131–45.
47. Michael C. Banner, *The Justification of Science and the Rationality of Religious Belief*. Oxford: Oxford University Press, 1990, 67–118.
48. Richard Swinburne, *The Existence of God*. Oxford: Clarendon Press, 1979, 277–90.
49. T. F. Torrance, *Theological Science*. London: Oxford University Press, 1969, 216.

4. Theory

1. Irenaeus, *adversus haereses*, IV.xx.7.
2. Wlad Godzich, 'Foreword: The Tiger on the Paper Mat', in Paul de Man (ed.), *The Resistance to Theory*. Minneapolis: University of Minnesota Press, 1986, ix–xviii.
3. C. S. Lewis, *Mere Christianity*. London: Collins, 1952, 130.
4. Vladimir I. A. Propp, *Morphology of the Folktale*, 2nd edn. Austin, TX: University of Texas Press, 1968, 99.
5. Victor Shklovsky, 'Art as Technique', in *Russian Formalist Criticism: Four Essays*. Lincoln, NE: University of Nebraska Press, 1965, 3–24, at 7.
6. Shklovsky, 'Art as Technique', 8.
7. Frank Lentricchia, 'On Behalf of Theory', in Gerald Graff and Reginald Gibbons (eds), *Criticism in the University*.

Evanston, IL: Northwestern University Press, 1985, 105–10, esp. 108.

8. Larry Laudan, *Progress and its Problems: Towards a Theory of Scientific Growth*. Berkeley: University of California Press, 1977, 31.

9. Hilary Lawson, *Closure: A Story of Everything*. London: Routledge, 2001, 4.

10. Lawson, *Closure: A Story of Everything*, 21.

11. P. T. Forsyth, *The Person and Place of Jesus Christ*. London: Independent Press, 1909, 213–14.

12. Forsyth, *The Person and Place of Jesus Christ*, 15.

13. T. F. Torrance, 'Athanasius: A Study in the Foundations of Classical Theology', in *Theology in Reconciliation*. London: Geoffrey Chapman, 1975, 215–66, at 241.

14. Augustine, *Sermo* 117.

15. T. S. Eliot, *Burnt Norton*, V.13–17.

16. Giambattista Vico, *The New Science*. Ithaca, NY: Cornell University Press, 1968, 60.

17. Janet Martin Soskice, 'Theological Realism', in W. J. Abraham and S. Holtzer (eds), *The Rationality of Religious Belief*. Oxford and New York: Clarendon Press, 1987, 105–19, at 110.

18. T. F. Torrance, 'Divine and Contingent Order', in A. R. Peacocke (ed.), *The Sciences and Theology in the Twentieth Century*. Notre Dame, IN: University of Notre Dame Press, 1981, 81–97, at 84.

19. Arthur Peacocke, *Intimations of Reality*. Notre Dame, IN: University of Notre Dame Press, 1984, 51.

20. Karl Barth, 'Schicksal und Idee in Theologie', in *Theologische Frage und Antworten*. Zurich: Evangelischer Verlag, 1957, 54–92, at 80.

21. Wolfhart Pannenberg, *Systematic Theology*, 3 vols. Grand Rapids, MI: Eerdmans, 1991–8, vol. 1, 249.

22. James Barr, 'The Concepts of History and Revelation', in *Old and New in Interpretation: A Study of the Two Testaments*. London: SCM Press, 1966, 65–103, esp. 67–8.

23. Alan Richardson, *History, Sacred and Profane*. London: SCM Press, 1964.

24. Richardson, *History, Sacred and Profane*, 294.

25. Richard Swinburne, *The Existence of God*. Oxford: Clarendon Press, 1979, 136.

26. Pierre Duhem, *La Théorie physique: son objet – sa structure*, 2nd edn. Paris: Vrin, 1997, 284.

27. Alasdair MacIntyre and Paul Ricoeur, *The Religious Significance of Atheism*. New York: Columbia University Press, 1969, 14.

28. Otto von Neurath, *Empiricism and Sociology*. Dordrecht: Reidel, 1973, 198.

29. Walter Bauer, *Orthodoxy and Heresy in Earliest Christianity*. London: SCM Press, 1972.

30. This is the position developed in the classic study of H. E. W. Turner, *The Pattern of Christian Truth: A Study in the Relations between Orthodoxy and Heresy in the Early Church*. London: Mowbray, 1954, 81–94.

31. Edward Schillebeeckx, *Jesus: An Experiment in Christology*. London: Collins, 1979, 439–515.

32. Gordon D. Kaufman, 'Metaphysics and Theology'. *Cross Currents* 28 (1978), 325–41.

33. David Hume, *Enquiries concerning Human Understanding and concerning the Principles of Morals*, 3rd edn. Oxford: Clarendon Press, 1975, 165.

34. Otto Neurath, 'Protokollsätze'. *Erkenntnis* 3 (1932), 204–14.

35. V. F. Lenzen, 'Procedures of Empirical Science', in O. Neurath, R. Carnap and C. Morris (eds), *Foundations of the Unity of Science: Toward an International Encyclopedia of*

Unified Science, 2 vols. Chicago: University of Chicago Press, 1955, vol. 1, 279–339.

36. Michael Redhead, *From Physics to Metaphysics*. Cambridge: Cambridge University Press, 1995, 87.

37. John Milbank, *The Word made Strange: Theology, Language, Culture*. Oxford: Blackwell, 1997, 44.

38. Milbank, *The Word made Strange*, 44–5.

39. See the careful study of Kristian Jensen, 'Protestant Rivalry: Metaphysics and Rhetoric in Germany, *c.*1590–1620'. *Journal of Ecclesiastical History* 41 (1990), 24–43.

40. John Macquarrie, *Jesus Christ in Modern Thought*. London: SCM Press, 1990, 344.

41. Eberhard Jüngel, *Gott als Geheimnis der Welt: Zur Begründung der Theologie des Gekreuzigten im Streit zwischen Theismus und Atheismus*, 4th edn. Tübingen: J. C. B. Mohr, 1982, 146–67.

42. Jüngel, *Gott als Geheimnis der Welt*, 200.

43. Richard Bauckham, *God Crucified: Monotheism and Christology in the New Testament*. Grand Rapids, MI: Eerdmans, 1998, 41.

44. Bauckham, *God Crucified*, 42.

Conclusion

1. This idea has already been explored to some extent in Stanley Hauerwas, *In Good Company: The Church as Polis*. Notre Dame, IN: University of Notre Dame Press, 1995. It needs much more rigorous application.

2. John Donne, 'Sermon No. 1', in *The Sermons of John Donne*, ed. E. M. Simpson and G. R. Potter, 10 vols. Berkeley/Los Angeles: University of California Press, 1954, vol. 7, 51–71.

Index